The 2000 election sh___ ___ ___ mechanics of voting, such as ballot design, can make a critical difference in the accuracy and fairness of our elections. But as Dennis F. Thompson shows, even more fundamental issues must be addressed to insure that our electoral system is just.

Thompson argues that three central democratic principles—equal respect, free choice, and popular sovereignty—underlie our electoral institutions and should inform any assessment of the justice of elections. Although we may all endorse these principles in theory, Thompson shows that in practice we disagree about their meaning and application. He shows how they create conflicts among basic values across a broad spectrum of electoral controversies, from disagreements about term limits and primaries to disputes about recounts and presidential electors.

To create a fair electoral system, Thompson argues, we must deliberate together about these principles and take greater control of the procedures that govern our elections. He demonstrates how applying the principles of justice to electoral practices can help us answer questions that our electoral system poses: Should race count in redistricting? Should the media call elections before the polls close? How should we limit the power of money in elections?

In answering these and other questions, Thompson examines the arguments that citizens and their representatives actually use in political forums, congressional debates and hearings, state legislative proceedings, and meetings of commissions and local councils. In addition, the book draws on a broad range of literature: democratic theory including writings by Madison, Hamilton, Tocqueville, and contempo-

Just Elections

JUST
ELECTIONS

CREATING A FAIR
ELECTORAL PROCESS IN
THE UNITED STATES

Dennis F. Thompson

THE UNIVERSITY OF CHICAGO PRESS • CHICAGO AND LONDON

DENNIS F. THOMPSON is the Alfred North Whitehead Professor of
Political Philosophy at Harvard University and director of the Center for Ethics
and the Professions. Among his books are *Democracy and Disagreement* (1996,
with Amy Gutmann), *Ethics in Congress: From Individual to Institutional
Corruption* (1995), and *Political Ethics and Public Office* (1987).

The University of Chicago Press, Chicago 60637
The University of Chicago Press, Ltd., London
© 2002 by The University of Chicago
All rights reserved. Published 2002
Printed in the United States of America
11 10 09 08 07 06 05 04 03 02   1 2 3 4 5

ISBN: 0–226-79763–5 (cloth)

Library of Congress Cataloging-in-Publication Data

Thompson, Dennis F. (Dennis Frank), 1940–
Just elections : creating a fair electoral process in the United States / Dennis F. Thompson.
p. cm.
Includes bibliographical references and index.
ISBN 0-226-79763-5 (cloth : alk. paper)
1. Elections—United States.   2. Representative government and
representation—United States.   3. Election districts—United States.   I. Title.
JK1976 .T47 2002
324.6'3'0973—dc21   2002005405

Contents

Preface

The presidential election of 2000 stands as a durable reminder that the way democracies conduct their elections makes a difference. That is why I begin each chapter of this book with lines from some of the major characters in this electoral drama. But if that election demonstrated that procedures matter, it also showed that mere procedures can matter too much. The public debate and much of the scholarly discussion it stimulated have focused on the techniques of counting votes and the strategies for contesting the results. The more enduring lessons of this election concern the principles that underlie the procedures. That is why I devote more attention to the values the procedures express than the mechanics they require, and why I give greater consideration to elections in general than to any particular election or its results. My subject is not just the election of 2000, but just elections. Specifically, I focus on electoral practices in the United States that could be more nearly just.

The practical aim of this book is to encourage more serious and sustained deliberation about the moral foundations of electoral institutions. To appreciate the significance of those foundations, we need to examine the principles that sustain those institutions and assess the conceptions of democratic representation they presuppose. The character of our democracy is at stake in how we elect our representatives as much as in which representatives we elect and what laws they enact. This is partly because the procedures of elections influence the results of elections. More fundamentally it is because the procedures express political values that underlie our common life as democratic citizens. My hope is that by more clearly understanding the connections between our electoral practices and democratic principles, we can more critically appreciate the ways in which our electoral institutions fall short of the demands of justice. We can then more constructively seek ways to make the institutions more just, or at least less unjust.

The primary theoretical aim of the book is to develop principles of electoral justice and show their relation to electoral institutions. Anyone who cares about elections should take an interest in this kind of theory. Almost any criticism or defense of an electoral practice, whether in the public forum or the scholarly literature, presupposes theoretical views and often invokes fragments of theories if not theories themselves. We cannot effectively assess those criticisms and defenses without engaging in theoretical inquiry. By undertaking that kind of inquiry in this book, I seek to show why theorizing about electoral justice cannot be avoided, and how it might be carried on productively.

A more general (though less explicit) aim of the book is to suggest that the kind of theory deployed here to examine electoral justice should be more widely practiced in the academy. My hope is that this approach—institutional political theory—can be extended beyond electoral justice to many other questions that political theorists address. The value of the approach is better demonstrated by applying its methods to specific problems than by expounding its virtues in a general manifesto. For that reason, I concentrate on showing how it can illuminate the problems of electoral justice rather than on explaining how it should affect the practice of political theory more generally. Nevertheless, to make clear at the outset that the relevance of institutional political theory extends beyond electoral institutions, I call attention to three general implications of the approach. They take the form of methodological precepts that should guide the choice of the context, content, and level of analysis in the study of political principles.

The first precept affirms that interpreting political principles requires attending to institutional context. The meaning of principles such as equality and liberty cannot be adequately understood apart from the institutions in which they are realized. Until we examine the ways they play out in political institutions, not only can we not decide what kind of equality or liberty we wish to promote, we cannot even determine what the principles mean. What equality means varies, depending on, for example, the system of representation in which it is realized. To be sure, if we state the principles at a sufficiently abstract level, we can find some general meanings common to many of their applications. But such meanings are not only incomplete but often misleading. Abstracted from institutional context, principles sometimes seem indeterminate when they actually have definite political conclusions, or—what is less appreciated—they often seem determinate when they actually leave open significant choices among competing political alternatives.

The second precept suggests broadening the content of political theory to include the arguments that citizens and their representatives present in public forums. If the meaning of principles depends on their institutional context, then the arguments that political agents themselves make in this context should be relevant to interpreting those principles. Theorists do not of course have to accept these arguments at face value, but they need to take some of them seriously. When they fail to do so, their theories fail to connect appropriately with political practice. Without an appreciation of the public values that the arguments express, theorists cannot effectively justify or criticize the institutions that embody those values. They cannot successfully carry out one of the essential tasks of theory—assessing the reasons that political agents themselves give to justify or criticize political practices. These reasons are to be found in the fragments of theories implied by the arguments that citizens and their representatives present in public forums. The reasons are presented not only in theorists' favored forum of principle, the Supreme Court, but in many other sites of deliberation—congressional debates and hearings, state legislative proceedings, meetings of commissions and local councils. The province of political theory should include not only the manifestly theoretical, but also the incompletely theoretical.

Finally, institutional political theory favors a level of analysis that lies in the midrange of political argument. Instead of comprehensive theories such as libertarianism and egalitarianism or all-embracing ideologies such as liberalism and conservatism, it concentrates on principles that operate closer to the political ground. It seeks principles informed enough by actual practice to connect to political agents, but detached enough to provide a critical perspective on their actions. Because midrange principles may be common to several comprehensive theories, the point of institutional theorizing is not to force choices among such theories, but to facilitate interpretations of the principles themselves. It seeks to identify conflicts within and between the principles, and to determine whether they can, or even whether they should, be resolved. This kind of theorizing may lack the drama of a grand clash of worldviews, but it offers the prospect of a more meaningful engagement with the views of political agents—the citizens and their representatives, who argue about, take part in, and try to improve the institutions of democracy.

Acknowledgments

Anyone who practices institutional political theory must be prepared to learn from the previous work and current wisdom of scholars in other disciplines. In writing this book, I benefited greatly from the counsel of not only political theorists, but also political scientists, historians, constitutional theorists, and scholars who specialize in election law.

Several colleagues in political theory and philosophy temporarily set aside some of our theoretical disagreements and helped make my arguments stronger or at least clearer. My single greatest intellectual debt is to my longtime colleague and sometime collaborator, Amy Gutmann, who nearly every week for the better part of a year subjected my developing ideas to constructive criticism, and later commented on nearly every section of the manuscript. Charles Beitz, Stephen Macedo, Nancy Rosenblum, and T. M. Scanlon also gave me valuable advice and creative suggestions for improving many of the arguments in the book.

On the more empirical aspects of the book, I benefited from the astute comments of several political scientists—notably Mark Hansen, Thomas Mann, Sidney Verba, and Raymond Wolfinger. I also received discerning historical instruction from Alexander Keyssar. Two constitutional theorists—Frederick Schauer and Sandford Levinson—contributed thoughtful criticism on an early draft of the entire book.

When I began this project, I had not expected to find the literature on election law to be as theoretically fertile as it is. I learned much especially from the work of Samuel Issacharoff, Pamela Karlan, and Richard Pildes, whose casebooks are indispensable guides to this literature. Pildes himself gave me extensive and insightful comments on the entire manuscript. So did another election law scholar, Heather Gerken, who encouraged me to rethink several key arguments. Also, Lani Guinier offered some helpful criticisms on a draft of chapter 1.

An institutional theorist especially should not fail to acknowledge support received from institutions. I conducted the research and wrote a draft of most of the book at the Center for Advanced Study in the Behavioral Sciences in Stanford during 2000–2001. The director, the staff, and the other fellows helped make the year both productive and enjoyable. While devoting themselves mainly to subjects other than electoral justice, the faculty and fellows in the University Center for Ethics and the Professions at Harvard have over the years encouraged me to believe that an institutional approach to political theory may be fruitful, and helped me to think more deeply about the relation between theory and practice.

No author could ask for more capable research assistants than Simone Sandy and Maria Catoline, both of whom worked diligently on this project from its beginning. Judy Hensley, Allison Ruda, and Kim Tseko also provided assistance along the way. Jean McVeigh and Carrie Vuori contributed to the project indirectly but essentially by keeping the rest of my complicated professional life from collapsing into chaos. At the University of Chicago Press, John Tryneski and his staff, including Anne Ford, Leslie Keros, and Monica Holliday, showed what a difference excellent editorial support can make. The manuscript was copyedited by David Bemelmans; the index was prepared by Margie Towery.

My wife, Carol, while carrying on her own career, somehow managed to provide the sympathetic support that enabled me to carry on mine. Her good cheer and wise advice sustained me during even the most challenging periods of working on this book.

INTRODUCTION
Electoral Justice

> Now that George W. Bush has been declared the winner and
> will be inaugurated next January, will you accept him as the
> legitimate president or not? Yes—83 per cent, No—16 per cent.
> GALLUP POLL, 15–17 DECEMBER 2000

Elections can occur without democracy, but democracy cannot endure without elections. They are not the only method of maintaining popular control of government, but they are the essential one. They directly serve what the framers of the U.S. Constitution saw as the chief aims of any respectable constitution: to obtain rulers who possess the "most wisdom" and "virtue to pursue the common good," and to keep the rulers virtuous while "they continue to hold their public trust."[1] Expressed in less noble language, these remain the central purposes of elections today. Prospectively, voters try to choose an acceptable representative from among the competing candidates, and retrospectively they try to hold the successful candidates and parties accountable in subsequent elections.[2]

As American society has become more pluralist in its interests and its citizens more diverse in their views, voters disagree more than ever about which if any candidates are wise and virtuous—or merely which if any are sensible and honest. Voters therefore more than ever need to be able to judge the process of elections independently of the outcomes. They need principles to determine whether elections are right when they disagree about whether the leaders they elect are good. The disagreements about electoral justice go as deep as those about electoral outcomes, but they are not the same. They are disagreements not about the positions of candidates and parties or even about the meaning of the results, but about the procedures of the elections themselves.

Electoral justice thus is a species of procedural justice. It seeks fair terms of cooperation, a set of practices that all citizens could accept as an equitable basis for making collective decisions. Just procedures are not merely the practices that citizens happen to accept or that their representatives happen to establish. Procedures are just to the extent that they realize principles that could be freely adopted under conditions of equal power. In the case of electoral justice, the principles express the values of equal respect, free choice, and popular sovereignty. An election is just to the extent that it satisfies these principles. This book interprets and develops these principles through an examination of some leading controversies about electoral practices in the United States in recent years.

LEGITIMACY

Electoral justice clearly does not require a just outcome. The candidate who most deserves to win—the most qualified according to whatever standard one chooses—may well lose a just election. Even if the candidate most likely to promote just policies is defeated, the election may still be completely just. While most people recognize that electoral justice demands less than a just outcome, many do not appreciate that electoral justice demands more than a legitimate one. The results of an election may be accepted as legitimate because the procedures are regarded as legitimate, but the procedures may still not be just.

Nothing illustrates more vividly the difference between a legitimate and a just election than the reactions of Americans to the controversy over the presidential contest of 2000. Not only did an overwhelming majority accept George Bush as the legitimate president, a substantial majority of those who voted for Al Gore did too. This was so even though a majority of the electorate still preferred Gore (by greater margins than the votes he received in the election), and even though a still larger majority favored the abolition of the electoral college (which brought about Bush's victory despite his loss of the popular vote).[3] Many voters disapproved of the outcome but accepted Bush as the legitimate winner because they accepted the election as a legitimate procedure. The losers may have been disappointed, even angry, but they did not take to the streets, threaten to defy executive orders, or refuse to cooperate in making new laws and policies. They accepted Bush's authority to issue orders and execute laws that they considered themselves obligated to obey. They recognized the winner's right, not merely his power, to take office.

An election is legitimate to the extent that is conducted in accordance with rules established through the appropriate legal and political process of a society. This is not a high standard. The process by which the rules are established must itself be legitimate, but almost any process that is minimally democratic and accepted by a substantial number of citizens is sufficient. Moreover, the conduct of the election itself does not have to follow the rules perfectly. Electoral legitimacy is elastic, and can survive in the face of significant violations. Only if the violations are widespread, deliberate, and consequential do they undermine legitimacy.

However widespread the violations may have been in the 2000 election, most were probably not deliberate, at least not in any organized way. Perhaps more important, the very closeness of the outcome—amounting to a statistical tie—made it difficult to show that the violations were consequential in the sense that they changed the result. The closer an election, the greater the difference any single violation can make, but also the harder it is to show that a particular violation or set of violations was the factor that made the difference. If the violations had turned a Gore landslide into a Bush victory, they could have made the election illegitimate. But in this election, no one could say for sure that Gore would have won if there had been no violations.[4]

Modest though its demands are, the value of legitimacy should not be underestimated. The viability of democratic government depends on it. In elections in the United States it has not always been the case that winners could count on losers' accepting the results. Many democracies are still struggling to create enough legitimacy to sustain a stable political system. Even in well-established democracies, electoral legitimacy facilitates political cooperation after a hard-fought campaign, and enables the winners to serve without facing persistent challenges to their authority. Especially after a close election, if the electoral process did not come to a legitimate conclusion in a timely manner, the protests could continue indefinitely, and the business of government would suffer.

The moral force of legitimacy is limited, however. A legitimate election may be unjust, or less just than it should be. That possibility is realized in our electoral life more often than is usually recognized. In the 2000 election, many of the voters who accepted Bush as the legitimate winner did not consider the process fair. Although nearly 70 percent of Gore's supporters were prepared to accept Bush as the legitimate president, even more of his supporters thought the Supreme Court decision that put Bush in office was "unfair."[5] Nearly a quarter of Bush's supporters also had doubts about the fairness of the process. Still more significant, two-thirds of black voters felt they had been "cheated" by the electoral process even though a majority of them accepted the outcome. If voters see an election as unfair and feel cheated by the process, they also presumably believe that the procedures are less just than they should be.

Thus we can criticize the procedures of an election as unjust even while accepting the outcome as legitimate. This kind of criticism—and any defensible normative judgment about the electoral process—presupposes a set of principles of electoral justice. In contemporary debates the most common approaches to developing those principles are what may be called the individualist and the competitive views of the electoral process. The individualist view emphasizes the rights of voters, and the competitive view the claims of candidates. But neither captures the full range of considerations that electoral justice should recognize because both neglect, in somewhat different ways, the institutional dimension of the electoral process.

INDIVIDUAL RIGHTS

At the birth of the Republic, most Americans were not entitled to vote. The Constitution granted individuals the right to vote only in elections for the House of Representatives and only if they were qualified to vote in the popular branch of their own state legislature.[6] John Adams warned that if the restrictions on the franchise began to be removed, "there will be no end of it."[7] He was essentially correct in his prediction if not in his attitude. Recognizing the moral right of some new groups to vote created an historical dynamic that led, if not inevitably then compellingly, to universal suffrage. First propertyless men, then black men, women, blacks again, and finally those eighteen to twenty years old won the right to vote. The progress was not steady—periods of contraction followed periods of expansion—and some obstacles to the exercise of the right have still not been overcome. But throughout the struggle, the appeal to individual rights played a central role.[8] Earlier grounded more in natural law, later based more on notions of human dignity, the right of each citizen to participate in choosing the representatives who make the laws by which all citizens are bound still stands at the moral core of any adequate conception of electoral justice. The individualist approach rightly emphasizes that moral worth inheres in each individual citizen, not in the collective outcome of the election, and not in the representatives and the laws they enact.

Nevertheless, the individualist approach is at best incomplete and can often be misleading—even as a guide for recognizing the moral worth of individuals.[9] By emphasizing the independent actions and discrete claims of individual voters, the approach neglects the interactive effects and structural patterns of the institutions in which elections take place. It is in this institutional dimension that some of the most significant problems of electoral justice arise.

Consider the problem of exit polls, the surveys in which voters leaving the polling stations are asked for whom they voted. In recent elections the media has increasingly used these polls to predict the outcome of various races. Television commentators report the results and "call" the election often before the polls close. The forecasts probably discourage some citizens from voting, and thus distort the electoral process in a way that may be unfair to citizens who do vote and the candidates who lose votes that would have been cast for them. Defenders of the media's election projections appeal to individual rights: "it is up to a voter to vote. [It is] their responsibility whether or not to be influenced" by the reports of exit polls.[10] But to leave the choice to the individual is not only to neglect the effects on the other citizens and the candidates in a particular election, but also to restrict the range of choice for all citizens in other elections. As individuals they do not have the option of voting in a system without exit polls. In this individualist regime, citizens have no way to prevent the dissemination of the collective results of their individual votes if they believe that no one should have such information before everyone has voted. They could, acting together through their representatives, change the rules, and establish a different regime. Or they could— again acting together—decide to maintain the current regime. Either way, they would not be simply exercising an individual right. They would be using institutional means to choose just ends for their electoral institutions.

This example illustrates only one kind of institutional issue that electoral justice should consider. The chapters that follow call attention to a wide variety of those issues and argue that they should have a more prominent place in deliberation about principles of electoral justice. The rights that individuals claim have different meanings and different effects depending on the nature of the institutions in which they are to be exercised. Some of the effects involve the familiar problems of collective action: no individual's vote is likely to make a difference to the outcome, but if no one voted, everyone would suffer. Other institutional effects become clear only when we consider the wider political context of elections. Creating districts in which blacks are in the majority may put more blacks in Congress, but "bleaching" other districts may reduce the number of white representatives who would support black causes. Is it more important to have more black representatives or more representatives who will pay more attention to blacks in the legislature? Is it more important to encourage cross-racial coalitions in the constituency or in the legislature? The disputes turn not only on the rights or actions of individual voters but on how representative institutions should function. What is at stake in many disputes about electoral justice is the conception of democratic representation itself.

Finally, the institutional approach emphasizes that, whether or not caused by specific institutions, most problems can be resolved only by structural changes. Citizens now vote alone, one by one, in the polling booth, and their ballots are counted, one by one, in the precincts. But the conditions under which they vote, and the procedures by which their ballots are counted, can be changed only by citizens acting together. When they do, they need to appreciate the broader institutional effects of changes in seemingly discrete electoral practices. They need to act and think institutionally.

FAIR COMPETITION

The other leading approach to electoral justice—the competitive view—pays more attention to institutions but mostly only to those that create the conditions for electoral competition. "A competitive struggle for the people's vote" is for many political scientists and political theorists the very definition of democracy. This influential view of democracy has stimulated a fruitful line of research in political science. In a more sophisticated form (which draws on economic models) it remains one of the dominant approaches to the study of elections.[11] Transposed into a normative key, the view makes fair competition the chief criterion of just elections. According to this approach, an election is just to the extent that the electoral process gives candidates a fair chance to compete for office: comparable opportunities to raise resources, unbiased rules for conducting primaries and elections, and impartial procedures for resolving disputes. As in a game, contestants may bring different talents to the field, but the rules and customs of the competition should treat all the same.

The competitive view, often embellished with sporting metaphors, figures prominently in contemporary controversies about elections and campaigns. Several states take the view so literally that they actually decide close elections by a game of chance. In New Mexico, when the results of an election are a virtual tie, the candidates face off in a poker game.[12] During the controversy over the results of the 2000 election in Florida, Bush supporters continually objected that Gore was trying to change the rules of the game. Gore supporters replied that they were merely attempting to determine who had really won the race. They said that what they were doing was not like trying to add or subtract a mile in a marathon while it was being run, but only like asking officials to look more closely at the film of a photo finish.[13]

The competitive view pervades debates about campaign finance reform. In a Senate debate after the election, members repeatedly appealed to the need for a "level playing field." The current system is "unfair," Senator Jeff Sessions complained, because "it makes it difficult for candidates to run on a level playing field."[14] Independently wealthy candidates can spend unlimited amounts of their own money, while their less fortunate rivals can spend only what they can raise from supporters who are limited to contributions of only one thousand dollars each. Speaking in favor of an amendment that would have raised the contributor limits for candidates competing against wealthy candidates who rely on their own money, Senator Michael DeWine argued: we must "begin to level the playing field, making it easier for that candidate running against the millionaire to raise money" and making "the race a lot more competitive."[15]

This debate exposes one of the difficulties of the competitive view as a basis for electoral justice. It tends to focus on the claims of candidates to the neglect of the interests of voters. Voters have an interest in seeing that campaigns and elections are competitive, but their interest does not always coincide with that of the candidates. The millionaire amendment would certainly help less wealthy candidates, and probably make the competition fairer. But it would do so at the price of further increasing the influence of money in campaigns. It would permit the less wealthy to raise more money, but it would do nothing to address the general problems of campaign finance, which affect all candidates and ultimately all citizens. An election may be quite competitive—the candidates may be evenly matched because they are both well financed by special interests—but voters may still reasonably object to both the candidates and the process. Any candidate for whom they vote may turn out to represent special interests instead of their own interests. Voters may rightly prefer a process in which money plays a less significant role, whether or not it is more competitive.

The academic versions of the competitive view rely more on the analogy with the market than the metaphor of a game. They do not neglect voters, but they liken them to consumers. Treating voting as an act that expresses only partisan preferences, similar to purchasing products, neglects other kinds of claims the act may express—most significantly, political principles. The market analogy can illuminate the interplay of interests, but it obscures the interaction of ideas in the political process.

More generally, the fixation on competition, whether between interests or ideas, distorts electoral justice. Competition in elections is not an end in itself; fair competition is neither the same as or the main aim of electoral justice. In the current system, in which two parties dominate in most jurisdictions, and most incumbents in legislative races are reelected, the goal of increasing competition may often be appropriate. But to decide whether more (or less) competition is desirable, we need to balance a number of different values. Too little competition may make legislators less accountable than they should be. Too little turnover may block necessary and desirable change. But too much competition may distract legislators from the business of government. Too much turnover in office may deprive government of the benefits of experience, and discourage leaders from pursuing just but unpopular causes.[16] The goal should be not to maximize competition, but to find the optimal level for sustaining a just democratic process. Competition can be a means to this end, but only one means among many. All should be judged by principles of justice that consider the electoral process as a whole—including conceptions of democratic representation.

PRINCIPLES OF ELECTORAL JUSTICE

Like principles of justice generally, the principles of electoral justice rest on the fundamental idea that the democratic process should regard citizens as free and equal persons. This idea expresses a conception of persons as agents who have the capacity to exercise control over their lives but also the need to cooperate with others to accomplish their individual and collective goals. As independent agents capable of reason, they must find a basis for cooperation—including a method for choosing leaders—that can be justified to each as free and equal persons.

In our time this idea has been most fully elaborated in contractarian theories of justice, most notably in the work of John Rawls, but its core is compatible with a wide variety of conceptions of democratic justice.[17] The essential requirement—that the laws must be mutually justifiable to the persons bound by them—should be part of any conception of justice that bases the exercise of power on reason, not on force. To recognize this moral status of citizens, the principles of electoral justice, again like those of justice generally, express the values of equality and liberty. In the case of elections, these principles need to be supplemented by a third, the principle of popular sovereignty, which addresses the question of who should decide the rules that govern elections.[18]

The principle of equality takes the form of a principle of equal respect: the electoral process should provide citizens with equal opportunities to have their votes counted equally, unless respectful reasons can be given to justify unequal treatment. The reasons, which are part of the meaning of the principle, must express equal respect for persons. Because each citizen is equally bound by the laws and by the authority exercised by the leaders chosen in elections, each citizen should have the right to take part in making those laws and choosing those leaders on an equal basis. The principle was violated in the past when poll taxes prevented poorer citizens from voting, and is disregarded now when registration requirements burden some groups of citizens more than others. It is also breached when some votes are not counted because some districts cannot afford to buy accurate voting machines and provide adequate assistance at the polls.

The principle does not demand literal equality, even in the act of voting, the least hierarchical activity in democratic politics. Complete equality is not only impracticable, but also undesirable. Consider redistricting, now subject to the constitutional requirement of one person, one vote. Officials are supposed to keep districts approximately equal in population when they redraw the boundaries of legislative districts every ten years, but within this constraint they are permitted to give more weight to some groups of voters than others. They do not have to treat all groups equally if they can offer respectful reasons for the treatment. They may favor rural over urban citizens, members of one political party over another, supporters of incumbents over challengers, or black over white voters.

All of these pose problems of justification, but racial redistricting most sharply reveals the conflicts that arise when inequalities need to be justified. Those who oppose racial redistricting argue that drawing districts on the basis of race, manifested in the bizarre shapes that such districts often have, expresses disrespect toward black citizens. The practice sends the message that citizens should be politically divided along racial lines; it says that racial differences matter more than equal citizenship. Those who favor racial redistricting argue that, on the contrary, the practice often provides the only available means of recognizing the basic claims of equal citizenship of black citizens. In a society where voting is still racially polarized, creating majority-minority districts may be the only way to give black voters any chance at all to elect representatives and influence legislation. If justified in these terms, the practice expresses equal respect. Both opponents and proponents of racial redistricting thus appeal to a principle of equal respect, but interpret it in contrary ways. Explicating these conflicting interpretations, and the further assumptions about the democratic process they presuppose, can clarify the meaning of the principle of equal respect.

"Free elections" is a rallying cry of democrats throughout the world. The United States has been fortunate to have finally established electoral institutions that enable most citizens most of the time to vote without fear of intimidation or concern about bribery and extortion. That is no minor achievement. But even in an electoral process that is relatively free, the value of liberty can still be at risk in at least three different ways. First, if the slate of candidates presented to voters includes none whom they find acceptable, they may reasonably think that they do not really have a choice at all. While no system can guarantee that all voters will find a candidate on the ballot whom they favor, it can give voters a voice in the process that determines who wins a place on the ballot. A just system should at least provide adequate opportunities for voters to influence who is nominated. The fewer such opportunities, the less free their choice. Free choice is impaired when a political party makes it difficult for citizens to participate in the nomination process, or when a dominant party places obstacles in the way of third-party challengers.

Choice is also less free to the extent that it is less informed. If voters do not have appropriate information about the candidates, they cannot know whether the vote they cast truly expresses their own view of the candidates. If the media deny candidates adequate opportunities to present their messages, voters' choice is less free. Choice is also less free to the extent that voters are subject to undue pressures. Although the most blatant forms of coercion are now less prevalent, a more devious kind prospers: the influence of political money. The pecuniary pressures on both the selection of nominees and the flow of information create a serious threat to free choice in elections.

Combining these three aspects, we can express the value of liberty in the electoral process by this principle of free choice: the process should give citizens adequate opportunities to put an acceptable set of alternatives on the ballot, acquire appropriate information about the candidates, and make their decisions without undue pressure. The principle does not imply, as might at first appear, that choice is freer to the extent that voters have more alternatives, more information, and more insulation from external pressures. Less of some of these may sometimes actually enhance free choice.

Consider information on the ballot. Placing a notation on the ballot that indicates what position a candidate takes on the issue of term limits gives voters more information. It is also a kind of information that by popular initiative a majority of voters in many states have declared they want. Yet providing this kind of information encourages voters to decide on the basis of a single issue. The notation gives them more information about one issue, but is likely to lead them to pay relatively less attention to others. Arguably, their judgment would be better informed if the information they received were less in total amount but more evenly distributed across issues. Furthermore, this single-issue information comes at a substantial cost: it promotes a particular form of representation—what the framers knew as "instructed" representation—which may unduly limit the discretion of legislators. Even voters who prefer this form of representation for one issue may find their future choices too constrained if the practice spreads to other issues. It could, for example, discourage candidates from running whom these voters would otherwise favor, and could prevent their own representatives from forging the compromises needed to pass legislation in their interest.

Whether more information promotes free choice, then, depends not only on whether citizens want more information or whether they favor term limits (or any other policy that might be featured on the ballot). It depends more fundamentally on what forms of representation citizens may wish to choose for their democracy.

Who should finally decide the rules that govern elections and the disputes they sometimes generate? The principle of popular sovereignty has a definite answer: the majority. If the majority should choose who governs them, they should have the right to determine how they choose who governs them. The answer affirms the value of popular sovereignty, a defining feature of democracy in contemporary societies. It also captures the essential majoritarian character of elections in the United States. Candidates sometimes win with only a plurality, and sometimes lose with a majority of the popular vote. Some political procedures require supermajorities, and some permit minority vetoes. But the expression of a majority will remains the central meaning of popular sovereignty. Despite the persistence of devices such as the electoral college, which dilute the power of majorities, elections remain the most important institutional expression of their will.

Because American democracy does not endorse absolute majority rule, the principle of popular sovereignty cannot rule absolutely. Principles of equal respect and free choice protect individuals and minorities against the tyranny of majorities even while majorities exercise their right to regulate the majoritarian electoral process. But on questions about electoral practices that do not raise such issues—on questions about which majority should rule—the principle of popular sovereignty reigns supreme.

The main challenge of interpreting the principle is to adjudicate the competing claims of various majorities—local versus national, and present versus past and future. Should a majority in a state legislature resolve disputes about the election of the president? On the one hand, compared to other bodies such as the courts or other elected officials such as the governor, the legislative majority is more likely to reflect the will of the electoral majority in the state. The Constitution therefore gives state legislatures considerable power in the selection of presidential electors. On the other hand, granting state majorities full authority over presidential electors ignores the claims of the national majority, who may reasonably prefer a uniform method based on a shared conception of representation. The president, after all, represents everyone. Moreover, because legislators do not always face the voters at the same time as do presidential candidates, and because the partisan division in the legislature may not reflect the division in the presidential vote, the state legislature represents a majority slightly out of sync with the electoral majority. In these ways, the principle of popular sovereignty poses but does not resolve the conflicts between the authority of state and national majorities, and between past, present, and future majorities.

The principles of electoral justice thus deal not only with clear injustices such as intentional discrimination against minorities, but also with contestable injustices such as biases in methods of representation and state sovereignty over national elections. The clear injustices create significant practical problems and indirectly raise important theoretical issues. But the contestable injustices—the apparently reasonable disagreements about what electoral justice should require—pose the greater theoretical challenge. In these cases, the very meaning of the principles is problematic. The principles admit of more than one interpretation, and the interpretations give rise to conflicts not only between the principles but also within the principles themselves.

The analysis here pays more attention to the conflicts within principles because they have been neglected and because they need to be clarified before the conflicts between principles can be critically discussed. As long as the principles are taken as simple statements of single values such as liberty or equality, the conflicts between them tend to be seen as stark ideological oppositions. Turning the conflicts into a confrontation between full-blown theories—libertarianism versus egalitarianism, or republicanism versus liberalism—obscures the tensions within the theories. Such confrontations also make it appear that to resolve questions of electoral justice we have to choose one side or the other in a grand theoretical debate. Electoral justice requires choices among theoretical principles, but not necessarily among comprehensive theories. The democratic principles we are most likely to find justifiable do not inevitably fit together in a coherent whole. They usually operate, one at a time, in what may be called the midrange of political deliberation—between the abstract concepts of philosophers and the concrete proposals of politicians. They stand between theory and practice, informed by both, but identified with neither.

The scope of this book is limited to the United States because its electoral institutions are in many ways distinctive and the meaning of electoral justice depends critically on institutional context. For similar reasons, the merits of alternative electoral systems such as proportional representation, which are more widely used in other nations, do not receive much attention here. These alternatives certainly raise questions of justice, and proposals to adopt some of them in the United States deserve serious consideration. But the more pressing task is to expose the critical issues of justice in our existing electoral practices. They have been neglected not only by those who assume legitimacy is sufficient, but also by those who think justice refers mainly to whole political systems.[19] We should not suppose that the only important questions of justice involve differences between systems or even types of institutions rather than differences within them. Even if we accept the two-party system, for example, we can try to make it more or less favorable to equal respect, and more or less friendly to free choice.

DELIBERATING ABOUT ELECTORAL JUSTICE

Because the principles of electoral justice contain within themselves fundamental conflicts, they do not provide ready-made standards that would enable citizens to decide when an election is just or unjust. But properly understood, they can clarify the choices that citizens need to make about what kind of justice they wish to establish in their elections. In the case of many of these choices—what kind of information voters should have, for example—a number of different choices, within a fairly wide range, may be justified. In other cases—whether obstacles to registration and voting should be eased—electoral justice gives a more definite answer. In these kinds of cases, the principles express requirements that the electoral process must fulfill. The more nearly the process fulfills the requirements, the more nearly just it is.

Because the principles pose choices, citizens themselves should have a voice in interpreting the principles. They should have the opportunity to deliberate about the meaning and application of those principles.[20] Elections embody and shape fundamental values of democracy, and the values they express are contestable. Decisions about electoral procedures involve choices among substantive values no less than do decisions about who should win an election and what legislation they should enact. The continuing deliberation that a healthy democracy encourages about the substance of its policies should extend to the substance of its procedures.

Deliberation about electoral justice is already taking place. Many citizens recognize the moral stakes involved in disputes about electoral rules and procedures, and press their views in many different public forums. They argue not only about highly contentious issues such as racial redistricting, but also about seemingly mundane matters such as what notations should appear on the ballot and whether candidates may be listed as representing more than one party. The content of these deliberations provides the raw material for interpretations of electoral justice developed here. That material comes from a wide variety of sources—the views of the framers, commentary by theorists, the Constitution, court decisions, legislative debates, and commission hearings.

None of these sources should be regarded as finally authoritative. The Constitution, as interpreted not only by the courts but also by other institutions, provides the starting point for much actual deliberation about electoral justice. Because it also expresses in various ways the values of equal respect, free choice, and popular sovereignty, it is an important source for any conception of electoral justice, including the principles developed here. But the principles of electoral justice are not primarily intended as interpretations of the Constitution. They are meant as guides in an ongoing search for the broader meanings of these values in our democratic culture. They can support not only interpretations but also criticisms of the Constitution as well as the other laws that govern our electoral institutions.

The episodes of deliberation considered in the chapters that follow show that electoral justice is a work in progress. The principles of electoral justice, like the deliberations about it, allow for reasonable disagreement, and invite continuing dialogue. The most instructive sources take the form, not of statements of positions, but of exchanges of views. That is why references to the oral arguments and testimony in court proceedings play as prominent a role here as the final opinions. That is also why general indications of the direction of desirable change are more important than specific proposals for reform.

Despite the increased interest in electoral practices, deliberation about electoral justice has not spread as far as it should have, and is not as substantive as it should be. The 2000 election brought electoral problems to the attention of a wider public, and showed that even such minor matters as the design of a ballot could make a difference (recall the notorious "butterfly ballot"). But much of the response has centered on improving the efficiency and accuracy of the electoral process. The discussion has dwelt on the technical means to accomplish this end—for example, to what extent optical scanners should replace punch card systems.[21] These efforts are no doubt important. Making sure that all votes are accurately counted is a worthy goal, one supported by fundamental values such as political equality. But insofar as this or any of the efforts have been challenged, the controversy has centered not on fundamental values, but on questions such as who should pay for the reforms and whether they disproportionately benefit one political party. The deeper disagreements about the meaning of equality or liberty implied by the various reforms have been less often joined.

Nor can we count on philosophers to restore the moral dimension in the discussion of electoral justice. The suggestion that political procedures raise issues of substantive justice that are as contestable as ordinary legislation runs against the grain of the leading philosophical theories of justice. The most prominent philosopher of justice, John Rawls, defends a version of pure procedural justice that would place questions of electoral justice beyond the reach of ordinary political decision making.[22]

Rawls seeks agreement on broad procedural principles to establish the basic structure of society, and lets the remaining disagreements about substantive legislation work themselves out in the regular political process. As long as the basic structure is just, any outcome arrived at within it is just.[23]

The procedures defining the basic structure are substantive in the sense that they rest on fundamental moral values of the kind described earlier (free and equal personhood). But for the purposes of political deliberation, they are taken as given; they are not subject to contestation because they create the framework in which contestation takes place.[24] Rawls recognizes that the electoral process must satisfy basic standards of justice. Political justice requires that all citizens have "the right to take part in political affairs," and that elections are "fair and free, and regularly held."[25] But how these requirements are fulfilled—the specific rules that govern elections and the particular institutions in which they take place—should be considered matters of "political judgment" and best left to "political sociology."[26] This sharp dichotomy between rights and institutions, implicitly accepted by many theorists of justice, distorts electoral justice, both in what it excludes and what it includes.

By excluding questions of institutional design, the dichotomy obscures the fact that many decisions about procedures involve choices among fundamental values of justice. Many of the controversies analyzed in this book show how the choice of institutions depends on what conception of liberty or equality we adopt. Should candidates be permitted to be listed on the ballot under the label of more than one political party? That depends on whether in realizing free choice we should give priority to expanding the range of alternatives from which a voter chooses, or increasing the likelihood that the alternative the voter chooses will prevail. The controversies also often depend on larger institutional questions such as whether it is more important to encourage third parties or to preserve the two-party system. These decisions do not always involve a choice between just and unjust institutions, but they often pose a choice between institutions that are more or less just.

On the other side of the divide—the rights required by justice—the philosophical theories neglect the significance of the fact that the principles that express these rights call for interpretation. The interpretations often involve choices among conflicting values and usually turn on institutional considerations. The meanings of the principles, as well as their institutional implications, are largely indeterminate until we decide what kind of equality or liberty we wish to promote. Does political equality require that government take positive steps to provide incentives for citizens to vote, or only that it ensure that citizens are not denied the opportunity to vote? Does political liberty require that candidates should be free to spend whatever they wish on campaigns, or does it demand that campaign expenditures be limited so that voters and the electoral process are free from undue financial pressures? On both sides of the divide that these philosophers of justice assume, the electoral process poses substantive problems of justice. Any adequate set of principles of electoral justice will encourage citizens to choose among conflicting interpretations of equality, liberty, and sovereignty.

Democratic theory as deployed here in the midrange of political deliberation cannot resolve most of these conflicts. But it can identify the issues that should be subject to deliberation, clarify the moral values at stake, distinguish good from bad reasons offered in support of electoral practices, and establish some common ground for compromise or at least for more fruitful controversy. This kind of democratic theory can show that an institutional approach is more productive than others, and that criticisms that consider conceptions of representation are more justified than those based narrowly on individual rights or candidate competition. Finally, the principles of electoral justice can also support specific conclusions: registration procedures should be eased, campaign expenditures controlled, regulatory authority strengthened.

Some of the arguments in the chapters that follow are intended to show that a conclusion is subject to reasonable disagreement. Others are meant to demonstrate that even if a conclusion is subject to reasonable disagreement, it is on balance more justifiable than the alternatives. Still others aim to establish that a conclusion is the only reasonable alternative. All of these arguments, even those that support a single conclusion, should be considered part of an ongoing deliberation about electoral justice. They are reconstructions of deliberations past, contributions to deliberations present, and invitations to deliberations future.

The principles of electoral justice examined here furnish content for the deliberations in which citizens should engage, and provide a framework for the mutually justifiable reasons that citizens should give to one another. The interpretations of those principles challenge citizens and their representatives to face up to the conflicts of value that their electoral practices manifest, and to find ways to deal with the conflicts on terms that are mutually justifiable to all those who are bound by the results. Fully developed and reliably applied, the principles can afford a sound basis for criticizing and improving the procedures that constitute elections—whether they be unjust, or only less just than they could be.

ONE

Equal Respect
Why Votes Count

No American will ever be able to seriously say again,
"My vote doesn't count."
PRESIDENT BILL CLINTON, NOVEMBER 8, 2000

The presidential election of 2000 is destined to become a parable for civics classes and a chestnut in debates about rational choice approaches in political science. Neither role is fitting if the lesson is that any voter might decide the outcome of an election. Even in this election, the chances that any particular voter could make a difference were low, hardly great enough to be a compelling reason to vote. The deeper significance lies elsewhere: citizens certainly wanted their votes to count but many also simply wanted them counted. A week after the national election, the Palm Beach County canvassing board in Florida considered whether to conduct a recount. Outside the board's operations center a chanting crowd in the parking lot brandished signs that read "Count my vote" and "Why don't I count?"[1] No doubt some hoped that their votes might determine who would be president, but many also evidently were offended by the prospect that their ballots might be completely ignored. They seemed to feel that a refusal to count their votes would amount to a declaration that they did not count as citizens. It would be an affront to their civic standing. The signs were pointedly personal: count *my* vote; why don't *I* count?

The civic alienation that comes from having one's right to vote disregarded has been a potent force in the history of political movements seeking to extend the franchise. An important study of American thought on citizenship concludes that "[t]he deepest impulse for demanding the suffrage arises from the recognition that it is the characteristic, the identifying, feature of democratic citizenship in America, not a means to other ends."[2] The right to vote as an expression of civic standing remains a powerful part of the meaning of elections in this country. It provides the basis for the principle of equality that should govern the electoral process.

The value of political equality in the electoral process is best conveyed by a principle of equal respect. The principle rests on the fundamental idea (presented in the introduction) that the democratic process should respect all citizens as free and equal persons. The full meaning of the principle can be understood only by analyzing its applications in various institutional contexts, such as those examined in this chapter. But the core of the principle can be simply stated: the electoral process should provide citizens with equal opportunities to have their votes equally counted, unless respectful reasons justify unequal treatment. The reasons are respectful if they could be mutually accepted by free and equal citizens, and thus only if they affirm, or at least do not deny, the equal civic standing of citizens. For example, inequalities that result from geographical variation are acceptable to the extent that they do not create or reinforce other, unjustifiable social inequalities. Citizens have more control over where they live than over who they are, and where they live does not necessarily carry any irremediable stigma. But inequalities based on ascriptive characteristics such as race and gender are not acceptable unless they can be shown to benefit citizens disadvantaged because of their race or gender.

The principle of equal respect requires less than do the ideals of equality that theorists typically propose to define electoral justice.[3] The principle does not demand that all citizens have an equal right to determine the outcome of the political process. Nor does it require that electoral institutions grant citizens equal prospects of electoral success or even that all votes have equal weight, provided the unequal treatment can be justified.[4] The principle demands less because the meaning of electoral justice is less fixed than many theorists assume. Any adequate principle should make room for the possibility that the inequalities inherent in institutions such as the electoral college, the Senate, and more generally the federal structure of the American polity can be justified in terms that free and equal citizens could accept. By keeping this possibility open, the equal respect principle recognizes that reasonable disagreement about electoral justice is not only inevitable but also desirable.

Although it sets what might seem a minimal standard, the principle has significant substantive implications and considerable critical power. It draws attention to inequalities in the electoral process and demands that citizens and their representatives justify them if they can. It requires that departures from equality be justified in terms of equal respect. The justifications are part of the meaning of the principle and therefore part of the public meaning of institutions that promote or impede equal respect. Although the meaning of equal respect is not completely fixed in advance, disagreements about how it should be interpreted take place within a framework that recognizes the equal civic standing of all citizens.

We can begin to see the force of the principle of equal respect by examining some of the disagreements that arise in three different phases of the electoral process—casting votes, drawing districts, and counting ballots. Because the principle leaves open the possibility that inequalities may be justified, the disagreements focus more on the reasons that may be given for inequalities than on the inequalities themselves.[5] The central question is the meaning of electoral inequalities, not simply their presence or absence. Thus, in order to see what equal respect requires of our electoral institutions and how they fall short, we need to consider not merely what the institutions do, but what they express. We need to give attention to the public meanings of electoral institutions.

CASTING VOTES

The Constitution, a salient source of public meanings in the United States, does not grant anyone a right to vote. That is not a surprising omission in a document framed for a nation that restricted the franchise to white male property owners. But as the franchise was extended, the omission persisted. None of the amendments dealing with the voting rights of blacks, women, or those eighteen to twenty affirms a positive entitlement. They simply prohibit the states from using certain kinds of reasons to exclude such individuals from voting. In a landmark decision in 1966 banning poll taxes in state elections, the U.S. Supreme Court held that the equal protection clause of the Fourteenth Amendment prevents states from placing any restrictions on the franchise unless they can be justified by a compelling state interest.[6] Since few state interests can pass that test, few if any restrictions on voting can survive constitutional scrutiny. Yet even this decision did not establish an affirmative right to vote. The Constitution and its amendments still do not require the states to hold an election for any particular office except Congress. The Constitution in effect only says to the states: if you hold an election, you cannot exclude anyone unless you have a compelling justification.

The structure of public deliberation about voting rights mirrors that of constitutional discourse. The public debate centers on the meaning of equality, and its focus is on the reasons for excluding individuals from voting, rather than the reasons for including them. Although this negative orientation neglects the important positive values of the act of voting, it has the advantage of directing attention to the most appropriate subject for a principle of justice—the worst-off citizens. At least with respect to voting, those who are denied the vote are manifestly the worst off. More broadly, concentrating on the reasons for exclusion brings out what is distinctively wrong about being denied the right to vote or having one's vote disregarded. The wrong comes not only from the loss of benefits—the chance to influence the outcome or the satisfaction of fulfilling a civic obligation. Exclusion is unjust even if the excluded citizens never intended to vote in the election in question, and even if they did not expect their votes to make any difference to the outcome. Exclusion is unjust because it expresses a denial of equal respect. To see why this so, we need to examine the expressive dimension of both the act of voting and the institutions in which it takes place.

Expressive Voting

Why do people vote at all? Most citizens know that even in a close contest like the 2000 election, their own vote is not likely to determine the outcome. The most plausible explanations portray the decision to vote not as a rational calculation about the effects on the outcome, but as an "act of social participation or civic involvement."[7] The act of voting can be valuable for citizens, quite apart from its consequences for choosing or controlling representatives. Voters may take satisfaction simply in knowing (and perhaps in showing) that they have done their civic duty. The more that people participate in the process, the more likely they are to consider it fair.[8] More broadly, voters can find value in the act itself if it is part of a wider process of participation in which they constitute their identities as citizens.[9]

Beyond promoting these intrinsic values for the individual and society, elections serve important expressive purposes.[10] In two different but related ways elections express civic attitudes that are distinct from views about individual candidates and parties. First, they enable citizens to express attitudes about the political process. Whether and how citizens vote sends messages about what they think not only of the candidates, but also of the electoral institutions. Second, elections and electoral procedures also express the polity's attitude toward its citizens. The electoral process can be not only individually but also institutionally expressive.[11]

The expressivist view explains why citizens care about what happens to their vote even when they know that it will not make any difference to the outcome. The view may also explain why citizens who do not take the trouble to vote in an election would strenuously object if they were denied the opportunity to do so. But as a normative standard for individual voters, the expressivist view has been sharply criticized. Voting as self-expression seems to endorse the idea that giving vent to one's personal views and displaying a "righteous sense of commitment" is more important than caring about the substance of politics, the qualifications of candidates, or the merits of issues.[12] Responsible citizens, the critics say, should not regard their vote as an opportunity for self-expression but as an occasion for careful reflection on the consequences of the collective results of the election. Although an individual vote may not have significant consequences, voters have a duty to do their part in the collective enterprise. They are obligated to consider conscientiously the qualifications of the candidates and the substance of the issues.

The critics of the expressivist view are right to resist the implication that voting should in general be an occasion for venting personal feelings or registering protests. Some individual voters may be justified in using their vote for such purposes. Electoral justice requires that citizens have an opportunity to register protests. But voters are justified in using their votes in these ways only if most other voters are using it for the more conventional purpose of choosing among candidates. Protests lose part of their point—to challenge the attitudes that most citizens hold—if most citizens are protesting. More fundamentally, elections would cease to serve their primary purpose if most voters cast their ballot without regard to the comparative merits of candidates and parties. Elections are an "instrument of democracy" for choosing governments.[13] Providing the means for selecting representatives from among a slate of a candidates is one of their essential functions. If we were to adopt only one general prescription for individual voters, a decision-oriented perspective provides the better counsel: citizens should take their voting as seriously as if they were deciding the outcome of the election themselves. This perspective has the further advantage of emphasizing that voting is as much a duty as a right—a neglected aspect of its normative status considered later in this chapter.

Although the expressivist view is not the best guide for specifying the general duties of individual citizens, it is an indispensable approach for understanding the justice of electoral institutions. Elections are not only instruments for choosing governments; they are also media for sending messages about the democratic process. We can bring out more clearly the significance of the expressivist function of elections by looking at the constraints that institutions place on what voters can say on their ballots, and then in more depth at the restrictions on who can vote and how they are represented.

Consider an electoral practice that constrains what voters can express—prohibiting the counting of write-in votes. Why shouldn't a voter be able to record a write-in for anyone at all—even (say) Donald Duck? The question is not as fanciful as the character: Donald Duck has "a long and distinguished history as the exasperated voter's candidate of choice."[14] Yet the Supreme Court upheld a Hawaii prohibition on write-in votes that prevented a voter from declaring Donald Duck as his choice for the state's House of Representatives. The voter wished to protest the actual choices he was offered. (Typically, the Democratic candidates in Hawaii run unopposed, and many voters cast blank ballots.) When state officials told him that his write-in vote for Donald Duck could not be counted, he sued.

One reason that a prohibition on write-ins is objectionable is that it restricts voters' choice. As the dissenting justices in the Hawaii case wrote, because "late-breaking" information may become available too late for other candidates to qualify for the ballot, "allowing write-in voting is the only way to preserve the voters' right to cast a meaningful vote in the general election."[15] The next chapter returns to the issue of restricting voters' choice. But the dispute about write-ins also turns significantly on the role of expressive voting. In upholding Hawaii's prohibition, the Court majority argued that "the function of the election process is to 'winnow out and finally reject all but the chosen candidates,' not to provide a means of giving vent to 'short-range political goals, pique or personal quarrels.'"[16] This argument sounds like the same objection to the expressivist view mentioned earlier, and therefore might seem to have the same force. The Court majority, however, make a broader claim. They are not arguing merely that voters should not generally use the ballot to express protests. They are supporting an institutional practice that prevents all voters from expressing any protests of this kind. Further, they are defending a practice that sends a message about institutional priorities—that preserving an existing party system has priority over publicizing the views of dissenting minorities.

If we recognize the expressivist function of elections, we can object to the Hawaiian write-in prohibition on two grounds (corresponding to the two expressivist purposes mentioned earlier). The prohibition prevents voters from expressing their views about institutions, and it supports an institution that itself expresses an objectionable view about institutions. The prohibition and the institutional message it sends are objectionable because they disregard the requirements of equal respect. Restricting write-ins and reinforcing dominant parties over disaffected minorities fail to respect disadvantaged citizens. In this case, the disaffected minorities were citizens frustrated by the long-standing dominance of the Democratic party in their state and the almost impossible hurdles that independent candidates faced. In general, ballot constraints of this kind disproportionately burden minorities who are usually already disadvantaged in other ways. They also deprive the political system of information that can reveal legitimate discontent among minorities and that can help initiate needed policies to rectify unequal opportunities in the society.[17]

Even more important than the institutional meaning of restrictions on what can be expressed is the meaning of restrictions on whose expression should be recognized. Rules that make people ineligible to vote call into question their status as full members of the polity. Electoral institutions signal not only whose votes should count, but who should count. When citizens or people who should be citizens are formally excluded, they are stigmatized. Reflecting on his efforts to end the disenfranchisement of blacks in the nineteenth century, Frederick Douglass wrote: "To rule us out is to make us an exception, to brand us with the stigma of inferiority."[18] Rules that exclude, implicitly or explicitly, tell the excluded they do not count.

Lingering Inequalities

The end of formal exclusion finally came, but only after a long struggle. The history of suffrage in the United States is not a story of gradual reform and inevitable progress, as it has often been portrayed in patriotic speeches and even in scholarly works.[19] The movement for universal suffrage did not precisely observe Alexis de Tocqueville's "invariable rule of social behavior," which predicted that once concessions are made to one group, they "follow one another without interruption."[20] The progress was fitful: gains won in one decade were sometimes taken away in the next.[21] But if Tocqueville was wrong about the contours of this historical curve, he was right about its endpoint: "sooner or later" the people would completely abolish the "voting qualification" (though the end came later rather than sooner).

Tocqueville was also right about the moral logic of the movement toward universal suffrage. The fewer the people who continue to be excluded, the harder it is to justify their exclusion. "The ambition of those left below the qualifying limit increases in proportion to the number of those above it."[22] The progress is driven not by power alone, for in his account the success of the excluded mounts as their numbers decline. An essential factor must be the moral force of their claim—the increasing difficulty of finding respectful reasons for exclusion. We can see something of this same moral dynamic at work in the more subtle forms of exclusion that persist in the electoral process today.

Now that universal suffrage has generally triumphed, our electoral process no longer blatantly "rules out" the largest groups directly or indirectly excluded in the past—women and blacks. Its rules of eligibility no longer declare that women and blacks do not count at all. Two significant groups nevertheless remain disenfranchised. The largest group of citizens still denied the right to vote is convicted felons.[23] One study estimates that the laws excluding felons disenfranchised nearly 5 million citizens.[24] The traditional justifications for their exclusion—felons have broken the social compact and they are not virtuous citizens—do not seem compelling.[25] They do not support the permanent ban that many states, including Florida, have enacted. Once felons have served their sentences, they should surely regain their right to vote.

Even if some restrictions on felons could be justified in principle, the effects in practice are likely to violate equal respect. The ban on felons falls disproportionately on blacks and Hispanics. In Florida as many as 30 percent of all black males in the state may have been denied the right to vote because of their criminal records.[26] Many other citizens who had no criminal records were denied the right to vote in 2000 because their names mistakenly appeared on lists of felons compiled by private corporations and used by state officials to purge the voting roles.[27] Again, blacks suffered disproportionately.

Another large group affected by the outcome of elections but excluded from participating is resident aliens.[28] Their claim to participate is challenged because citizenship is generally assumed to be a prerequisite for voting. To enjoy the right to take part in making decisions for the community, it is said, one should be a full member; one must accept the responsibilities along with the rights of membership. Neither the federal government nor the states permit noncitizens to vote in their elections.

Yet resident aliens pay taxes, hold jobs, own businesses, and sometimes even serve in the military. In some cities they are permitted to vote in school board elections. Several towns in Maryland, notably Tacoma Park, have extended the franchise to resident aliens. In Europe where nations once jealously reserved the vote for their own citizens, the growing interdependence and increasingly porous borders have loosened the connection between citizenship and the franchise. Citizens of any member state in the European Union can now vote in most local elections of any other member state in which they reside.[29] In the Scandinavian countries immigrants who meet rather minimal residency requirements may vote in local elections. As the number of resident aliens increase and their contributions to the economy and society grow, the United States will find it harder to justify denying them the right to participate in choosing the leaders who govern them.

Exclusion persists not only in the laws that deny some individuals the right to vote, but also in the practices that discourage the exercise of that right. Now that poll taxes and language tests are prohibited, the most visible barriers to the exercise of the right to vote have disappeared. But the message the electoral process sends is not yet one of equal respect. In most elections less than half the electorate turns out. More disturbing from the perspective of equal respect, those who do not vote come disproportionately from socially and economically disadvantaged groups.[30] The poor, the young, and those who did not finish high school vote less often than the well-to-do, the retired, and the college educated.

But do these turnout patterns prove that the electoral process itself fails to show equal respect toward specific groups of voters? Some defenders of current practices may object that the patterns show only that some citizens do not wish to exercise their right to vote. The objection implies that even if the disparities in turnout lead to public policies that disadvantage some groups, we should not blame the electoral system. To suppose otherwise— to suggest that the problem is the system rather than the citizens who fail to vote—is to show disrespect toward the nonvoters. Citizens are responsible for exercising their right to vote. If they choose not to vote, their decision should be respected. We acknowledge their standing as equal moral agents, their equal capacity to make choices equally as their fellow citizens, by accepting their decision not to participate.

This objection has the appropriate moral form, but it neglects a salient empirical fact. The opportunities to exercise the right to vote are not equal—and not only because the general background conditions in society enable some groups to participate more easily and effectively than others. If this general injustice were the only problem, it could not be attributed to the electoral process alone. But the rules governing the process themselves undermine equal opportunity and create barriers that disproportionately affect certain groups. The most significant formal barrier is one of the seemingly most innocuous—the requirement that each citizen must register before voting. A perfectly reasonable rule, it is intended—let us charitably assume—to make elections more honest and efficient.[31] But the rule may also make elections less inclusive. Some evidence indicates that registration requirements contribute to low turnout.[32] More important, the burdens they create fall disproportionately on citizens who are poorer, less educated, and in other respects less well-off—the same people who are already less likely to vote.[33]

If the rules of the electoral system themselves are partly responsible for these unequal patterns of voting, then the system cannot be said to express equal respect for all voters. The disrespect is not explicit, as it is when the system formally excludes some citizens. But implicit messages are no less a significant part of institutional meanings. The implicit message of these patterns of voting is clear enough if we consider the institutional context in which they occur. The unequal voting is the product of rules that could be changed. They violate equal respect not only because they deny some citizens equal opportunities to participate, but also because they send the message that their fellow citizens are indifferent to the persistence of this inequality, and do not care enough to try to remove the barriers that sustain it. (The expressive argument thus goes beyond the objection based on the value of participation: the institution expresses disrespect toward disadvantaged citizens even when they manage to overcome the barriers and cast a vote.)

To avoid sending a message of disrespect, why not simply abolish registration? Most other democracies have far fewer requirements than the United States, and higher turnout. Several smaller U.S. states have same-day registration, and one state (North Dakota) has no registration requirement at all.[34] Even if we grant that registration may serve a valid function in preventing fraud, or at least providing greater assurance that all the votes cast are valid, we may still ask why registration should not be made more convenient.

Making registration more convenient and voting thereby more prevalent is the aim of the National Voter Registration Act, the so-called motor voter law. Since 1995 this law has required states to give citizens the opportunity to register when applying for a driver's license or visiting any of several types of government offices, such as those dealing with welfare, disability services, and military recruitment.[35] The Act was finally passed only after months of partisan squabbling, and only after overcoming both a presidential veto and a Senate filibuster. Why should such a seemingly high-minded, good-government reform provoke so much acrimony? Even Senator Mitch McConnell, the Republican from Kentucky who led the opposition to the bill, declared: "The concept of motor voter, as we all know, is noble."[36]

The concept may be noble, but the consequences most members expected were not so welcome to Republicans. Most Republicans believed, along with most Democrats, that the Act would lead to higher turnout— but mostly of Democratic voters. The belief that higher turnout would help the Democrats more than the Republicans has little basis in experience, and runs contrary to the findings of most political scientists.[37] Nonvoters are not very different from voters in partisan allegiances or political opinions. Also, newly registered voters in the south tend to be more Republican than long-time registered voters; more generally, they tend to be more independent (which does not favor the Democrats) and younger (which favors the Republicans).[38] Nevertheless, the assumption that easing the registration requirements would advantage the Democrats has influenced the dynamics of electoral reform since the nineteenth century, and continued to shape the partisan positions in the motor voter controversy. Some Republicans voted for the final bill, but only after they secured major concessions that they hoped would diminish the Democratic gains from the reform. Welfare and unemployment offices were removed from, and military recruitment offices were added to, the list of government agencies at which voters could register.

Yet it is not the partisan motivations but the justifications partisans gave for their positions that are significant for interpreting the meaning of the equal protection principle. Not surprisingly, members did not want to have to appeal to partisan advantages to justify their positions. In fact, few accused their opponents of having partisan motives, presumably because their opponents could have easily turned the charge back against them. In the Senate debate, only Phil Gramm explicitly made the charge, and even he limited it to only one aspect of the bill—the proposal to include unemployment and welfare agencies but not tax agencies on the list.[39] Deprived of the partisan arguments, both sides faced a problem of justification: neither wished to give the other side a partisan advantage, but neither wished to imply that it was against equal participation by all citizens.

The Republicans in Congress initially faced the greater challenge: How could they possibly justify opposing a bill that would allow more citizens to exercise their right to vote? They offered two main arguments. First, they revived the traditional concern about fraud—but now directed it against illegal aliens. Illegal aliens have a strong incentive to commit fraud, they said, because a voter identification card is especially valuable to people without adequate documentation, who can use it to apply for many other benefits.[40] The fraud argument was less persuasive than it had been in the past. As several senators pointed out, many states had eased their registration requirements (some had even adopted a motor voter plan), and none (even those with relatively large numbers of illegal aliens) had reported any increase in electoral fraud.

But to the extent that the fraud argument carried any weight, its proponents evidently did not think it could stand alone. They felt it necessary to add an objection of inequality to the charge of corruption. It is not the fraud as such but the "dilution" of the votes of honest legal citizens that they found most objectionable. The "plundering of the voting rolls by those who are not entitled to vote" denies those who are so entitled their equal standing under the law.[41]

Members seemed even less comfortable putting forward their second argument by itself—the claim that the reforms would impose excessive costs on the states. The claim was credible enough: the reforms would cost more money, the federal government would not pay any of the costs, and many of the states had already found alternative ways to accomplish the same objective. But simply to declare that protecting the opportunity to vote was costly did not seem sufficiently high-minded. So Senator McConnell argued that funds allocated to voter registration would have to come from other programs, especially those that benefit the disadvantaged. Invoking the words of a former Democratic governor (Bill Clinton!), McConnell implied that the states may find themselves "cutting back on important educational initiatives, closing county hospitals, unable to fund increases in cash assistance levels and slashing . . . programs that provide . . . services to our low-income citizens."[42]

Democrats had the advantage of seeming to be on the side of expanding voting opportunities for all citizens, but the Republicans spotted an opening to challenge their opponents on their own ground. Democrats found themselves struggling to find reasons to oppose some Republican-inspired extensions to the bill—in particular an amendment that would require automatic registration of military inductees. (Both Republicans and Democrats assumed military personnel were more likely to vote Republican.) Senator John McCain, the sponsor of the amendment, argued: "The men and women who serve in the military should be given every opportunity to register to vote and to vote. The same opportunities that any nonserving citizen of this country will possess under this legislation."[43] How could anyone oppose this appeal to equal opportunity? Senator Wendell Ford, the sponsor of the main bill, admitted that opposing voting opportunities for the military would be like "voting against heaven, home, motherhood, and apple pie."[44]

Senator Ford found what he may have thought an apple-pie argument of his own against this amendment. Automatic registration "takes away from individuals their choice of whether to register or not. It takes away . . . responsibility."[45] The value of individual or personal responsibility underlying this argument is widely accepted and often invoked by advocates on both sides of public policy disputes. As we have already seen, it can and has been used to oppose any easing of registration requirements. It also reared its head in the legal controversies over the 2000 presidential election. An unusually strong assumption about the value of individual responsibility lay behind the claim that only votes not recorded because of mechanical failure should be recounted. Voters who did not remove the hanging chads, who were confused by the butterfly ballot, or in other ways did not follow instructions should not have their votes counted, even if their voting intentions could be clearly discerned. They were deemed to have disqualified themselves "by their own actions."[46]

In the motor voter debate, Senator Ford's appeal to individual responsibility served his purpose—to defeat the special provision for military inductees. But the appeal is justified only if it is coupled with an equality principle. The fact that the amendment would have limited the choices of only a certain class of citizens (military inductees) is critical to the argument. Individual responsibility cannot stand alone, and indeed is misleading without an equality principle.

Consider more closely the steps in the argument from individual responsibility. The argument begins with claims about moral agency. We respect persons as free and equal moral agents by granting them the opportunity to make choices on their own. We disrespect persons by depriving them of the opportunity to make choices, even if the choices we make for them are for their own good, and even if they are likely to make the wrong choices. If we prevent them from choosing not to register, we in effect act as electoral paternalists; we violate their autonomy as moral agents.

If the proponents of the argument were to stop at this point, they would have proved too much. The conclusion would risk undermining any attempt to ease registration requirements and would call into question most efforts to expand voting and other forms of participation. The argument seems to imply that the more individual responsibility we permit our fellow citizens to exercise in overcoming obstacles, the more respect we show toward them. The implication may even follow that we show disrespect toward our fellow citizens if we seek to remove barriers to their exercise of voting rights. This begins to sound like a "tough love" theory of moral respect.

To be sure, there is a difference between eliminating some obstacles to voting (for example by abolishing poll taxes) and eliminating all obstacles (by instituting automatic registration). But the difference is a matter of degree. Citizens are not deprived of any important choice by a system of automatic registration. Such a system still gives voters choices: they can renounce their registration, and they also can decline to vote. Even if automatic registration is considered an interference with moral autonomy, its effect seems minor compared to the increase in autonomy that comes from removing a structural obstacle to voting. Some of the measures required to implement automatic registration, such as national identity cards, may pose a threat to personal privacy and therefore to autonomy, but effective protections could be designed specifically to protect against such consequences.

The more general problem with the argument is that it interprets individual responsibility too narrowly. Exercising individual responsibility is not only a matter of acting alone, overcoming difficult challenges, or making hard choices. Individual responsibility can be demonstrated by choosing to act together with other citizens to restrict some of one's choices for the sake of expanding others. The next chapter considers whether such restrictions on choices can actually promote the value of free choice, but it should be clear that even if automatic registration eliminates a choice, it does not eliminate individual responsibility. Citizens can responsibly decide together that preserving the option not to register is less important than facilitating the opportunity to vote. In this way, citizens can be individually responsible by making their democracy more institutionally responsible.

Had Senator Ford (and the other opponents of the automatic registration for military inductees) explicitly invoked an equality principle instead of the value of individual responsibility, they would have been on stronger moral ground (and at less risk of undermining the general effort to ease barriers to voting). The objection should have been to the unequal application of the rule. If automatic registration is considered an advantage to citizens, then providing it only to some citizens (even those as worthy as military inductees) is inequitable. Even if automatic registration were to be regarded as a disadvantage because it takes away individual responsibility, then providing it to only certain groups in effect declares that some citizens are less equal as moral agents, and less capable of carrying out their responsibilities as citizens. In either case, an appeal to a principle of equal respect is necessary.

The difficulty that both sides in this debate found in opposing the easing of registration requirements shows the power of the principle of equal respect. Neither the arguments from corruption and cost nor the argument from individual responsibility could alone justify this opposition, and the opponents recognized the need to appeal to the value of equality. Even with an equality principle the opponents' arguments were not sufficient. The principle of equal respect, we have seen, most readily lends itself to justifying the expansion of opportunities to vote. Compared to previous practices, simplified registration is more consistent with a principle of equal respect. The motor voter law is surely justifiable from the perspective of that principle.

Yet the principle of equal respect demands more than either side in this debate was willing to support. The motor voter law may in fact still be biased against less advantaged citizens. Because lower class citizens in some urban areas are less likely to hold drivers' licenses, "motor voter programs . . . expand the electorate without overcoming its upward class skew, a feature that may explain why both Republicans and Democrats sometimes support them."[47] Offering registration at public assistance agencies partly compensated for the class bias, but racial disparities remain.[48] Also, some states have moved more aggressively in making registration available at motor vehicle departments than they have at public assistance agencies.[49] Restoring welfare offices to the list of agencies where citizens may register could help alleviate this bias. A national system to maintain the registration of people who move would increase turnout generally, and reduce somewhat the bias against younger citizens.[50] But more radical measures—such as implementing automatic registration in both federal and state elections—may also be necessary.

Beyond Registration

The motor voter law and other efforts to relax registration requirements have not stemmed the decline in voting turnout.[51] Many reformers therefore seek to go beyond registration, and make voting itself easier. We should not, however, try to imitate the registration reforms too closely. Increasing opportunities to register by mail or on the Internet, provided that sufficient protections against fraud are in place, is a sensible reform. Increasing the opportunities to vote by mail or on the Internet, even with adequate protections, is more questionable.[52]

Opportunities for early voting have significantly increased in recent years. Voting before election day has nearly doubled since 1980.[53] In Oregon all statewide elections have used a mail-in ballot since 1995. In the 2000 presidential election, a quarter of the California vote and two-fifths of the Texas vote was by absentee ballot. Absentee voting can promote equal respect insofar as it facilitates participation by citizens who would otherwise have difficulty in going to the polls on election day—especially some older voters, disabled persons, and members of the armed forces. It also gives voters more time to mark their ballots, and thus enables them to think more carefully about their decisions, enhancing free choice.

However, the availability of absentee voting increases turnout only modestly if at all.[54] Moreover, unrestricted absentee voting could reduce voter participation by discouraging efforts to mobilize voter turnout. Also, the effects are not equally distributed. Whites are twice as likely as blacks to vote by absentee ballot. Even if absentee voting generally increased turnout, expanding the practice significantly would still be problematic. Unlike registration, voting should take place more or less simultaneously. When citizens go to the polls on the same day, visibly and publicly participating in the same way in a common experience of civic engagement, they demonstrate their willingness to contribute on equal terms to the democratic process. Walking to the polling station and standing in line with one's neighbors may not be one of the most exciting moments in life, but election-day voting serves an important expressive purpose. It enables citizens to express their commitment to a common project in which they participate on equal terms—the process of choosing the leaders who will represent them. The public affirmation is quite different in meaning from the private transaction of filling out and mailing in an absentee ballot. In addition to this expressive value, such activities can contribute in modest ways to the development of the capacities of equal citizenship. Participating openly with others is more likely to reinforce civic attitudes than is voting alone at home.

Early voting could weaken equal respect in yet another way. Equal respect implies that voters should have access to more or less the same kind of information when they make their choices. Although absentee ballots are sealed until election day, absentee voters usually mark their ballot much earlier than everyone else. They have less (or different) information than election-day voters have. No doubt many election-day voters make up their minds early, but they at least have the opportunity to change them. Perhaps absentee voters themselves should not be said to suffer any harm, since they choose to vote early. But some election-day voters may be disadvantaged by the actions of the early voters. If some of the early voters would have voted differently in light of late-breaking information and changed the outcome of the election, the like-minded regular voters might well complain that their own votes did not count as much as they would have. The next chapter further explains the importance of the simultaneous character of elections, but it should be clear that a broad expansion of absentee voting could erode that character and undermine equal respect.

If the electoral system is to realize more fully the value of equal respect, we need to find ways to increase not only the opportunities to vote but also the incidence of voting among groups who now disproportionately fail to participate. Equal respect is more likely to be fulfilled insofar as the actual distribution of voting is more equal. Yet in the debate about registration, as in virtually all the earlier controversies about the expansion of the suffrage, both sides assumed that the law should seek to make opportunities for voting, not actual voting, more equal. Almost no one has seriously proposed compulsory voting, as in Australia and Belgium, where turnouts of over 90 percent are common. No one has strongly pressed for payments to voters, or even government-sponsored get-out-the-vote campaigns.[55] No one has actively explored the proposal to increase turnout by offering inducements such as lottery tickets.[56] We have not even been willing to take the simple step of declaring election day a national holiday or holding elections on weekends, as many other democracies do.[57] If we are committed to equal respect, why do we not take such proposals more seriously?

In the American political culture, proposals of this kind have not won much support partly because voting is still considered more an individual right than an institutional duty or public trust. On this view, citizens should have the right to vote, but no one, certainly not the government, should compel, induce, or even actively encourage anyone to vote. This view contrasts with the classic liberal view expressed John Stuart Mill: voting is not a right but a "trust" because it is the exercise of "power over others." If we treat voting as a right, he asks, "on what ground can we blame [the voter] for selling it?"[58] We might reasonably resist Mill's view if it implies, as he seems to suggest, that everyone's votes should be public and better educated citizens should be granted extra votes.[59] But these implications do not necessarily follow from the view of voting as a public trust. As Mill himself recognized, the open ballot and plural voting may not be necessary or desirable in some social and political circumstances.[60] We can regard voting as both a right and a trust: citizens have a right to vote, but they should exercise it responsibly.

Recognizing a right to vote might still seem to entail that citizens have a right not to vote. If so, some critics would object that compulsory voting undermines individual responsibility. This objection is similar to the argument already considered against easing registration requirements, and can be answered in a similar way. Compulsory voting removes one opportunity for exercising responsibility (deciding to vote), but replaces it with another (deciding how to vote). Citizens can reasonably determine together that requiring everyone to accept the responsibility for deciding how to vote is more important than permitting some to exercise their responsibility in deciding whether to vote at all. Compulsory voting does restrict choice, but (as the next chapter shows) the principle of free choice does not preclude deciding to limit some choices for the purpose of enhancing others. Furthermore, compulsory voting provides an opportunity for expressing a stronger protest than is possible in a voluntary system: citizens can more clearly demonstrate their opposition by publicly accepting a penalty for not voting.

The proposal to pay people for voting (directly or indirectly) raises a further issue—what is sometimes called the commodification objection. Commenting on a lottery a candidate offered as a way of increasing turnout, a state supreme court observed that "such a scheme encourages the electorate, whose motivation to vote should be a sense of civic duty, to go to the polls out of an ignoble desire for short-term financial enrichment."[61] The vote is turned into a commodity, something to be bought and sold on the market, and the act of voting marks the conclusion of a market transaction rather than the fulfillment of civic responsibility.[62]

The commodification objection is overstated. Paying citizens to vote is not the same as permitting them to sell their votes. It does not turn the act of voting into a commodity that can be bought and sold on the market. A citizen does not have any choice about where or when to sell the service or on what terms. Payments in the amounts (or lottery tickets with the odds) that are usually offered are not likely to be great enough to cancel out the civic motive. Most payments do not radically change the meaning of the act; compensated voting still expresses a willingness to participate in a common enterprise on equal terms with one's fellow citizens. Citizens are compensated for jury duty, but they are still praised for doing their civic duty. Indirect compensation for voting is already common, and does not seem adversely to affect its civic meaning. Many states give public employees time off to vote, and some require private employers to do the same. Political parties provide in-kind compensation for voting—transportation, child care, and even tickets to postelection entertainment.[63] Like most acts, voting is done with mixed motives, and it may express many different attitudes. If a scheme on balance enhances equal respect, we should not reject it simply because part of the motive or part of its meaning is pecuniary.

None of these objections is fatal to proposals that promote equal respect by easing registration requirements or mandating voting. Neither does the principle of equal respect require any of these particular schemes. Other better ways of achieving the same objective may be found. Furthermore, reasonable differences of opinion exist about how much equality the government should promote. How much more than mere opportunity should be sought? What kind and degree of incentives are appropriate to offer voters? These and similar questions cannot reasonably be decided without further empirical inquiry and political deliberation.

The principle of equal respect can play an important role in assessing whether elections are just in the United States. On the most plausible interpretations of the principle, registration practices and turnout patterns fall short of what equal respect requires. The principle rules out some common practices, such as burdensome registration requirements, and it looks with favor on others, such as a national holiday for elections. Even when the principle does not dictate any particular solution to problems it identifies, it sets some of the terms of the ongoing democratic deliberation. More generally, it reminds us that in defending or criticizing the electoral process we should take into account its institutional as well as its individual dimensions. The reasons given to justify or criticize proposals to change the process should recognize that individual responsibility does not preclude individual collaboration in designing shared institutional practices. Our justifications should also recognize that electoral institutions, as well as the act of voting itself, are not narrowly instrumental devices for choosing and controlling political leaders, but also broadly expressive structures for creating and sustaining political meanings. The meanings the institutions express become more transparent the more we deliberate together about their justice.

DRAWING DISTRICTS

Most citizens in the United States vote in districts, which must be more or less equal in population. This requirement of just elections has been recognized since the earliest days of representative government. Writing in the seventeenth century, John Locke observed that "in tract of time this representation becomes very unequal and disproportionate to the reasons it was at first established upon," and counseled that the electoral system be reformed from time to time so that the "people shall choose their representatives upon just and undeniably equal measures."[64] Locke argued that even in a parliamentary system where the legislature is sovereign, the executive (which in his theory included the judiciary) should have the authority to carry out such reforms if necessary to achieve justice.

The American judiciary did not immediately accept Locke's counsel. It was not until 1962 that the Supreme Court ventured into the political thicket of reapportionment, but once inside, the Court created a revolution. In a series of bold decisions beginning with *Baker v. Carr* in 1962, the Court established clearly and decisively "one person, one vote" as the standard for assessing the justice of electoral districts.[65] The malapportioned districts, whether the result of population shifts or deliberate design, violated the equal protection clause of the Fourteenth Amendment. Virtually every state was forced to redraw its electoral boundaries.

As significant as this standard has been for the American electoral system, it raises more questions than it answers. It has been more readily accepted than might have been expected because it says less than might have been hoped. Contrary to what some critics charge, it did not replace the Madis-

onian with a majoritarian conception of democracy in which a single faction (the majority) makes the laws.[66] Madisonian interest group politics—
factions checking factions—thrives no less in a system of equal districts
than in a system of unequal districts, though some groups may do better
in one than in the other.[67] The equal population standard can also encourage partisan gerrymandering, another manifestation of factionalism. More
generally, the standard as applied does not say that every vote should count
equally in all elections. It does not call into question, for example, the individual inequality produced by the equal representation of the states in the
Senate, or the institutional inequality inherent in the electoral college.[68] But
even limited to redistricting, it contained within itself the seeds of another
electoral revolution. As the debate turned again to race, the shape of the districts became the focal point for the continuing conflict over the meaning
of electoral equality, and how electoral institutions express it.

The Shape of the District

Once officials must redraw the boundaries of districts to make them more
equal in population, they need a standard for choosing among the almost
indefinite number of ways of carving up a state that are consistent with this
aim. "One person, one vote" is not very helpful in making these choices.
Strictly interpreted as requiring every vote to count equally, it would prohibit patterns that give any category of voter more weight than any other;
only a random distribution would be acceptable. Even in random redistricting, votes would not be weighted equally for most categories because
people do not distribute themselves randomly among districts. Interpreted
more permissively, as it has been in practice, the standard allows officials to
take into account some of the factors that have traditionally determined the
boundaries of districts—such as geographical features, historical communities, partisan advantage, and even incumbency protection. Armed with
powerful computer technology scarcely imagined at the time the standard
was proposed, politicians can now create equal districts that give more
weight to any of a wide range of different categories.

The courts have usually not found fault with redistricting plans that took
these traditional factors into account, even when the result clearly advantaged some groups. The Supreme Court has said that partisan gerrymandering might violate equal protection, but set the standard for a violation
so high that no complaint is ever likely to succeed.[69] Racial gerrymandering is another matter, however. No one today would defend deliberately

designing districts to disadvantage blacks or other minorities. That would be rightly accepted as a clear violation of any plausible principle of equal respect (as well as the Constitution). The more controversial issue—and much of the electoral litigation of the past decade—turns on the question of the extent to which states may create districts with a majority of black voters.[70] To avoid the racially discriminatory results prohibited by the Voting Rights Act, racial districting is sometimes necessary.[71] But courts forbid using race as the predominant factor in drawing districts. States must use race, but not too much.

The litigation has therefore been exquisitely complex; most of the decisions have been closely divided. Much disagreement remains not only about the right conclusion but also about which considerations should be relevant in reaching a conclusion. As the state officials undertook the challenging task of redistricting after the 2000 census, many believed that the court decisions had "created confusion, uncertainty and immense new difficulties."[72] Judicial opinions therefore cannot be taken as an account of an emerging consensus, or a guide to what most Americans think equal respect means in redistricting. But along with democratic theory they provide some indication of the range of reasonable disagreement about its meaning, and what issues should be addressed as citizens continue to deliberate about its meaning.

From the perspective of democratic theory, the factors that officials consider when creating electoral districts fall into three distinct groups. First, territorial factors (such as geographical divisions) are legitimate criteria because districts should be compact enough to enable representatives to meet in person with their constituents.[73] These criteria have less weight than in the past, when travel and communication were more difficult. Another reason for deferring to geography—to preserve the sense of community and common interest that some districts enjoy—has also become less relevant as citizens move easily in and out of districts and live and work in different districts. Indeed, some theorists question whether territorial divisions are relevant any more at all. Those who favor systems of proportional representation in legislative elections would completely eliminate districts, and permit citizens in effect to form their own constituencies.[74] Other writers suggest that the Internet opens new possibilities for political representation by enabling people to become "more connected with one another along dimensions other than physical proximity."[75] Nevertheless, it would be difficult to argue that equal respect actually prohibits territorial divisions. On their face, they do not declare some people less worthy than others. Treating people differently who live in different places does not usually deny them equal respect. Nor do territorial divisions restrict anyone's liberty. The very mobility that makes them less relevant also makes them less oppressive.[76]

The second set of factors are partisan: districts are drawn to protect the party in power and the seats of incumbents. Historically, the party fortunate enough to control the state legislature controlled the redistricting required after each decennial census. In most states, the legislature still has the most important role; even in most of the states that have created redistricting commissions, parties choose at least some of the members.[77] What is wrong with partisan gerrymandering? In some circumstances, arguably nothing. Control over redistricting is one of the fruits of political victory, and a party's using the control to its advantage is no more objectionable than its using majority power to appoint permanent judges, enact laws with long-term effects, or commit the government to binding contracts.

But the acceptability of partisan redistricting depends on its taking place in a fluid political process in which those out of power can effectively challenge those in power. The assumption is that the opposition has a fair chance to win control later and, if they succeed, then to take their turn at redrawing the district boundaries to their advantage. If the assumption does not hold—if the opposition's chances are indefinitely blocked by partisan gerrymandering—the vitality of the political process suffers. The potential ailments are several: less accountability as representatives take their reelection for granted; less responsiveness as representatives discount the demands of constituents identified with the rival party; less diversity as single parties, ideologies, or groups dominate; and less legitimacy as the permanent losers become increasingly alienated. Electoral institutions become congested, desirable change is impeded, and democratic representation is impaired.

Individual citizens generally experience these infirmities as a diminution of their political liberty. Partisan gerrymandering thus can breach the principle of free choice (the subject of chapter 2). It may also undermine popular sovereignty (the subject of chapter 3) insofar as it involves politicians' choosing their own constituents. But for all its ills, partisan gerrymandering does not by itself violate the principle of equal respect.[78] As long as more than one party exists, the parties are open to all members, and none of the major parties is exclusively identified with a minority group, gerrymandering that makes some parties temporarily more powerful than others does not declare some citizens less worthy than others.[79]

The third set of factors—often called ascriptive—do raise problems of equal respect. Ascriptive characteristics such as race differ from geographical location and partisan affiliation in two respects. First, they are morally arbitrary in the sense that they are the product of natural processes over which the persons to whom they are ascribed have little or no control. Using such characteristics as a basis for assigning any kind of status within the political process runs the risk of transmitting the arbitrariness to the process itself. Without a compelling further argument, the process would treat some people differently from others for no respectful reason.

Second, some kinds of ascriptive characteristics have been the basis for persistent and systematic discrimination in the past. Again race is the most prominent example.[80] Past racial discrimination could supply the reason that removes the arbitrariness of using this ascriptive characteristic. But that reason cuts in two directions, and thereby poses a dilemma. If we use race for designing electoral districts, we perpetuate racial stereotypes and thereby send the message that race matters more than common citizenship. But if we refuse to use race, we perpetuate the disproportionately white racial composition of the legislature and thereby send the message that one race deserves to have more political power than another. Unless we resolve the dilemma by rejecting one of these interpretations, our electoral system will fail to show equal respect toward some of its citizens.

Which Message?

The dilemma shows itself clearly—and in its expressive form—in *Shaw v. Reno*, the first in a series of cases in the 1990s that confronted the question of the constitutionality of majority-minority districts. Writing for the Court's five-member majority, Justice O'Connor held that redistricting may be challenged as a violation of equal protection if it can only be rationally interpreted as a scheme to "segregate voters" on the basis of their race.[81] At issue were two bizarrely shaped districts in North Carolina, both created to increase the chances of electing black members to Congress.[82] To explain what is wrong with such schemes, she in effect invoked the expressive function of the electoral system.[83] Racial redistricting carried to such extremes "reinforces the perception" that blacks "think alike" and thus perpetuates "racial stereotypes." Furthermore, "the message that such districting sends to elected representatives" is that "their primary obligation is to represent only the members of that group, rather than their constituency as a whole. This is altogether antithetical to our system of representative democracy."[84]

How can the mere shape of a district send such a message? Although "appearances do matter," they cannot alone constitute the expressive meaning of an action or, in this case, an electoral scheme. O'Connor comes close to saying that the bizarre shape alone sends the message, but her interpretation of the meaning of the scheme must take for granted some knowledge of why the scheme was created and how it is likely to work. The electoral scheme is not visible in the way that segregated swimming pools or drinking fountains are. Most citizens never know what the shape of their districts are, and cannot suffer the kind of "stigmatic harm" that segregated facilities cause.[85] Furthermore, if representatives in majority-black districts are inclined to represent only blacks, it is not because of the shape of the districts as such but because of the concentration of blacks in the districts.

A bizarrely shaped district might be plausibly interpreted as expressing racial stereotyping and an affinity for single-group representation, but only if the appearance is combined with a story about how the district was created. The shape of the district is a visual statement of the whole set of actions that created the scheme and together express its meaning. If the shape of the district had resulted from random procedures or unforeseeable coincidences, we might still think it objectionable, but we would not say that it sent any message or carried any meaning in itself.

More than mere appearances are necessary to interpret the expressive meaning of an electoral scheme. To interpret the scheme as sending the message that O'Connor reads in it, we may not need to know the actual intentions of the officials who devised the scheme, as we would if the question were racial discrimination. But we do need to know that officials took race into account in drawing the boundaries for whatever motive.[86] We also need to know that officials assumed that blacks would be more likely to vote for black representatives. In general, to discern the expressivist meaning of an electoral scheme, we need to know quite a bit about its institutional context.

The dissenters in *Shaw* took institutional context seriously—up to a point. In their view, racial districting can be challenged only if it "substantially disadvantages certain voters [those who had "essentially been shut out of the political process"] in their opportunity to influence the political process effectively." They criticized the majority for "focusing on looks rather than impact," and emphasized that the impact of the scheme was beneficial for blacks.[87] The redistricting therefore could not be said to disadvantage a group that was already disadvantaged. Although they did not explicitly use the expressivist language of the majority, they in effect maintained that the message the North Carolina redistricting scheme sent was one of equal respect. As Justice Stevens concluded: "If it is permissible to draw boundaries to provide adequate representation for rural voters, for union members, for Hasidic Jews, for Polish Americans, or for Republicans . . . it is permissible to do the same thing for members of the very minority group whose history in the United States gave birth to the Equal Protection Clause."[88]

Despite the many references to "impact," the dissenters did not go very far in exploring the likely consequences for black representation. They took for granted that "adequate representation" means simply electing more black representatives to the legislature. They did not consider that the redistricting might have other less favorable consequences for black interests.

One consequence is that concentrating black voters in a few districts "bleaches" adjacent districts, increasing the proportion of white voters in those districts and thereby enhancing the electoral prospects of candidates less sympathetic to black interests. Some studies show that redistricting had these bleaching consequences in the 1990s. Racial redistricting in the south (though not in the north) seems to have contributed to the tendency of the House to reject legislation favorable to blacks in the 1990s.[89] Nor do the majority-black districts created in the process expand political participation by black citizens, as some of their advocates hoped. Black turnout rarely grows, and white turnout often declines, after a district becomes majority-black.[90]

A second more general consequence neglected by the dissenters is that racial redistricting discourages the building of cross-racial coalitions. Critics of racial redistricting raised this concern early in the legislative debate, well before the courts confronted the issue in the rush of cases in the 1990s. Testifying at a Senate hearing in 1982 on the amendments to the Voting Rights Act, a political scientist who conducts research on ethnic conflict argued that "assured minority representation" encourages white majority politicians in effect to say to minority communities: "You have your own representatives. Don't come to us with your problems; speak to them."[91]

On its face, the minority representation that majority-minority districts supposedly guarantees does seem less desirable than the more fluid, collaborative politics that racially mixed districts are assumed to promote. Guaranteed minority representation sends the message that minorities are on their own and should not expect much help from their fellow citizens or representatives from other groups. The collaborative politics associated with mixed districts offers minorities the chance, at least occasionally, to become part of the majority. It holds out the hope that some whites will join with black members of the legislature to promote causes that black citizens favor and that might otherwise fail to receive a fair hearing.

Whether the institution of racially mixed districts sends that hopeful message depends on whether white representatives actually act in this collaborative way. In a notable case challenging the racial redistricting in the Tennessee legislature in the mid 1990s, the federal district court went beyond the prima facie message of racial districting, and sought evidence about whether white representatives from mixed districts actually reach across racial lines and try to build coalitions.[92] The evidence, admittedly more anecdotal than systematic, consisted of testimony from prominent white members of the Tennessee Senate—Stephen Cohen, a veteran legislator from Memphis whose district was about one-third black, and John Wilder, the Senate Speaker whose district was about one-fifth black.[93]

During the trial, the chief judge repeatedly pressed the witnesses to address what he called the "political science reason" for preserving white majority districts in which blacks have substantial influence (so-called influence districts). Why, he asked, are black voters "better off in that situation" than in a system with more majority-black districts?[94] The senators explained that, though the legislature might have fewer blacks, it would have more representatives (like themselves) who were sympathetic to black interests. Cohen proudly pointed out that the law declaring Martin Luther King's birthday a state holiday would never have passed without the support of the representatives from white-majority districts like his, which have substantial black minorities.[95] In case that achievement was not sufficiently impressive, Wilder cited dozens of other bills that representatives like him supported and that benefited blacks in more material ways ("what some people call the pork barrel").[96] Wilder also stated that he had appointed blacks to major chairmanships in the Senate: "they have a third of the chairman. They have had a strong voice, it was due them."[97]

Cohen and Wilder had creditable track records of promoting black interests and helping their black colleagues. Their testimony, based on their own experience, was not seriously challenged. The court relied heavily on their statements in rendering its final judgment. Reversing its own previous decision of just two years before, the court held that "influence" districts (now defined as those in which blacks comprise at least a quarter of the voting-age population) could count in satisfying the requirements of the Voting Rights Act (provided that some majority-minority districts already exist).[98]

By taking seriously this testimony and other evidence about the effects of the redistricting on the legislature, the court in effect showed that the meaning of a redistricting scheme cannot be read by looking at only districts—whether it be their shape, their composition, or even their distribution. The meaning depends in part on the consequences that redistricting would have on the dynamics of the politics within the legislature. Encouraging cross-racial cooperation in the legislature can be one of the purposes, and therefore part of the meaning, of a redistricting scheme. The district court thus went further than the *Shaw* Court—further than either the majority or the dissenters—in considering the institutional context of redistricting.[99] In this respect, the district court's approach moved closer to a fuller interpretation of the meaning of the Tennessee redistricting scheme and toward a more complete understanding of the message it sends about equal respect.

The district court stopped short of exploring one important institutional feature of the legislature. The "brooding omnipresence" in the case was an institutional "fact that appears nowhere in the published opinion: the partisan composition of the Tennessee Senate."[100] Wilder, Cohen, and their Democratic colleagues controlled the Senate, and hardly needed to be pushed to place their black Democratic colleagues in committee chairmanships and in other ways to work with them to advance their legislative goals. The partisan dynamics of the legislature, quite apart from any constituent pressure, were sufficient to encourage cross-racial cooperation. The senators who testified also neglected to mention that a majority of the senators who voted in favor of Martin Luther King Day were from districts that did not have a substantial number of black constituents. This and other legislation that blacks favored seem to have passed in part by means of old-fashioned logrolling and traditional party politics. The black representatives, even though small in number, were able to gain support for some of their agenda because they were critical to the Democrats' control of the Senate. In this episode, then, having majority-black districts was at least as important for black influence in the legislature as preserving unbleached districts.

The point is not simply that the partisan dynamics of the legislature produced consequences favorable to blacks, but that given those dynamics the institution of majority-black districts sends a different message than it otherwise would. It expresses a conception of representation more like the collaborative politics usually associated with racially mixed districts, and more consistent with equal respect, than the message it sends when considered in isolation from the legislative process.

A further indication of the ambiguity of the message that majority-black districts send can be seen in the striking shift in the attitudes of the parties toward racial redistricting in recent years. As Republicans watched their prospects brighten in the bleached districts, some became ardent supporters of affirmative action in redistricting. As Democrats saw their safe seats increasingly threatened, some lost their enthusiasm for the practice. In one of the first major redistricting cases following the 2000 census, the New Jersey commission as usual split along strictly partisan lines.[101] But this time the Democrats favored, and the Republicans opposed, a plan that "unpacked" three of the majority-minority districts, transferring some of their black and Hispanic voters to mostly white districts. The commission's nonpartisan chair and the courts upheld the plan. Majority-minority districts seem to send a different message now than they did when first created.

It turns out, then, not to be so easy to decipher the expressivist meaning of an electoral scheme. To resolve the competing interpretations of its meaning, we must examine its institutional context. Once we undertake that task, we are likely to find that, as in the Tennessee case, the story is quite complex, and is itself contestable.[102] As the chief judge in that case remarked: "[I]sn't it a fact that when you start doing things in politics you can't ever tell what can happen in terms of influence? [O]ver time it is hard to predict who is going to influence whom in politics."[103] Even if we could settle on a definitive account of the context, the meaning of an electoral scheme is likely to be too specific and contingent to be expressed as a general conclusion about using race as a factor in redistricting. The kind of dilemma posed by the majority and the dissenters in *Shaw* is simply not resolvable in those terms. What message the use of race sends depends on what conception of the representative process we accept, and what conception our electoral institutions realize.

Conceptions of Representation

The justices in *Shaw* seemed to recognize that competing conceptions of representation were at issue. Is racial districting "antithetical to our system of representative democracy," or is it necessary for "adequate representation" of minorities?[104] Some commentators have also seen a clash of conceptions of representation in this dispute. But neither the justices nor the commentators distinguish the conceptions in a way that captures the conflict.

One common distinction is between descriptive and substantive representation. In the former legislators represent constituents by sharing ascriptive characteristics such as race; in the latter legislators represent constituents by promoting their material interests.[105] Descriptive representation can be significant, and some voters might reasonably prefer to have a representative of their race or ethnic origin, even at the sacrifice of some material benefits for their group.[106] But in the redistricting debates, the advocates of majority-black districts generally believe that more black descriptive representation is also the best way to increase black substantive representation. They may be wrong about their expectations, but they are not committed to electing more blacks to the legislature regardless of the consequences for passing legislation favorable to blacks.

Another familiar distinction is the contrast between individual and group representation.[107] In individual representation, legislators represent their constituents without regard to ascriptive characteristics. Electoral majorities are composed of whatever groups of individuals happen to vote for the representative. The majority who elect the member from the second district of Ohio are identified as simply those who voted for him. In group representation, legislators have a primary obligation to some ascriptive group, and districts are judged according to whether they advantage or disadvantage groups. The problem with this distinction is that all redistricting, in principle and practice, is driven by group politics—whether the groups are defined by partisan affiliation, economic interest, or ethnic origin. Even geographical boundaries are not random, and were never assumed to be. Rural and urban constituents can constitute groups too. One of the most compelling arguments made by the defenders of racial redistricting is that, because officials take into account other kinds of group identity in drawing district boundaries, equal respect requires that they also be permitted to take into account racial identity.

Yet another distinction is between territorial and proportional representation. In the former, a legislator represents a single geographical district, responding to whatever combination of interests it happens to produce. In the latter, legislators represent the salient groups in the society in proportion to their numbers in the electorate. This distinction may have been what O'Connor had in mind in her criticism of racial districting. The "primary obligation" of legislators in such a system "is to represent only the members of that group, rather than their constituency as a whole."[108] It was certainly on the minds of some senators during the hearings on the amendments to the Voting Rights Act. They feared that the amendments would undermine territorial representation by encouraging demands for proportional representation of groups.[109]

The contrast between territorial and proportional claims constitutes a real tension in our system of representation: the more we seek representation for various groups, the more we have to discount the geographical boundaries in drawing districts. But accepting the tension as given begs the question of why geography should have such weight in defining a constituency. To answer that question, we would need to consider whether geographical districts fulfill the values of community that Tocqueville and earlier theorists assumed. To the extent that they are only administrative conveniences, they can be justifiably modified to serve other values.

A more fundamental contrast cuts across the others because it applies to districts however they are defined. It distinguishes what may be called discretionary and mandatory representation.[110] In the discretionary conception, representatives have considerable autonomy in their legislative actions. They can more readily build coalitions, engage in logrolling, and forge compromises with their colleagues to achieve their constituents' goals. These collaborative aspects of legislative politics play a more significant part for the representative who acts on the discretionary conception.[111] In the mandatory conception, representatives are more constrained by the positions they have taken in winning election and reelection. They devote more attention to building coalitions within their constituency. Once they fashion the compromises necessary to win office, they are more bound in their legislative actions to represent the positions those compromises represent. In the mandatory conception, the politics of constituency service is a more salient part of the representative process.

Majority-minority districts might seem to favor mandatory representation. Legislators elected from such districts are usually more bound to support causes that favor blacks, and in that respect they seem to be acting in the spirit of mandatory representation. But the idea of majority-black districts actually fits better with discretionary representation. On most issues that do not specifically affect the interests of blacks, legislators from such districts have more discretion and therefore more room for making compromises and engaging in logrolling. Majority-black districts also tend to be safe, and the safer the seat, the more discretion the representative has. (Many other districts are also safe, especially those designed by the parties in control of the redistricting.) Legislators from more diverse districts are more likely to make commitments to their constituents on a wider range of issues, and may find it more difficult to sustain stable coalitions. They therefore are likely to have less scope for changing their positions in the legislature (unless they too hold safe seats).

The principle of equal respect does not declare one of these conceptions of representation definitely superior to the others in all circumstances. The more robust constituency politics that goes with mandatory representation can strengthen local participation, encourage cooperation among contending ethnic and other groups in the district, and produce more competitive elections. These effects could help disadvantaged groups where their numbers or their support are too small to elect more than a few of their own representatives. The more fluid legislative politics that accompanies discretionary representation can produce more open and visible bargaining, permit more flexibility and change, and encourage more political deliberation. These effects could help disadvantaged groups who send a critical mass of representatives to the legislature, especially if their party controls it.

It would be useful to examine to what extent these forms of representation produce these consequences in practice. For example, do representatives of majority-black districts actually have more discretion in making legislative action?[112] It would also be important to compare the effects on black representation with the effects on other racial and ethnic groups. Equal respect applies to all such groups but probably in different ways, depending on these effects and the nature of the past discrimination the group has suffered. But for the purposes of assessing how these conceptions relate to equal respect, we need recognize only that the conceptions mark distinct institutional choices, which affect important political values including equality, and which vary in ways that cannot be determined in advance of political deliberation.

Deliberating about Districting

If we cannot say in advance whether the principle of equal respect requires a particular conception of representation, we cannot conclude that racial districting violates equal respect—even if racial districting seems to fit better with one conception of representation rather than another. Racial redistricting does not send a message for all seasons. This negative conclusion has an important positive implication. Because the electoral system has significant though variable effects on equal respect, citizens should have an opportunity to take part in deciding what kind of representative system they wish to have. They should have a voice in determining the balance among the various conceptions of representation the system expresses, and in deciding the uses of race and other categories in redistricting.[113] Neither unaccountable courts nor unreconstructed legislatures should be the only forums for such deliberation. The challenge (which chapter 3 further explores) is to find a way for citizens to be represented in deliberations about what form representation should take.

Wherever this deliberation takes place, the principle of equal respect provides several constraints on how it should be conducted. First, the principle shows that some claims are not decisive. We should challenge both the assertion that a redistricting scheme is "antithetical" to our system of representative government and the assertion that it is absolutely necessary for "adequate representation." What representation requires is contestable and variable, and a claim that it requires one scheme rather than another should always be questioned. Specifically, we should consider its meaning and its consequences for disadvantaged citizens as well as its broader implications for the democratic process as a whole.

Second, it should not be a decisive argument against a redistricting scheme that it benefits some groups more than others. We should always examine whether equal treatment actually produces equal respect. Racial preferences in districting may be justified because racial discrimination took place in the past. Partisan preferences may be justified to promote a two-party system. But it should not be acceptable to conclude that partisan gerrymandering is justified but racial gerrymandering is not—simply by appealing to a principle of equality.

Third, in designing districts we should not presume that all members of an ascriptive group "think alike," but neither should we deny such groups opportunities to express their common interests. Assigning blacks to their own electoral district may be attributing electoral opinions to some blacks that they do not have. This practice could disrespect some citizens' capacity for free choice. But refusing to create majority-minority electoral districts denies disadvantaged groups one of the most important means they have to compensate for their lack of equal opportunities in other parts of the political process. Here as in some other disputes about electoral justice, there may be a tension between free choice and equal respect. But the tension could also be understood as arising within the value of equal respect itself. Respecting citizens as equal persons requires treating all as equally capable of exercising free choice, but it also requires granting all equal opportunities in the political process.

We should not assume in any particular dispute that basic tensions of this kind must be resolved by choosing one or the other competing value. Instead, we should seek institutional solutions that might promote both. For example, we should take more seriously proposals to establish a system of cumulative voting, in which each citizen may cast as many votes as there are seats to be filled.[114] Cumulative voting would require multimember districts, which would break with tradition in federal elections. Although the Constitution does not require single-member districts for Congress, federal law does. This objection from customary practice should not be decisive. The method is increasingly used in local jurisdictions, such as school boards and municipal councils.[115] A bill that would permit states to use it in congressional elections has been introduced in the House. The method enables voters in effect to form their own electoral groups. It thus respects free choice. But at the same time, it increases the chances that members of minority groups can elect their own candidates if a sufficient number so choose. It thus values equal respect.

A fourth implication is that the deliberations should focus not mainly on the meaning for individual voters (or even groups of voters), but rather on the meaning for institutions, specifically those that constitute the democratic process. Equal respect refers ultimately to respect for persons, who are of course individuals. But the harms that unjust elections create are not limited to the individuals whose votes the electoral system fails to weight fairly. The democratic process as a whole suffers. Individuals are harmed because institutions are harmed.

These institutional harms have been obscured because so much of the debate has taken place in judicial forums, where only individuals have standing to sue. The democratic process cannot be a party to a suit. Despite the sharply divided decisions and shifting rationales for the voting rights cases in the 1990s, the Supreme Court justices have been unanimous on one conclusion: only the voters in a district have standing to complain about a redistricting scheme.[116] The justices sometimes disagree about which voters in the district have standing, but they all agree that no voter outside it can complain. This view of standing does not comport well with the expressivist conclusions of some of the Court's opinions, most notably the majority's view in *Shaw*.[117] If racial redistricting is wrong because it perpetuates racial stereotypes or because it sends a message to elected representatives that is "altogether antithetical to our system of representative democracy," then the harm falls not only on the citizens in the district in question, not even only on blacks, but on all citizens who depend on "our system of representative government."[118]

It does not follow that the Court should radically change its doctrine on who has standing to sue. Some broader rules of standing might be desirable (for example, permitting citizens in other directly affected districts in the state to sue). But it would hardly be practical to grant standing to every citizen who wished to sue for damages resulting from defects in the system of representative government. Nevertheless, we should not let the limitations of judicial discourse dictate the content of the continuing deliberation about redistricting and electoral processes. We should recognize that equal respect is as much a question of institutional health as individual harm. Citizens have views not only about the persons who would be their representatives, but also about the kind of legislature by which they would be governed, and more generally about the nature of the democratic process under which they would live. Citizens may not be able to express these views in any particular election, but they should be able to insist that the views be considered in the design of their electoral institutions.

COUNTING VOTES

The Voting Rights Act defines voting as not only casting a ballot but "having such ballot counted properly and included in the appropriate totals of votes cast."[119] This provision has triggered few lawsuits and attracted little public attention. Most citizens and officials have evidently assumed that once votes are cast and districts determined, the electoral process will run smoothly on its own. If it occasionally goes awry, the mistakes do not matter either because the election is not close or because a recount readily resolves the dispute. In close elections, recounts are common enough, and a few have generated litigation, sometimes forcing the courts to count the votes themselves.[120] But in most disputes over vote counting the issue has been simply whether the votes have been accurately counted. Occasionally, fraud, bribery, or partisan bias has been charged, but rarely have matters of high principle been raised.

The dispute about the presidential election of 2000 dramatically raised the stakes. As a result of the Supreme Court's decision in *Bush v. Gore,* and the challenges to the electoral process by minority groups, we can see more clearly that disputes about counting are not merely about counting but about fundamental principles of democracy—specifically about what equality requires.

Recounting the Count

Seven justices of the U.S. Supreme Court declared that the recount underway in Florida in December 2000 denied the state's voters equal protection of the laws because the officials counting the ballots were applying different standards in different districts.[121] Palm Beach County began by not counting hanging chads, switched to counting a vote if any light could be seen through the chad, changed back to counting hanging chads, and then was ordered by a court to count dimpled chads.[122] Only five justices of the Supreme Court thought the variation in standards here and elsewhere in Florida was a sufficient reason to stop the recount, but five were quite enough to give Bush the verdict and finally the election.

The Court had never before found an equal protection violation in an election case of this kind, and the reasoning surprised even some of the Court's most ardent defenders.[123] (Whether the Court was justified in intervening on grounds other than equal protection is considered in chapter 3.) Local variation in the electoral process has long been common in the United States. It has been assumed to be necessary and arguably desirable for promoting local control and civic involvement. Today many counties in the same state—even precincts in the same county—still use different ballots, instructions, machinery, as well as different standards for the regular counting of ballots. In the Florida case, the differences in accuracy between punch-card systems and the optical scanners used in some counties were much greater than any differences in the standards applied in conducting the recounts.[124] No one had claimed before that local variation in election procedures of this kind violated equal protection or any other principle of equality.

What troubled some of the justices was not the variation per se, but the variation in the application of what seemed to be an objective standard (the test of whether the ballot was punched through). This first became clear in the oral argument. After David Boies, the attorney for the Gore campaign, pointed out that the law accepts considerable variation among jury verdicts and decisions of public officials, Justice Souter replied: "[I]n jury to jury cases, we assume that there is not an overall objective standard . . . but [in this case] what is bothering . . . me and others, is [that] there is no [basis for a] subjective appeal. All we have are certain physical characteristics [which] are being treated differently from county to county."[125] Souter seemed to be suggesting that unequal treatment may be acceptable if there is some scope for judgment or discretion (the "subjective appeal"), but is not permitted if there is no basis for disagreement (an "objective standard").[126]

This is a potentially significant distinction for understanding equal respect, but it needs to be elaborated and even then used only with qualifications. Equal respect requires that citizens be treated equally unless there is a respectful reason for the differences. Obviously, much depends on what counts as a respectful reason. Souter's distinction does not provide a criterion for such a reason. Subjective reasons are not necessarily better than objective reasons for unequal treatment. They may be worse because they risk arbitrariness.

But the distinction does point to a significant consideration in assessing whether an institution is likely to have respectful reasons for unequal treatment, especially in cases where no reason is or can be given by the responsible officials.[127] If officials treat citizens differently according to a subjective standard, such as "ascertain the intent of the voter," they may be justified in reaching different conclusions. By their nature we expect subjective standards to produce variation, and do not necessarily ask for any further reason. Disparate treatment by itself does not signal lack of respect for some citizens. Other facts, such as independent evidence of bias on the part of the officials, would be required to demonstrate a violation of equal respect. In contrast, if officials treat citizens differently according to an objective standard (such as "count no ballots with hanging chads") or according to different objective standards at different times, they are less likely to be able to provide an acceptable reason. The disparate treatment directly expresses lack of respect for some citizens.

Equality versus Locality

We may be able to find justifiable reasons for some disparate treatment—if not for using different standards in the same county for the same election, at least for using different standards in different counties and different states. Local variation is likely to give citizens more control over the electoral process, encourage political participation, increase partisan competitiveness, and enable districts to experiment with different procedures that if successful may be more widely used. Provisional voting, statewide registration, and the motor voter law gained national support because they could be shown to have worked well in several states. These benefits may be worth the sacrifice of uniformity not only because they may outweigh the costs of unequal treatment, but because the unequal treatment itself is not so objectionable.

Local variation may result in weighting some votes less than others, but the unequal treatment itself does not call into question the civic standing of any individual or group, disadvantaged or not. If you happen to live in a county that did not count hanging chads in this election, you are just unlucky compared to someone who lives in a county that does. You are not likely to regard the disparate treatment as an assault on your civic dignity. More important, if you do not like the standard your county uses, you can, with the help of your fellow citizens, change it. Neither the standard nor the likelihood of its being applied to you rests on ascriptive characteristics beyond your control such as gender or race, or deeply held identities beyond your desire to change such as religious and cultural beliefs. Local variation in this way could be seen as recognizing individual responsibility, respecting citizens' capacity for choice rather than denigrating their equal standing.

One might have expected some of those who objected to local variation in the Florida case to have shown more appreciation for this kind of argument. Some of the justices had in the past given great weight to the value of state and local control, and even in this case some went out of their way to stress the importance of individual responsibility.[128] But the majority in this case insisted that the Florida situation was exceptional: the case involved a "special instance" of "a statewide recount under the authority of a single state judicial officer." Because the Florida supreme court had taken it upon itself to order a statewide recount, it should have exercised its "power to assure uniformity" in the process.[129] Once the court took control, the benefits of local control were no longer relevant. In one simple order, the Florida court had disabled any Tocquevillian appeal to the value of local variation.

The great advantage of the Supreme Court's argument (for those who value local control and individual responsibility) is that it is not easily generalized. Unlike a broad holding that the variation by its nature violates equal protection, an argument limited to the circumstances in which a state court takes charge of a statewide recount does not immediately invite challenges to the many different variations in electoral procedures in Florida and throughout the United States.

The disadvantage is that the argument is so resistant to generalization that it appears unprincipled. The conclusion is so closely tailored to the specific circumstances that it seems more like edict than law. Reaction to the decision in the legal community reflected this tension between the advantage and disadvantage, and in ways that reveal an important feature of the dynamics of equality claims. Those who seek to expand the scope for equality in the electoral process seized on the decision to mount more radical challenges and to call for more extensive reforms in the future.[130] Those who wish to resist such expansion insisted that the decision is "not that significant" and predicted that in a few years it will not even be taught in many law schools."[131]

Equality claims have a tendency to expand simply because their form is general: they call for equal treatment unless relevant differences can be justified. This is a problem not only for those who fear the expansion (forcing them to impose what may seem to be arbitrary limits) but also for those who welcome it (tempting them to disregard the value of local control). What both need are some principled limits. The distinction cited earlier between ascriptive and other characteristics is a plausible place to start developing such limits. We can say that, to the extent that differences in counting procedures do not have and are not intended to have the effect of discriminating against disadvantaged ascriptive groups, they do not violate equal respect. So far, that seems a familiar criterion, parallel to the standards used to assess violations of voting rights in general. But the criterion is somewhat more complex here because the effects are generally less obvious and occasionally more contestable.

Consider differences in voting machines. Optical scanners are more accurate than punch-card systems but they are also more expensive.[132] Does equal respect require equal accuracy? Some localities may decide to spend less on electoral machinery and more on other needs they regard as more urgent (such as education or welfare). If the decision is arrived at democratically, why should localities be prohibited from establishing their own priorities? If the election is state or national, citizens beyond the locality of course have a legitimate interest in how the votes are counted. They deserve some assurance that the counting, the outcome of which will also affect them, satisfies some minimum threshold of accuracy. But it is not obvious that the accuracy of the punch-card system falls below a reasonable minimum. Certainly citizens have accepted the results of such systems for many years in many jurisdictions.

Nevertheless, if the disparate results produced by voting machines reinforce ascriptive inequalities, then any adequate principle of equal respect must take notice. In Florida the counties that could afford optical scanners were somewhat wealthier and whiter, and the votes of their residents were more likely to be recorded accurately. The poorer and blacker counties tended to have punch-card systems, and the votes of their residents were more likely to be discarded because of error. However, the disparity in the availability of accurate machines was not great in Florida.[133] Nationwide, the distribution of machines was evidently not biased at all against blacks and the poor, but counties with higher percentages of minority residents tended to have higher percentages of uncounted presidential votes.[134] The disparities in the accuracy of the count, which were much greater, probably resulted from differences in the way the machines were used, and therefore partly from differences in the resources available to help voters use the machines properly.

In Florida (as in most states) the resources available to counties vary greatly, and follow the pattern of existing class and racial inequalities. Criticism of this disparity, explicitly distinguished from the charge of overt discrimination, was prominent in the testimony presented to the Civil Rights Commission during its hearings on the Florida election. One witness concluded: "Florida's election was not necessarily a conspiracy against African-Americans to diminish their impact in the state's electoral process. [T]he real scandal in Florida [resulted from] the inequities that existed from county to county . . . disparities between wealthy and poor counties. [P]oor counties, whether in Florida or elsewhere, have always had a disproportionate number of votes not counted."[135]

One of the most important—and neglected—types of resource is the availability of competent staff. Most of the proposals for reform of vote counting have focused on technological fixes—especially improvements in voting machinery. No doubt such improvements would be worthwhile, but as with most technologies, people need assistance in using the machines, coping with the inevitable breakdowns, and challenging eligibility rulings that deny their access to the machines.[136] Also desirable is making the option of provisional voting available to voters whose eligibility cannot be verified at the time they arrive at the poll.[137] With this option, they go ahead and cast their ballot, and if officials later confirm their eligibility, their votes count as usual.

The disparity in resources to recruit and train people who can provide assistance to voters on election day is especially significant because critics of the Florida recount (and others who stress the individual responsibility of voters) make much of the distinction between tabulation errors and voter errors.[138] The former are the fault of the system and may warrant a recount, the critics say, but the latter are the fault of the voters and do not. The appeal to individual responsibility appears again. One prominent critic writes: "If the punchcard machine doesn't work and as a result the voter does not emerge with a fully punched-through ballot, he should know, if he's read the directions, that he has a spoiled ballot and he should request a fresh ballot and a properly operating voting machine."[139]

But many voters in Florida complained that they could not find anyone able or willing to respond to their complaints.[140] In understaffed and over-worked precincts—especially in urban areas as closing time approaches, when more working class people vote—many voters may not realize that they have spoiled their ballots, and when they do are not likely to find anyone to assist them. Inadequate staffing tracks other inequalities. The disparities that citizens face as they go to the polls are reminiscent of those that children confronted in the era of "separate but equal" schools.

The reference to schools is apt for another reason. Like many other states, Florida leaves voter education mostly to local districts, and does little to make sure the districts provide adequate instructions to voters in advance of the election. Yet many citizens, especially those voting for the first time or those voting infrequently, lack basic information about such simple matters as how to mark a ballot. Some commentators are not troubled by this, and see it as a way of reducing the influence of less educated citizens on the outcome of the election. One argues that most invalid ballots result from the failure of voters to follow directions, which are "simple and clear at least for anyone who could read." He observes, with evident sympathy for the thought: "[S]ome conservatives may think it rather an excess of democracy for illiterates to hold the electoral balance of power."[141]

If we know that some modest improvements in voter education could decrease the frequency of voter error and fail to take steps to implement them, we are in effect denying less experienced voters the opportunity to cast a valid ballot. Equal respect demands more than that. Some of the deficiencies in voter education could be readily remedied, but state officials have not shown much interest in addressing them. The neglect of voter education was dramatically revealed in this exchange between Secretary of State Katherine Harris and Chairperson Mary Frances Berry during the Civil Rights Commission hearings:

> *Chairperson Berry:* . . . Were there voter education materials prepared and distributed on the mechanics of how to vote?
>
> *Witness Harris:* That's a day-to-day operations type of thing . . . since all voting systems are determined by the county supervisors of elections, they provide their own instructions for each of the counties. It is not as though we could in one media market have voting information that would explain how to vote because . . . there would be a number of different systems that might be employed.
>
> *Chairperson Berry:* And you don't know whether your office provided information or marketing information or education help to the counties on the mechanics of how to vote. . . .
>
> *Witness Harris:* Again, that would be a day-to-day operational question that you could address to Mr. Roberts [Director of the Division of Elections] if you would like.
>
> *Chairperson Berry:* Why don't you ask him? You're sitting next to him. He works for you, ask him. Why can't he whisper in your ear and tell you the answers?
>
> *Witness Harris:* I just thought it would be more expeditious if you had him answer it.
>
> *Chairperson Berry:* I see. Are you interested in the answer to the question, Madam Secretary?
>
> *Witness Harris:* I'm extremely interested—
>
> *Chairperson Berry:* I see. Is your interest engendered by my asking you the question or were you interested before you came here?
>
> *Witness Harris:* Actually, I was very interested. [142]

Harris went on to explain that while campaigning for the secretary's office, she had gathered many ideas for voter education (among them, working with "some of the fast food restaurants" to put messages "on their paper mats encouraging voter turnout, voter education"). But she found that her office lacked resources to pay for most of them, and in any case local districts had "complete autonomy" to decide whether to implement them. [143]

Thus, while equal respect does not call for an optical scanner in every district, it does demand an equitable distribution of electoral resources among districts. Equal respect is concerned with comparative accuracy among districts, not absolute accuracy. All districts should be able to provide tabulation systems that are not systematically biased against any ascriptive groups, and ensure sufficient staff support to give voters assistance at the polls if they need it. They should support educational campaigns to help citizens, especially first-time and infrequent voters, understand how to cast valid ballots that accurately record their choices. Districts should find efficient ways to permit voters to correct mistakes they may make in casting their ballots. Providing opportunities for correcting mistakes need not be at the cost of increasing the waiting time for other voters.

CONCLUSION

Electoral institutions speak to citizens, and they do not say simply: you have a right to vote. They express messages about civic standing. The messages are not only about individual rights but also about institutional responsibility. This responsibility falls on individuals—on citizens who should consider the vote to be a trust as well as a right, but even more on officials who should make sure the institutions send the right messages. The principle of equal respect developed in this chapter provides a standard for assessing whether institutions are sending the right messages—more generally, whether they are recognizing the equal moral standing of each citizen as democratic justice requires. Electoral institutions should provide citizens with equal opportunities to have their votes equally counted, unless respectful reasons can be given to justify unequal treatment. Appeals to equal respect play an important role in the continuing debates about electoral institutions. Even critics of egalitarian reforms such as easing voter registration find themselves invoking some form of a principle of equal respect.

Any principle of equality calls for interpretation. The analysis here is intended as a contribution to an interpretative project that should continue within the democratic process itself. The reasons that citizens give for criticizing or justifying inequalities in the electoral institutions become not only part of the public meaning of the principle of equal respect, but also part of the expressive meaning of the institutions themselves. To make and keep those institutions just, citizens need to deliberate together to understand those meanings, and to work together to change the institutions themselves when they fail to express equal respect.

The principle of equal respect is framed to capture a wide variety of meanings of electoral equality, but it is not completely open ended. Any adequate interpretation of the principle should take place within a framework that recognizes some important methodological and substantive standards that are often neglected by other approaches and principles.

Methodologically, even while recognizing that individuals are the fundamental moral subjects in democratic theory, we should assess equal respect, and locate any justifications for unequal treatment, in the context of institutions. This prescription is generally accepted when the subject is social justice in society as a whole. Most discussions of justice deal with social and political institutions, however abstractly described. But although voting obviously takes place in institutions, the reasons usually given to justify or criticize electoral practices focus on the individual right to vote. This individualist orientation obscures the institutional dimension of voting in at least three ways.

First, it neglects the worth of opportunities. The equal opportunity to vote is assumed to be satisfied as long as individuals can exercise their right to vote, as long as the rules of eligibility do not exclude any individual or any group. But even seemingly neutral rules governing registration often systematically treat some citizens differently without respectful reasons, and thereby fail to express equal respect.

The individualist approach also obscures the complexity of the meanings expressed in the electoral process. It encourages the belief that the meaning of an institution can be read from its relationship to voters, considered one at a time. But the meaning often depends on a complex set of relationships, not only among voters or between voters and their representatives, but also among their representatives in the legislature. Whether racial districting sends a message of equal respect cannot be determined by looking only at the shape of the district, the distribution of the majority-minority districts, or even the composition of the legislature alone.

The third way in which the individualist perspective neglects institutions is by misrepresenting the consequences of violations of equal respect. The harm that comes from the failure to express equal respect falls not only on voters, as the individualist approach suggests, but also on all citizens and the democratic process as a whole. Legal standing, which shapes judicial discourse, restricts the range of harms that may be considered. Equal respect can damage civic standing as much through institutional as individual harm.

Substantively, a principle of equal respect should permit a range of reasonable disagreement about its own interpretation. A large part of the task of interpretation therefore should be devoted to identifying which reasons fall within, and which outside, the range of justifications that citizens could accept as free and equal persons. We saw that several major disputes about electoral justice cannot be resolved as readily as the advocates of the contending positions assume, but in each case some limits on what reasons should count as acceptable can be identified.

Disputes about what incentives voters may be offered, for example, cannot be resolved by a simple rule excluding all monetary inducements. Citizens may not sell their votes, but that does not mean that government or candidates may not pay them to go to the polls. Some kinds of incentives, whether financial or not, may improperly constrain free choice, but on their face most incentives do not offend the principle of equal respect. Nor do efforts to ease registration or otherwise remove disincentives necessarily undermine individual responsibility or violate individual autonomy. However, if incentives are intended to diminish, or have the effect of diminishing, the opportunities of already disadvantaged citizens, they breach the principle of equal respect.

A second set of disputes involve practices justified by appeals to ascriptive characteristics of voters, such as race or gender. These raise issues of equal respect in ways that practices based on other characteristics, such as geographical location or partisan affiliation, do not. That is why, in light of the principle of equal respect, racial districting—even when justifiable—requires more defense than partisan gerrymandering. But refusing to use ascriptive characteristics can also send a message of disrespect. The meaning of the message depends on a close institutional analysis of how the characteristics are used.

Local variation in electoral institutions raises another set of issues. Such variation usually violates strict equality, but it does not necessarily breach equal respect. Using different standards or different machinery in different electoral districts by itself does not assault civic dignity, and may help promote such other important values as local control and political participation. Contrary to what one might expect, subjective standards such as "intent of the voter" may be less objectionable than "objective" standards such as "do not count hanging chads," which allow for less variation. But when local variation produces standards or practices that fall below a reasonable minimum of accuracy, and when such variation reinforces ascriptive inequalities among disadvantaged groups, the principle of equal respect is offended.

Finally, disagreements about equal respect in electoral institutions often turn on competing conceptions of representation. One of the most significant though neglected conflicts is between discretionary and mandatory representation. With its emphasis on constituency politics, mandatory representation may help minorities who are unable to elect many of their own representatives make sure that those they can elect follow their will. Discretionary representation, which encourages coalition building in the legislature, may be preferable if minorities are able to send a critical mass of representatives to the legislature. Although equal respect does not decide the choice between these forms of representation, it shows why such a choice is necessary, and points to the key considerations that should influence it.

Democratic theory and its principles should not be expected to resolve these and similar disputes. Its task is to identify the issues that should be subject to deliberation, and to distinguish reasons that should be taken seriously from those that should not. The principle of equal respect makes some stringent demands on our electoral institutions. It points to ways in which they fall short and how they might be improved. It demands that citizens and their representatives take responsibility for shaping the meanings of their electoral institutions. In the spirit of equal respect, citizens should work together as free and equal persons to decide, in an ongoing process of deliberation, what the principle of equal respect means in the practice of electoral justice. Votes count when citizens count in the control of the electoral institutions that govern their democracy.

TWO

Free Choice
How Voters Decide

[V]oters who are longing for alternatives [are]
without any significant choice on the ballot.
RALPH NADER, NOVEMBER 2000

The choice is very clear. The contrast is very
stark. We have a choice between two candidates.
AL GORE, OCTOBER 2000

Voters often complain that they have no choice, and candidates just as often
claim that voters have a clear choice. Despite reaching contrary conclusions,
the complaint and the claim share the same premise: both assume that a
voter's choice is more valuable the greater the difference between the candidates. But it is not clear why this difference should matter so much. As long
as you can vote for the candidates you favor, why should you care about how
much they differ from the other candidates? And if you do not favor any of
the candidates on the ballot, why should it matter whether they differ from
one another? Free choice is promoted not so much by difference among the
candidates as by similarity between your ideal candidate and at least one
actual candidate on the ballot. How close the match is between ideal and
actual candidates depends on how a complex set of electoral institutions
shapes how voters decide.

In a pluralist society where voters have a wide range of views, no electoral system can guarantee individual voters that they will have the chance
to vote for their ideal candidate, or even a candidate about whom they are
enthusiastic. That would come close to embracing a principle of one voter,
one candidate. But an electoral system can provide opportunities for voters
to influence the array of choices on the ballot, and thereby to increase the
chances that they will find at least one candidate acceptable. The opportunities should extend well beyond the electoral process itself, but electoral

justice demands at least that citizens have a significant voice in nominating candidates. An important part of a principle of free choice in elections should therefore focus on the process that determines who the candidates are—specifically, how candidates win a place on the ballot, and what their place on the ballot means.

No less important than who is on the ballot is what citizens know about those who are on it. A principle of free choice therefore must also deal with the process by which citizens are informed about candidates. How much and what kind of information citizens need to make an informed choice is itself subject to dispute. To formulate an adequate principle, however, we do not have to decide whether voters can make do with shortcuts such as party affiliation, or whether they need more extensive knowledge of the candidates' positions on issues. Without presupposing any particular view of rational decision making, we can identify conflicts among various kinds of liberty that might arise in realizing even a minimally informed choice. The substance of these conflicts constitutes the second part of the meaning of a principle of free choice.

Choice is also less free to the extent that voters are subjected to undue pressure. Any adequate principle of free choice should therefore disapprove of the obstacles that discourage citizens from voting at all (such as those described in chapter 1). It should also condemn intimidation, extortion, bribery, and other manifestly improper forms of influence on candidates and voters. These overt forms of improper pressure are less prevalent than they used to be. Although occasional transgressions still occur, the systematic violations common in the past are rare. Thanks to the secret ballot, citizens cast their ballots without fear of retaliation (or hope of reward).[1] Thanks to the increased regulation of campaigns and elections, candidates and voters usually participate without fear of intimidation.

Other troubling influences remain, however—most conspicuously, political money. Poll taxes have disappeared, but questionable fundraising practices adversely affect both the selection of candidates and the flow of information. Money is not the only problematic influence on electoral choice, but it is so potent and pervasive in contemporary American politics that it warrants separate treatment. One problem with political money is that it creates and reinforces inequalities in the electoral process. Attempts to regulate these effects are often alleged to violate free speech, and in a contest between equality and liberty in our constitutional tradition liberty usually prevails. But money can also impair free choice itself, and efforts to control these effects can create a conflict with free speech. This kind of conflict, often overlooked in the debate about campaign finance, is between different kinds of liberty. Within our constitutional tradition, the adversaries in a contest between liberties are more evenly matched. The right of citizens to contribute to, and the right of candidates to spend on, campaigns are important liberties. But so is the right of citizens to make choices not determined by financial forces beyond their control.

A principle of free choice thus should cover three aspects of how voters decide: the objects of choice (how candidates are selected and presented on the ballot), the capacity for choice (the information voters are offered), and the pressures on choice (inappropriate influences on both the objects of and the capacity for choice). The principle of free choice developed here holds that the electoral process should provide citizens with an acceptable set of alternatives from which they can make an informed and unforced choice. The process should give citizens adequate opportunities to put an acceptable set of alternatives on the ballot, to acquire appropriate information about the candidates, and to make their decisions without undue pressure. Each of these aspects requires interpretation, and each embodies conflicts between different understandings of free choice.

The conflicting interpretations reflect the tension between an individualist and institutional approach. From an individualist perspective, choice may seem to be freer or more valuable the more alternatives voters have, the more information they receive, and the more insulation from external pressure they enjoy. But if we take a broader institutional perspective, we can appreciate the truth in a contrary interpretation. The principle of free choice should recognize that within a significant range of conditions choice may be enhanced by providing fewer alternatives, less information, and less insulation from pressure.

SELECTING CANDIDATES

The political party is the chief instrument for selecting candidates in most elections in the United States, as it is in most contemporary democracies. But unlike other democracies, the United States subjects parties to extensive regulation. Only a few other democracies control the selection of candidates at all. None mandates primaries, imposes strict rules about party labels, or regulates access to the ballot to the extent that the United States does.[2]

It may seem curious that a nation that prizes individual liberty and resists government regulation more than most other democracies should grant its political parties less freedom. But since the founding of the nation, political parties have been suspect. They were certainly not regarded as the friend of free choice: "The last degradation of a free and moral agent" was how Thomas Jefferson described party affiliation.[3] Madison's criticism of factions in *Federalist* No. 10 is directed as much against parties as any group; they are both "united by some common impulse . . . adverse to the rights of citizens . . . or the permanent and aggregate interests of the community."[4] With most of the other framers, Madison hoped that, like George Washington, leaders would stand above party. He never imagined that organized parties would become the main path to public office—certainly not for "enlightened statesmen." But Washington was the first and last president to stand above party. As soon as he had left the political stage, Jefferson, Madison, Hamilton, and their various supporters fell into partisan wrangling. Parties and party spirit were here to stay, and so were the original suspicions. As parties played a greater role in the selection of candidates, they also offered increasingly fertile opportunities for corruption. It was not long before it could be observed that "nowhere else in the western democratic world did parties looks so evil, at least to middle-class citizens, as they did in the United States."[5]

If parties were the main road to political office and if that road was not entirely straight, then parties could not be left to find their own way. They could not be considered mere private clubs, as free from government control as the voluntary associations protected by the First Amendment. In the last decades of the nineteenth and first of the twentieth centuries, courts repeatedly rejected the claims of parties to control the nomination process. They invalidated filing fees, candidate oath requirements, and even entire primary structures. Judges approached controversies about party regulation "with a profound suspicion of party leaders . . . and an expansive conception of the right to vote, which incorporated nomination and an effective . . . balloting experience."[6]

This history has left its mark on contemporary debates about the role of parties in the selection of candidates—but in somewhat divergent ways. In some respects, the decline of party autonomy has continued. The nominating activities of parties are now definitely considered the public's business; there is no question that parties can be regulated more than ordinary private associations. This legacy has persisted despite the recent judicial deference toward parties in the control of their own affairs. The disagreement now is not about whether parties are public, not even about whether public or private interests should prevail, but rather about the extent to which granting parties private autonomy will promote public purposes.[7]

In other respects, however, parties have benefited from this loss of autonomy. Many of the regulations imposed in recent years have actually strengthened parties—specifically, the dominant parties. Far from undermining the freedom of these parties, the laws that treat them as partially public entities protect them from challenge by minor parties. Some of these laws, such as restrictions on ballot access, came out of the turn-of-the-century reforms, championed by progressives and populists who had no intention of entrenching a two-party system. But even the laws intended to strengthen that system, such as the ban on fusion candidacies, did not immediately have this effect because they were adopted in an era in which minor parties and multiparty competition were flourishing.[8] Once the two-party system triumphed, however, the limits on ballot access increasingly served the joint interest of the major parties. They both now benefit, for example, from the provisions that give their candidates, but not those of minor parties, automatic access to the ballot. The debate has come to be framed as a conflict between the value of preserving the two-party system by protecting the autonomy of the major parties, and the value of encouraging broader participation by facilitating challenges from other parties and groups.

The public purposes of parties include two different ways of promoting the free choice of voters. The electoral process can give voters a voice in selecting candidates either through the dominant parties or through minor parties and other organizations. The advantage of working within one of the major parties is that its nominees are more likely to win elections. The advantage of supporting a minor party is that its nominees are likely to broaden the range of candidates, and thereby give voters a greater chance of finding at least one who is acceptable. Although the minor party candidates are less likely to win, they may influence the dominant parties and bring issues to public attention that would otherwise be ignored. A just electoral system should welcome both these ways of promoting free choice, but they are not always compatible. They express potentially conflicting interpretations of free choice. Controversies about fusion candidacies and blanket primaries illustrate the way these conflicts play out in contemporary politics.

The Function of Fusion

In many elections in the United States, voters who cast a ballot for a candidate who is not the nominee of one of the major parties are said to "waste" their vote. Third-party candidates usually have no chance of winning, and the expectation that they will lose further discourages potential supporters.[9] Voters who favor such candidates have a choice in this sense: they can cast a protest vote for their candidate, or they can vote for the major party candidate they find least objectionable. Although this choice seems less than genuine, it is not obvious why. It is not, as some critics suggest, a Hobson's choice, where the voter literally has but one alternative.[10] It is not the case that these voters have no opportunity to cast a meaningful vote because one of the alternatives is not real. Casting a protest vote does not contribute to the election of this candidate, but it is certainly meaningful, sometimes more so, than casting a vote for someone who has a chance of winning. Protest votes, in sufficient numbers, can send a powerful message, and can have an effect on campaigns and elections in the future. Voting for Donald Duck may not be pointless.

But the voters who decide they must choose the other alternative—the least objectionable major party candidate—have a more serious complaint. Their problem is not that they are forced to waste a vote, but rather that they are constrained to choose the lesser evil. Assume that they believe that both candidates would be bad for the country, but that one would be much worse. If they also accept that their duty is to vote as if they were deciding the election, they are obligated to vote for the least bad candidate. Their choice is still literally free; it could not be morally responsible if it were not voluntary. But the choice is less free (and to that degree forced) because they have only one morally acceptable alternative. Choosing that alternative, moreover, can have consequences that go beyond this particular election. Their votes could strengthen the claims of the candidate's party for public financing, ballot priority, and other privileges of major party status.

This kind of forced choice (as well as the hazard of a wasted vote) could be completely avoided only by adopting a different electoral system. The most appealing alternative is a form of proportional representation (PR), the system of a single transferable vote.[11] In a multimember district or national constituency, voters rank all candidates, and the votes are distributed proportionately to each candidate. With this kind of system, inferior candidates may still win, but no votes are wasted and no choices are forced. The system increases the proportion of voters who cast a ballot for a winning candidate, and the likelihood that individual voters will be represented by legislators they chose.

In these ways, this system could enhance free choice, but almost no jurisdiction in the United States has adopted it. Electoral justice certainly encourages experiments with this and other proportional methods. A close cousin of the single transferable vote, cumulative voting, has already proven its worth in local elections as a method for increasing minority representation without creating racial or ethnic districts. [12] These methods could mitigate some of the objectionable features of the current system, especially the winner-take-all rule, which arguably denies permanent minorities (in any district) a representative of their own. [13] But it would not be helpful, even if it were correct, to condemn the current system as simply unjust for failing to adopt some form of PR. [14] If the prospects of implementing the purer forms of PR more widely in the United States are as dim as they seem to be, we should devote more attention to mitigating the deficiencies in the existing system, especially the problem of constrained choice.

There is even less excuse for failing to consider methods such as instant runoff voting, which may be seen as a means to express the majority will more accurately. As its name implies, it simulates a runoff election. Its procedures are somewhat similar to those of the single transferable vote system, except that it is used to elect one representative in a single-member district. If no candidate receives more than 50 percent of the initial vote, the candidate with the fewest votes is eliminated and his votes transferred to the candidates designated as the second choice on these ballots. This process of elimination and transfer goes on until one candidate receives more than 50 percent of the vote, and can therefore be regarded as genuine choice of a majority. Some critics worry that the system may confuse voters, but it has been successfully used for many years in Australia, and is now in place in several U.S. states. [15]

But even if we accept the winner-take-all rule of the present system, we could mitigate the problem of constrained choice by a simple device called multiple-party nomination or fusion candidacy. [16] With this device, a minor and a major party can nominate the same candidate, who is then listed on the ballot as a nominee of both (either on separate lines or on one line indicating the two party affiliations). Ballots cast under either party label count toward the candidate's total.

In this system, voters casting their ballot for the minor party candidate do not necessarily waste their vote. With the major party endorsement, their candidate has a greater chance of winning. Their choice may also be less constrained because the major party may be less inclined to nominate a candidate they find unacceptable. With the prospect of minor party support, the major party is more likely to nominate a candidate who is attractive to minor party voters. Instead of being forced to vote for the lesser evil, minor party voters can have their electoral cake and eat it too. They can register their support for the minor party while voting for a candidate who is at least tolerable and may even be preferable. Furthermore, if the ballot lists the candidates on a separate line or otherwise allows for disaggregating the votes by party, the minor party voters are not forced to let their votes count as part of the major party's official totals for purposes of qualifying for public funds and maintaining the status as a major party. They are not conscripted to serve a party they do not support. They can unequivocally record their support for the minor party, increasing its political credibility for future elections. From the perspective of individual voters, then, fusion candidacies seem to enhance choice.

Nevertheless, fusion candidacies are now prohibited in most states.[17] Most of the antifusion laws were adopted for partisan reasons—to protect the major parties against alliances their rival might forge with other parties. As one Republican legislator explained in the heyday of fusion: "We don't propose to allow the Democrats to make allies of the Populists, Prohibitionists or any other party, and get up combination tickets against us. We can whip them single-handed, but don't intend to fight all creation."[18] The laws were enacted at the turn of the twentieth century, part of the "electoral system of 1896," which after the defeat of the Populists led to the decline of electoral competition.[19] Regional party monopolies grew stronger, partisan challenges became less frequent, and voter turnout fell to low levels from which it has never recovered. Although antifusion laws probably played only a small part in causing this general decline in competition, they seem to have had a more significant role in weakening third parties.[20]

It was the challenge of an emerging third party in Minnesota that put the issue of fusion candidacy back on the political agenda. The New Party— an assortment of labor activists, environmentalists, community organizers, and progressive academics—began its campaign against antifusion laws in 1990, established chapters in a dozen states, and achieved a notable if short-lived victory in federal court. In 1996, the Eighth Circuit Court of Appeals struck down the Minnesota law banning fusion candidacies. They declared the ban unconstitutional because it severely burdens third parties' associational rights.[21] The reasoning resembled the argument from forced choice mentioned earlier: the ban "force[s] the New Party to make a no-win choice . . . members must either cast their votes for candidates with no realistic chance of winning, defect from their party and vote for a major party candidate who does, or decline to vote at all."[22]

In 1997, the Supreme Court reversed, concluding that the burden imposed on the New Party is outweighed by the state's interests in "ballot integrity and political stability."[23] The burden is not heavy, the Court said, because the party remains free to endorse any candidate, ally itself with others, and nominate any other candidates for office. Without a ban on fusion, the Court feared that the ballot could be manipulated in various ways by any party. For example, minor parties could use it to "bootstrap their way to major party status" simply by nominating the major party candidate. Major parties could create numerous pseudoparties brandishing names like "No New Taxes" or "Safe Streets," who would turn the ballot into a "billboard for political advertising." But the Court's most significant concern was the preservation of the two-party system: "the constitution permits the Minnesota Legislature to decide that political stability is best served through a healthy two-party system."[24] Such a system may offer fewer alternatives to individual voters, but the alternatives it does offer are more meaningful. The candidates have a greater chance of winning office and carrying out policies that voters favor.

It may appear, then, that from the individualist perspective of voters, fusion enhances choice, and from the institutional perspective of the party system, fusion weakens choice. That is perhaps why the appeals court, which favored fusion, couched its analysis in terms of a "no-win choice" for individual voters and individual parties, and why the Supreme Court majority, which permitted the fusion ban, emphasized the importance of preserving the two-party system—an institutional claim. The difference, however, is not so sharp as this contrast suggests. The case for fusion at the individual level is more ambiguous, and the case at the institutional level stronger, than this contrast implies. Fusion can be defended, but more cogently by supplementing the individualist with institutional arguments.

Like the proponents of fusion, opponents also appeal to the value of choice, but emphasize a different aspect of it. Their first argument is not satisfactory, but their second has considerable force. The first argument is that fusion creates confusing ballots and leads to voter error. If a candidate is listed more than once, some voters, thinking that they should mark their ballot more than once, may cast an invalid ballot. Their choice is not free because they do not understand what they are doing. As a Minnesota state official commented: "When the name appears on the ballot numerous times— in fact, this happened in Connecticut in one of their elections where fusion was used—some of the voters thought that they had to fill in every line where the name appeared for the vote to count." [25]

This objection is paternalistic in a way that is inconsistent with the principle of free choice. The principle presumes that if voters are provided with adequate information, they should be responsible for making their own decisions. (Adequate information includes clear instructions, a well-designed ballot, and reliable guidance from election officials—ingredients that may be missing in some elections, as they were in some counties in Florida in 2000.) But the possibility of voter confusion should not be invoked as a general objection to limiting choice. Even the Supreme Court majority that permitted the fusion ban rejected this kind of paternalism. In oral argument, Justice O'Connor observed: "[W]hatever one might speculate about the lack of intelligence of the voters, we do have the State of New York, where this has gone on without huge confusion." (Justice Scalia remarked: "New Yorkers are smarter, I think. That's probably the answer.") [26] In its final opinion, the Court majority went out of its way to make clear that it did not rely on any paternalistic argument. [27]

Opponents of fusion have a second, stronger argument that appeals to the value of free choice. They point out that the range of choice is decreased if parties nominate the same candidate. Choice is restricted because voters have fewer candidates to choose from. In the Minnesota debate, the opponents of fusion argued that "a primary concern" should be to present "a diverse field of candidates to voters." A fusion ban does not "reduce the candidate choices available to voters or shrink the spectrum of ideas that opposing candidates are able to offer. On the contrary, it encourages minor parties to present candidates for election who may have been overlooked by the major parties." [28] Third parties serve an important function: they introduce "fresh faces" in the political race. When the parties perform that function, they deserve recognition on the ballot, but not when they simply endorse a candidate already nominated by one of the major parties. [29]

From the voters' point of view, the main contribution of third parties is not to increase the range of choices, however welcome fresh faces might be.

Rather, it is to increase the chances that voters will find at least one candidate on the ballot whom they regard as acceptable. Fusion opponents can argue that the best way third parties can serve this function is by offering citizens (and candidates) another path to nomination. If the party's nomination process is relatively open, then voters disenchanted with the major parties will have an additional opportunity to secure a place on the ballot for a candidate they prefer. What third parties most distinctively offer, and what the fusion ban may encourage, is not an increase in the number, range, or freshness of candidates, but an expansion of the opportunities for nominating different candidates. More choices may increase the chances that voters will find at least one candidate on the ballot they wish to elect. Whether this argument against fusion is ultimately correct depends on the nature of the nominating process in third parties, but the argument is sufficient to show that the case for fusion is not conclusive at the individual level.

Turning to a more institutional perspective and taking a longer-term view, we may assume that citizens in the United States have made their choice: they prefer the two-party system to multiparty systems (at least those of the European variety). If this assumption seems too much like a dubious form of tacit consent, then we might say that, in the absence of a compelling argument that justice requires a different system, we should not declare a particular election or a series of elections unjust simply because the electoral process is biased in favor of a two-party system. Under these circumstances, we should not object—and courts should not disallow—laws designed to support that system. Citizens could of course mount a challenge to the two-party system. There is no natural law that declares it the best of all systems, even for the United States. But if no such challenge presents itself, permitting legislatures to do what they think best to preserve the two-party system may best promote free choice.

Yet even from this institutional perspective, the case against fusion is not compelling. New York state permits fusion candidacies and has supported a robust third party, and yet the two-party system prospers. (Admittedly, the state's highly restrictive ballot access laws help the major parties maintain their dominance.) Even if we assume that citizens have chosen the two-party system over others, we need a further step in the argument to conclude that they have chosen to preserve the two existing parties as we know them. This further step requires some basis for claiming that these parties continue to fulfill the goals of the two-party system that citizens support. In practice,

that means that there must be institutional mechanisms for effectively challenging the parties. Their aim should be not to promote competition for its
own sake, but to keep the paths to nomination as open as possible.

If state regulation of the internal processes of the parties is rejected as
too intrusive, then state protection of the opportunities of third parties to
challenge the major parties becomes essential. Even those who give priority
to preserving the two-party system acknowledge that third parties deserve
some protection against the inherent major-party bias of the system. In the
oral argument in the Minnesota case, the state's assistant solicitor general
conceded that, though states should be free to favor the two-party system,
they may not "establish formidable barriers" or "go so far as to close the
door" to minor parties.[30]

This necessary concession prompted Justice Breyer to ask: "How do I
measure *how far?*"[31] Without an answer to this question, or at least without a principled distinction between the fusion ban and other impediments
to third parties, we cannot consistently tell states they may not ban fusion
candidacies. If we object to fusion, then we must object to many other long-
accepted elements of our electoral system:

> There are a lot of rules deliberately disadvantaging third and fourth and
> fifth parties—first past the post, single member districts. There are good
> arguments for and against such things. Proportional representation in
> many parties allows parties to grow more quickly and is a better represen-
> tation of people's views. On the other hand, two parties, which is a much
> worse representation, and interferes with people's ability to choose what
> they want, has the advantage that we know whom to hold responsible for
> good or bad government. Now . . . how can we say that a State doesn't
> have the right to choose between those two different views of democratic
> representation?[32]

If we can distinguish the fusion ban from other impediments within the
two-party system, we do not have to choose a wholly different view of democratic representation in order to defend fusion candidacies. The attorney for
the New Party suggested a distinction that goes part of the way toward resolving the difficulty Breyer raises. We can accept the "basic architecture"
of a system (such as the single-member rather than multimember districts)
but still reject the creation of "content-based rules" within that system.[33] We
should object to rules that dictate the content of choice—rules that tell voters and parties which candidates they may nominate—because they intrude

too deeply into free choice. That is in effect what the fusion ban does. Strictly speaking, the ban does not prevent a party from nominating anyone, but it does bar the minor party from placing its own nominee on the ballot if the person is already the nominee of another party. That may not seem like such a serious limitation; after all, the party can nominate almost anyone else in the district or state. But the ban is a limitation not only on the selection of a particular candidate but on the reason or rationale for the choice. It tells the party that it cannot choose a candidate for the purpose of forging an alliance with another party, or for the purpose of building public support for the party in future races. It in effect says "you can nominate anybody unless the person is popular enough that he might appeal to another party."[34]

The fusion ban is thus not only a limitation on the free choice of minor parties and their supporters, but also one that is in principle different from the relatively content-neutral limitations of the system as a whole. Single-member district and winner-take-all rules certainly affect the range of choice by influencing the number of parties and candidates, but they do not seek to regulate the reasons for choices as fusion bans do. These "architectural" rules provide the context in which parties and voters make their decisions, but they stop short of dictating the content of those decisions.

Although this distinction provides a basis for protecting third parties without challenging the whole edifice of the two-party system, it does not specifically answer Breyer's question: How far may states go in disadvantaging third parties? The question is not easy—perhaps not even possible—to answer in general terms in advance of considering particular institutional barriers in specific contexts. That is perhaps one reason that the Court has never been able to formulate a clear, easy-to-apply test for ballot restrictions.[35] A related reason is that any test should distinguish between single-issue groups, which seek ballot access only to advance a very limited agenda, and genuine political parties, which seek to build broader coalitions and promote general principles as the major parties do. From the perspective of discretionary representation and other collaborative conceptions of the democratic process, a party system that discourages single-issue groups and encourages broad-based parties is arguably preferable. Yet the distinction is hard to draw in practice, and courts especially would find it difficult to justify treating the two kinds of organizations differently.

The judicial forum is not well suited to considering the effects on the party system as a whole, as distinct from the effects on particular parties, whether major or minor. Courts are more comfortable adjudicating claims about individual rights than ordering structural changes. Procedural rules—such as the limits on the standing to bring suits and restrictions on advisory opinions—discourage challenges to large-scale institutions such as party systems. When the challenge to the fusion ban comes before a court, it takes the form of a conflict between the right of individuals to take advantage of a fusion option and the state's interest in preserving the stability of the political system. Framed that way, the individual's right pales in comparison with the state's interest. The broader institutional considerations that could strengthen the case for fusion are set aside. The courts do not provide the most suitable forum for considering the future of the two-party system.

Legislative forums may be even less suitable. Although legislatures are more comfortable with considering institutional design and structural change, they are also usually more partisan or at least more partial than courts. Most of their members have an interest in preserving not only the two-party system but the existing two parties. One party may see some advantages under certain circumstances in promoting the prospects of a third party, but over the long run each of the two major parties has a shared interest in discouraging challenges from minor parties. This common interest leads to what has been called partisan lockups, in which dominant factions within a party or the dominant parties erect entry barriers against nonmembers or third-party challengers.[36] In addition to imposing fusion bans, parties may implicitly conspire to discourage challengers by ensuring that party leaders hold safe seats and by preserving campaign finance regulations that benefit incumbents.

Consider the deliberation that took place in the Minnesota legislature when members were faced with the circuit court decision that temporarily overturned the fusion ban. They did not know that the Supreme Court would soon overrule that court, and they needed to act promptly to bring their electoral procedures into conformity with the law before the fall election. But their alacrity was not simply an eagerness to obey the law. If they did not act quickly, minor party nominees could be listed on the ballot several times and could use their vote totals to qualify for major party status and public financing. The main bill intended to address the problem created by the court's decision—introduced by a representative of one of the major parties—went no further than necessary. It permitted more than one party to be listed under the candidate's name on the ballot, but provided for no separate tally of party votes, and therefore no way for minor parties to demonstrate their actual support or their eligibility for major party status and public financing.[37]

In committees and on the floor, the New Party members objected that this minimalist approach violated the aim of enabling "the small party to establish itself as a durable, influential player in the political arena."[38] Sandra Pappas, a senator from one of the major parties, sought to come to their aid: she proposed an amendment that would permit voters to indicate their support for the party and for the fusion candidate. But her colleagues denounced the amendment: the floor manager, Senator John Marty, argued that "we basically have an election system where we elect candidates to office, not political parties. . . . this is a philosophical reason."[39] The New Party members and their sympathizers were outvoted at every stage, and the minimalist bill passed.[40]

The Minnesota experience underscores two different sets of institutional considerations that favor fusion, or at least weaken the case against it. First, the assumption that a two-party system promotes free choice depends on the possibility that the dominant parties are open to challenge, both from within and without. Such challenges can partially compensate for any lack of internal democracy within the major parties. The role of challenger is one that third parties are well qualified to perform, and can play more effectively if they can offer the option of a fusion candidacy. The New Party's failure to win even minor concessions on this issue weakened its capacity as a challenger on other issues and other candidates in the future. The second set of considerations refers to who should decide the question of fusion candidacies. The New Party's experience suggests that fusion may not always receive a fair hearing in legislatures because it is often perceived as a threat to the dominant parties. This case also shows that courts cannot be counted on to protect third parties. The judicial forum did not ultimately provide a friendly site for considering the merits of fusion.

The next chapter returns to the question of who should have the final authority to decide the merits of various electoral practices, but as far as the case for fusion is concerned, the analysis here shows that we can justify it as promoting free choice if we take into account these broader institutional considerations. The arguments from the perspective of the individual voter are not decisive: whether choice is enhanced depends more on the openness of the nominating process of the parties than on the range of choices or the likelihood of a nominee's winning office. The institutional arguments incline more toward fusion. The promise of the two-party system to serve the free choice of voters is less likely to be fulfilled to the extent that minor parties are denied the resources they need to influence the major parties' selection of nominees. Those resources include fusion candidacies. Because minor parties are less likely to secure such resources in a legislature dominated by two parties, legislative bans on fusion and other benefits for minor parties do not adequately respect the value of free choice.

The Security of Blanket Primaries

Fusion bans excite the opposition of minor parties and an occasional major party, but another electoral device, the blanket primary, rouses the ire of nearly all the parties. It is therefore typically adopted only by popular initiative, a process that bypasses the parties in the legislature and the state and national party organizations. In 1996 the voters of California approved Proposition 198, which replaced the state's closed primaries with blanket primaries. In a closed primary, only the members of a political party can vote on its nominees. In a blanket primary, any registered voter can vote for any nominee for any office. Although the California law was called the Open Primary Act, a blanket primary is actually more open than an open primary. In an open primary, a registered voter may request a ballot for any party, but then must choose among only candidates of that party.[41]

Both the proponents and the opponents of the proposition appealed to the value of free choice. The proponents of this initiative argued that the blanket primary would permit voters to vote for "the best candidate for each office, regardless of party affiliation, thereby giving voters greater choice."[42] Opponents defended the existing closed primary as providing "a real choice among candidates of different parties" and condemned the blanket primary as "an invitation to political mischief by special interests and political consultants."[43] They clinched the case (at least for certain voters) with this simile: "Allowing members of one party a large voice in choosing another party's nominee . . . is like letting UCLA's football team choose USC's head coach!"[44]

Political parties in the state, including the Libertarian Party and the Peace and Freedom Party, and the national organizations of both the Republican and Democratic parties publicly opposed the initiative. But no party undertook any significant effort to mobilize opposition. The Democrats declined to run a joint campaign against the initiative, evidently in the hope that the Republicans would mount their own. But after the polls showed that it was almost certain to succeed, the Republicans decided to devote their resources to other causes.[45] The parties did little more to support their own initiative two years later, which would have ensured that nonmembers would continue to be excluded from the elections that selected the party's delegates to the presidential nominating conventions. That initiative also failed, and the parties, now more in the mood to cooperate with each other, issued a joint statement and filed joint appeals in court.

The lower courts held that Proposition 198 did not violate the parties' right of free association.[46] The burden on the parties is not severe, and the state's interest in affording voters greater choice (among other goals) is substantial. But the Supreme Court overruled the lower courts, holding that California's blanket primary violates a political party's right of free association by forcing it to open up its candidate selection process—its "basic function"—to "persons wholly unaffiliated with the party, who may have different views from the party."[47] (The justices evidently assumed that imposing a nominee on a party is more intrusive than preventing a party from nominating its preferred candidate, as in a fusion ban, which they had upheld.)

Some important values are at stake on both sides of this disagreement, and they warrant further deliberation. Yet both sides made some claims that each mistakenly believed would resolve the disagreement straight away. Some opponents of the blanket primary argued that enhancing voters' choice is not a desirable goal. One of the expert witnesses testified at trial that giving voters more choice would benefit only the political elite. The "well educated, well informed, politically active" are the only voters who "will really be able to make good use of those extra choices," and they "already have disproportionate power."[48] Because of their "political ignorance," women, blacks, the poor, and the young would not be able to take full advantage of the greater opportunities for choice. This is a doubly spurious appeal to the value of equal respect. That value does not necessarily have priority over free choice in these circumstances. But even if we were to agree that it should take precedence, we should not accept the way it is deployed here. Equal respect does not require denying voters the opportunity to exercise choice on the grounds that they lack the capacity to do so.

Proponents of the blanket primary also make a claim that they mistakenly believe disposes of the dispute without further argument. According to exit polls, Proposition 198 had been supported by large majorities of voters of both major parties as well as by independents.[49] Should we not conclude, then, that the controversy is settled because the parties speaking through their supporters have endorsed the blanket primary? (Or at least that the dispute is simply between the party leaders and its supporters, and the only democratic resolution is to side with the supporters?) Even assuming that the polls accurately captured the views of supporters, we should not accept the results of an opinion survey as equivalent to a vote by the party. The parties have procedures for changing their common rules and for adopting official positions. Usually these procedures require a process of deliberation, which include soliciting recommendations from a central committee and permitting further discussion in party conferences or other similar forums. The party's view is thus not simply the sum of the views of its supporters or even its members considered as individuals. It is rather a collective outcome that results from following the deliberative procedures of the party organization.

Yet we should not accept the claim that parties should have the final word about what is in the interest of parties generally, even when the parties speak in their official voice after due deliberation. Party advocates, supported by several judicial rulings, seem to make such a claim. In response to the proponents of Proposition 198 who argued that the blanket primary would actually strengthen parties by making them more representative, the party advocates and their judicial allies maintained that it is for the parties to decide themselves what is in their interest.[50] To let authorities impose on a party their view of its interest is to practice a form of institutional paternalism. It is equivalent to interfering with the autonomy of individuals by forcing them to act on some authority's view of what is good for them. Parties, like individuals, should be free to choose what is in their own best interest, even if they are mistaken. That is supposedly part of what free choice should mean.

But parties are not individuals. To treat them as such, to regard them as having moral standing as collective entities, is a case of misplaced institutionalism. Treating institutions as individuals is as much a failure to appreciate the institutional dimension of politics as failing to recognize the institutional implications of individual actions (the kind of failure emphasized in chapter 1). Institutions have rights, but they should be derived from the rights of individuals. To determine what rights parties should have, we should decide what ends they serve for citizens.[51] Citizens join parties to pursue various ends, but at least as far as the nominating process goes, they participate in order to influence who the party puts forward in the general election. Their aim is to try to increase the chances that when they vote in the general election, they will have a more meaningful choice: they will find at least one acceptable alternative on the ballot. With respect to free choice, parties should be judged according to whether they contribute to an institutional process that promotes this aim of individual voters. We should assess the blanket primary, then, not according to how well it protects the autonomy of parties, as they or anyone else may define it, but rather according to how well it promotes the free choice of all citizens in the selection of nominees.

It might be objected that this way of framing the issue ignores the constitutional right of free association. The implication might appear to be that citizens have a right to form parties and to exclude those who do not share their views only if their doing so promotes the general interest. If the right were conditional in this way, it would hardly serve the purpose of a right. The point of a right is to prevent precisely this kind of justification; it is supposed to block any attempt to justify the restriction of individual liberty by appealing to social utility or the general interest. In striking down the blanket primary, the Supreme Court majority was seeking to protect the associational rights of parties against this kind of appeal.

But in the case of the blanket primary, the right of free association is not threatened so broadly as this objection implies (or as the Supreme Court majority claimed). The challenge is not to the whole of the party's autonomy. Parties remain completely free to determine their criteria for membership, their internal rules and procedures, their methods of campaigning, and their choice of candidates to endorse. Only the party's role in the nominating process is at issue. That role is admittedly important for the party, but it is also important for the polity. The reason that we must ask whether respecting the autonomy of parties in the nominating process benefits the process as a whole is that the process is mandated by the state. It is the only means of access that candidates have to the ballot, and therefore the only means citizens have to influence what their final choices will be in the general election.

That primaries are mandated by the state makes a critical difference. If parties could select their candidates through conventions or caucuses, they would be less subject to regulation because they would not be using a state-sponsored process. The right of free association would permit them to exclude anyone who did not support the platform or candidates a majority of members favor. A party would even be free to advocate white supremacy, select only racist candidates, and exclude members who refused to adhere to this party line.[52] The requirement that parties hold primaries, especially combined with the blanket provision, further limits the freedom of parties, but the question remains whether it limits the free choice of voters. Although not all states require primaries, there are good reasons for doing so. In many elections, the parties' nominations in effect narrow the voters' choice to two candidates, and in some elections, the party nomination determines the ultimate winner. But in any case, when a state requires that all candidates be selected in a primary, as California does, a political party's freedom (and that of its members) cannot be absolute.[53]

To conclude that a party's freedom may be restricted in order to enhance the free choice of all voters shifts the terms of the debate, but it does not determine how much or in what ways the choice may be restricted. The conclusion does not immediately justify blanket primaries: it leaves open the question whether they serve the value of free choice better than closed primaries do.[54] What remains at issue is a conflict between competing conceptions of electoral choice, neither of which can be completely rejected because each appeals to different reasonable conceptions of representation. This can be made clearer by considering the ways in which each kind of primary may enhance electoral choice.

The blanket primary provides opportunities for at least three kinds of choices lacking in a closed primary. First, and most obviously, voters have the chance to vote for nominees of different parties for different offices. This kind of primary maximizes what may be called the range of partisan choice. The range of choice is even greater because the primary is not a general election: voters know they have another opportunity to express their preferences among a (potentially) different slate of candidates. Second, the blanket primary benefits independents and minor party supporters who happen to live in the "safe" districts in which a major party candidate always wins the general election. They have no hope of electing their own candidates, and therefore have no influence at all in a closed primary. In the blanket primary, they at least have a choice among the nominees of the major party. Third, voters in a blanket primary have the option of voting strategically: they may vote for the weaker candidate in the opposition party in an effort to strengthen the position of the candidate of their own party in the general election. In the debates about the blanket primary, the dispute about this kind of cross-voting focused almost entirely on how common it is. Both proponents and opponents seemed to agree that strategic voting is less respectable than ordinary voting, and should not be encouraged.[55] But if the aim is to increase the range of alternatives from which voters may choose, then voting strategically is just another option that they should be offered.

A closed primary can also enhance the value of choice in several ways. First, instead of expanding the range of partisan choice, it increases what may be called the purity of partisan choice. It improves the chances of nominating a candidate who more closely reflects the views or preferences of the party faithful. A closed primary gives voters more choice among more purely partisan candidates. It thus offers a range of choices different from that offered in a blanket primary, which in this respect is more like a general election. Second, independents and minor party supporters in safe districts actually do have a choice in a closed primary. They can choose to join the major party. Admittedly, this may be a "hard choice," as Justice Scalia acknowledges, but it restricts their freedom less than the blanket primary constrains the freedom of party members, who may be forced to accept nonmembers' choice of a nominee as the standard-bearer of the party.[56] Third, a closed primary protects the faithful party members from "raiding" by strategic voters. It thereby increases the chances that their own sincere choices will not be rendered ineffective by the insincere choices of others. Even if strategic voting is rare, sincere cross-over voting is common (perhaps as high as 25 percent in some elections), and could limit the effect of the choice of party members. In the absence of a closed primary, "a single election in which the party nominee is selected by nonparty members could be enough to destroy the party."[57] Or if "being saddled with an unwanted, and possibly antithetical, nominee" would not completely destroy the party, it would "severely transform it."

Further analysis of the value of choice in each of the types of primaries might show that on balance one type is preferable to the other. (The contribution of each type to informed choice would also need to be considered. Blanket primaries potentially expose citizens to more information about more candidates, but closed primaries may permit citizens to use less information more effectively because they can have greater confidence that the nominees will follow the party platform.) On their face, the value of choice in each type of primary seems closely enough balanced that it would be difficult to reject one type because, from the perspective of the individual voter, it promotes free choice better than the other. The reason that it would be difficult, and the reason they seem closely balanced, is that they reflect different conceptions of representation. We need to move from the level of individual to institutional choice to see why this is so.

Blanket primaries tend to produce candidates who are more centrist. Officials elected under these systems stand closer to the median policy positions of their districts than do those elected under closed primaries.[58] Because candidates need to "attract support from the entire electorate, not simply from members of their respective parties," they are arguably more representative than candidates elected in closed primaries.[59] But they cannot be too representative of the center: if the nominees of the parties converge too closely, the blanket primary in effect becomes a general election. The aim should be to encourage parties to reach beyond the party faithful but to retain their distinctive party identities. If parties keep this aim in mind, the blanket primary can support the building of broader coalitions, and reduce the factionalism that Madison warned against in *Federalist* No. 10.[60] They can promote candidates and parties that adopt more comprehensive goals and more consensual programs.

Opponents of the blanket primary point out that this effect comes at a price, and one that Madison would not wish to pay: "In the Founders' view, factions were to be controlled not by seeking to eliminate them, but by ensuring a multiplicity of factions such that each would hinder the others from gaining a controlling majority."[61] The candidates selected in a blanket primary may be more representative of majorities, but they are less representative of minorities.[62] With blanket primaries, the parties, especially minor ones, find it more difficult to articulate a message of their own, recruit candidates committed to their platform, and mobilize interest groups to support their nominee.[63] (The party label of a candidate may therefore mean less, depriving voters of an important informational cue, and thus diminishing the value of free choice, as the next section suggests.) Our electoral system, with its single-member districts and plurality voting, already favors candidates and parties who stand close to the center of the electorate. Candidates who move too far toward either of the extremes risk successful challenges by a candidate who stands only slightly closer toward the center.[64] The blanket primary reinforces this tendency. As the multiplicity of factions merges into the unity of a two-party system, the distinctive voice of minorities is lost.

This contrast between two conceptions of representation is significant but still incomplete because it is largely static. We should be concerned with not only what groups are represented, but also with when in the process they are represented. The electoral process, like any political process, must resolve some disagreement at each stage by a final decision, but it usually leaves some to be resolved at later stages. Processes differ in how much disagreement they permit to go forward to each subsequent stage. Closed primaries leave more open for decision at later stages than do blanket primaries. The multiplicity of factions persists longer, and the distinctive voice of minorities continues to be heard longer. The persistence of disagreement does not mean that minorities necessarily have more influence. At each subsequent stage of a electoral process, more people participate, and any individual or group is likely to have less influence. What minorities gain from expressing their distinctive message longer, they may lose from influencing the electoral outcome less. Nevertheless, the closed primary does seem on balance to provide a more fluid and open form of representation. It can give minorities more influence in the nominating process, and can better promote the value of free choice for all voters.

We began with what seemed a simple question about a simple electoral practice: Does the blanket primary enhance the free choice of voters? Even without considering other values that such a practice might affect, we found that the answer is surprisingly complex. Some of the reasons offered to justify, and others to reject, the blanket primary can be discounted, but much of the core of both the arguments for and against remain. At the level of individual choice, the case for the blanket primary, though uneasy, is plausible. But when we consider the institutional context—in particular the kind of representation that each type of primary encourages—the closed primary looks more attractive. It can promote free choice more broadly.

More important than the resolution of this specific disagreement about primaries is a general implication for the principle of free choice. To interpret the meaning of the first part of the principle—to determine how the requirement of an acceptable set of alternatives should be understood—we need to look behind the range of alternatives offered on the ballot in the general election, and even beyond the correspondence between the alternatives and voters' preferences. We need to attend to the nominating process and the conceptions of representation that it expresses.

INFORMING VOTERS

Political science has amply confirmed what democratic theorists have long lamented: most citizens do not know much about most of the candidates for whom they vote, and even less about the issues on which the candidates disagree.[65] They know little about candidates and issues partly because they are not interested in acquiring political information, and partly because the political media do not present it in a helpful and reliable way. Although political scientists today describe the level of knowledge of the American voter somewhat more favorably than earlier studies did, they still paint a grim portrait: most cannot recall the name of their representatives, and many hold contradictory opinions about major political issues.[66] Their view of the American electorate does not seem very different from what Tocqueville saw nearly a century ago: "the people . . . are bound always to make hasty judgments and to seize on the most prominent characteristics" in choosing their representatives.[67]

Does political ignorance of this kind undermine the capacity for free choice, and thereby the justice of elections? Tocqueville himself did not think so.[68] He had no confidence that voters on their own would make wise choices. "I take it as proved that those who consider universal suffrage as a guarantee of the excellence of the resulting choice suffer under a complete delusion." Nor did he believe, as did theorists such as John Stuart Mill, that expanding political participation would eventually raise the level of political knowledge.[69] But he nevertheless accepted the desirability of universal suffrage. Among other advantages, it would prevent individuals and groups from falsely claiming to speak for the people, and thereby challenging the legitimacy of government.[70] More significant for our purposes, he accepted universal suffrage because he counted on what might be called institutional filters to provide a "partial corrective" for its defects. Two kinds of filters are especially important.

First, a habit of taking cues from better informed citizens—a habit Tocqueville thought then manifest only in the "mores" of New England—enables voters to make better choices. By better choices, he meant that voters would select men of "intellectual and moral superiority." That noble hope has all but vanished in modern elections, but the idea that voters need only minimal information if they take cues from better informed citizens or from other instructive sources remains very much alive. Indeed, it is a dominant theme in the studies of elections in contemporary political science. One variation emphasizes the two-step flow of communication: a division of labor enables ordinary voters to defer to opinion leaders who have been able to acquire the information necessary for making sensible voting decisions.[71] A more prominent variation points to "information shortcuts" and "cognitive heuristics," which voters use to make decisions that are similar to those they would make if they were perfectly informed. "People probably do not need large amounts of information to make rational voting choices. Cues from like-minded citizens and groups (including cues related to demographic characteristics and party labels) may be sufficient."[72]

To some extent, this minimalist literature is reassuring. It provides some basis for believing that voters' choices are free, or at least could be made freer without placing heroic demands on their political interest and competence. But we should not take too much comfort from these studies. They do not adequately distinguish shortcuts that are conducive to free choice from those that are not. Party identification under certain conditions may be a serviceable cue for many voters, but "likability" of a candidate even under favorable conditions is notoriously subject to manipulation.[73] The condition of the economy may be a useful if unfair heuristic, but a candidate's gaffe—even a culturally significant misstep of trying to eat an unshucked tamale—may be not only unfair but also misleading.[74] Missing in the optimistic readings of these studies are not only the distinctions that political scientists conducting further empirical inquiry might supply but, more important, some standards that citizens carrying on further political deliberation might themselves employ. There is no reason to discourage voters from using shortcuts, but there is good reason to encourage them to decide deliberately which shortcuts to use.

Another reason for caution is that the minimalist literature provides little evidence that the collective results produced by voters using these shortcuts are as satisfactory as the results realized by well-informed voters. The most systematic studies reveal substantial differences between the behavior of informed and uninformed voters.[75] These studies are consistent with the aim of increasing the level of information in the electorate. They do not suggest that more information, at least more information of the right kind, would be undesirable. As a normative ideal, we can still embrace a principle of free choice that encourages efforts to increase the level of useful information that citizens possess, even while acknowledging that levels less than the ideal may be adequate to enable citizens to make relatively informed choices—at least sufficiently informed choices to keep an election from being regarded as unjust.

Choice is freer when it is better informed, and voters could make freer choices if they acquired more reliable and relevant information than they currently possess. Normatively, that much seems unproblematic. The empirical challenges of creating a more informed electorate are more difficult. We need to know more about what kind of information voters actually need, what obstacles impede their acquiring it, and what measures could overcome those obstacles. In addressing these questions, political scientists have paid more attention to how individuals process information than to how institutions refine or distort it. In a criticism of his own and other earlier work on information shortcuts, one writes: "Citizens do not operate as decision makers in isolation from political institutions. If they are in a position to overcome their informational shortfalls by taking advantage of judgmental shortcuts, it is because public choices have been organized by political institutions in ways that lend themselves to these shortcuts."[76] In the spirit of the principle of free choice developed here, empirical inquiry would pay more attention to the institutional context of choice.

The institutions that most significantly shape information in political campaigns are the media. Critics charge that the media concentrate more on campaign tactics than policy issues, present sound bites rather than substantive debates, favor human interest features over hard political news, frame issues as discrete events rather than systematic patterns, dwell on personal failings of public officials more than their public failures, follow a herd instinct rather than their own independent judgment, and succumb to competitive pressures to report sooner rather than checking sources and facts more carefully.[77] The list goes on, and the indictment in many cases is no doubt warranted.

But with few exceptions (notably, campaign finance), the remedies proposed to deal with the failures of the media do not involve using the power of the state to limit anyone's free choice. Because freedom of the press carries such great weight in our constitutional tradition, the press itself—along with the forces of the market, and the pressures of private individuals and groups—is assumed to provide sufficient, and in any case almost the only acceptable, means of improving the media. This assumption is certainly questionable, but its constitutional respectability has the effect of preempting most conflicts of the kind that arise within the principle of free choice. Generally, if the question is whether the state should restrict the free choice of the press to enhance the free choice of others, the answer favors the press. That does not mean that the media have no responsibility for making the electoral process more just; on the contrary, the constitutional privileges they enjoy make their public obligations even greater.

The normative conflicts become more pressing when we turn to Tocqueville's second kind of institutional filter. To compensate for the inevitable deficiencies in political knowledge, he counted on certain "laws, democratic

in their nature, which nonetheless succeed in partially correcting democracy's dangerous instincts."[78] The laws he had in mind were those that established an institution—the indirect election of senators—that expired long
ago. Also his hope for the spread of two-stage elections has gone unfulfilled.
Indeed, the increasingly frequent use of referenda in recent years has taken
the electoral process in exactly the opposite direction. Referenda (discussed
in the next chapter) remove not only one but both "stages" of elections; they
circumvent the filter of legislative representation and permit voters to enact
laws directly.

Nevertheless, in a different form Tocqueville's concept of a filter remains
relevant. It suggests the unconventional thought that democracy may work
better if voters are denied certain kinds of information. If we cannot have
two-stage elections, perhaps we can create other filters, such as laws designed to insulate voters from information that might distort their decisions. The aim would be to discourage voters from making decisions on the
basis of information that in a less direct and more deliberative electoral process would not be so influential. In this spirit, we may ask: Can free choice
in democratic elections be enhanced by using the law to *limit* information
that voters receive?

The question points to a difficult normative problem—another conflict
between kinds of free choice. The conflict is between choice based on all
information that an individual voter happens to acquire, and a choice based
on a limited range of information determined in advance by law.[79] The first
kind of choice is free because individual voters themselves decide, without
legal restriction, what information they wish to consider. The second kind
of choice may also be regarded as free because voters cast their ballot on the
basis of information that is less likely to distort their choice.

The contrast between the two kinds of choice resembles the distinction
between negative and positive liberty.[80] Individuals are negatively free when
they are not constrained in selecting the information they use to make decisions. They are positively free when the information they use enables them
to make decisions that enhance their liberty. But to a greater extent than
the concept of positive liberty implies, the second kind of electoral choice
(decision with restricted information) is under the control of voters. They
can decide themselves what limits to place on the information they receive. They can decide in advance (indirectly through their representatives)
what types of information they wish to exclude. The process resembles a
precommitment device, such as a gag rule or secrecy order, which consti-

tutional assemblies and legislatures adopt to regulate their proceedings.[81] Like Ulysses, voters may bind themselves (with institutional wax in their collective ears) to avoid the temptation to listen to attractive but defective messages. They can protect themselves from voting on the basis of information they believe may distort their judgment.

Imposing restrictions on information in this way is not objectionably paternalistic, as is prohibiting fusion candidacies on grounds that they confuse some voters. Here the restriction aims at the good of those who are imposing it, and is intended to apply to all voters equally. Some citizens may still object to the restriction, but their situation is no different from that of most minorities who are outvoted in the legislative process. Legislation is paternalistic with respect to the minority only if the majority could promote their own good in some other fair way without coercing the minority, and if the justification for the legislation depends specifically on an appeal to the good of the minority.

The more serious problem with enhancing free choice by limiting information is the difficulty of determining which information should be restricted, and to what extent. If citizens confine their efforts to restricting only the most detrimental kind, they may avoid infringing free speech, and they may more readily reach agreement about what information should be restricted. Even some modest filters could improve the quality of the information that they use in deciding how to cast their ballot. They could then be better informed and their choices freer than they would otherwise be. To see how, with respect to electoral information, less can be more, consider two controversies that involve efforts to limit what voters can know at election time.

Informative Ballots or Scarlet Letters?

If you had wandered unprepared into the House gallery on February 12, 1997, you would have been perplexed by the proceedings on the floor. The House devoted the whole day to debating eleven different versions of a constitutional amendment intended to limit the terms of members of Congress. Most had been previously approved by initiative in the states.[82] You would not have been surprised that none of the versions of the amendment succeeded in winning the two-thirds margin necessary for passage. Incumbents usually do not vote themselves out of office. But you might have been puzzled by the pattern of voting. Many members voted for one version but consistently opposed other nearly identical versions. (Representative Barney

Frank, doubting that the members could distinguish among the versions, drolly proposed that members should be required to take a quiz on their differences.)[83] As a result of the dispersed support, no amendment gained even a simple majority, and only two received more than a hundred votes.

Why did the advocates of term limits scatter their votes among so many versions instead of concentrating their support on just one? Most of the amendments had been previously approved by initiative in the states, and many members believed that they had to vote only for the exact version adopted by their own state. In some cases they were instructed to vote against any other version. Representative Michael Crapo explained: "Last Congress I supported the . . . term limits bill. . . . However, in this Congress I must oppose this bill because of the initiative passed by the people of the State of Idaho which requires me to oppose any term limits measure that does not have the same set of term limit conditions [as] passed in the State."[84] Members were not literally required to vote as their state's initiative instructed, but if they did not do so, their name on the ballot in the next election would be accompanied by a notation like this:

DISREGARDED VOTERS' INSTRUCTIONS ON TERM LIMITS[85]

The notation came to be known as the "scarlet letter." Naturally, members sought to avoid such a stigma, but their rush to do so was not one of the House's most noble moments of deliberation. Representative Frank reproached his colleagues: you are performing "unbecoming parliamentary flip-flops" just so that "people will know the difference between you and Hester Prynne."[86] Even supporters of term limits feared that they would be branded with the scarlet letter unless they voted for only their own state's version. Just before his term limit amendment failed (and by a larger margin than in the previous session), the floor leader of the bill in the House, Representative Bill McCollum of Florida, blamed the expected defeat on the ballot notation laws: "I think there are far more . . . Members in this body who are for term limits, and if they had their free will and did not have the scarlet letters to be put beside their name . . . they would vote for this."[87]

The strongest argument for ballot notations is that they are informative. Whatever one thinks of term limits, they raise a significant issue about which voters should be informed. The notations tell voters something they want to know. No doubt there are other significant issues that also deserve the voters' attention, and if ballot notations were generally permitted, a fair process to determine which ones win a place on the ballot would need to be established. But proponents of ballot notations believe that creating such a process may be worth the trouble because of their potential for making voters better informed.[88] Ballot notations offer a unique opportunity to enlighten citizens because information presented at the moment of voting is more salient and likely to be more influential than information communicated during a campaign. That is why parties fight hard to get visible labels and prominent positions on the ballot. Simply having the first position on the ballot can make a significant difference.[89] So can having a name of another well-known figure. That is why some enterprising candidates change their names to convey a political message. Consider the Chicago alderman candidate who became "Carol Moseley-Braun" to exploit the popularity that the U.S. senator of that name then enjoyed, the Louisiana candidate who assumed the name "None of the Above," and the Tennessee politician who changed his middle name so that he would appear on the ballot as "Byron (Low-Tax) Looper."[90]

Ballot notations provide cues to more substantial information about a candidate than they explicitly state.[91] They directly respond to the need for simplification that the literature on voting heuristics shows is so important. "Supports a woman's right to choose" may reveal more than the candidate's position on the abortion question; it tells voters that the candidate probably supports a wide range of legislation to help women, and perhaps also other progressive social policies. Group affiliation (such as "Arizonans for Fair Tax Reform") is also an important cue for voters. It can be even more significant than party identification when the positions of parties converge on major issues. If party labels are permitted, why not other notations? Another virtue of ballot notations is that they broaden the political agenda. Because they are used mostly by grassroots organizations, they enhance the range of choice by directing attention to issues that the established parties tend to neglect, such as campaign finance and term limits.[92] They can aid in enforcing "clean election" rules by identifying candidates who stay within expenditure limits.

If ballot notations give voters more information, what reason is there to oppose them? It is easy to raise practical objections. The information they provide can be confusing. Some of the notations about term limits were misleading because they implied that the candidate opposed them in general when he was against only the particular form passed by the state initiative.[93] Who should decide what the ballot notations should say? If the candidates or the parties control the content, the notations may not raise the issues in which many voters are interested. If public opinion polls determine the content, minorities are likely to be slighted. If a nonpartisan commission or a panel of experts manages the process, the notations may be fair but bland. In general, if the practice became widely accepted, the pressure for more and longer notations would increase, and the ballot could become so cluttered that it would cease to be informative.

Nevertheless, most of these objections could be overcome or at least mitigated if we believed that informing voters in this way were a desirable goal in democratic elections. But many people—including all nine members of the Supreme Court—do not. Examining some of the objections raised by opponents of ballot notations can help suggest why providing more information does not always enhance free choice.[94]

The most common objection is that ballot notations—at least the ones deployed in favor of term limits—restrict the free choice of candidates and elected officials. The fear of having to wear the "scarlet letter" forces candidates to support term limits. The two Missouri congressional candidates who challenged the state's ballot notation law explicitly invoked the idea of coercion. They argued that "the public record confirms the obvious: that the ballot label can cost votes, and thus will have a coercive effect on candidates and their campaigns."[95] When the candidates' challenge reached the Supreme Court, much of the oral argument centered on the question of whether the "instruction" to the candidates to support term limits was enforceable and therefore coercive. In an exchange that illustrates the dispute, one of the justices asked:

> Is it accurate to call it an enforcement mechanism? [U]sually you enforce laws by punishing people who break them. . . . Here, the punishment is simply telling people that you ignored the instruction. Is that a punishment?

The deputy solicitor general replied:

> [I]t's an enforcement . . . because of the pejorative language . . . because it is a decision by the state legislature to focus the attention of the voters and judge candidates on a single issue. . . . And . . . because it is done in the voting booth and not in a public forum where there is an opportunity to respond and to debate.[96]

There are two difficulties with this emphasis on coercion. First, it is not clear that ballot notations are coercive in any relevant sense.[97] The notations do not prevent candidates from choosing to oppose term limits. Admittedly, the notations put pressure on candidates to support term limits, and may increase the chances that they will be defeated if they oppose term limits. But so does any kind of effective political communication, much of which also is "pejorative." The decision to put this particular notation on the ballot was made by the voters themselves, not only by the state legislature, and the issue had been fully debated in a public forum before the election. Furthermore, to the extent that coercion is involved, the agent is not the state, but the voters themselves; they are the ones who apply the "punishment." The state facilitates the electoral sanction by providing the information, but only in the way that it supports a similar sanction by requiring disclosure of the names of campaign contributors.

Second, even if ballot notations could be said to coerce candidates, they may still be justified by their effects in promoting the free choice of voters. Some of their critics argue as if the most important consideration is the right of candidates. Two justices declared that the Missouri scheme violates the "right of a political candidate, once lawfully on the ballot, to have his name appear unaccompanied by pejorative language required by the State."[98] Even the most thoughtful academic critics often emphasize the claims of candidates—for example, their "right to shape their own messages."[99] The persistent references to the "disadvantage" or "handicap" that some candidates suffer as a result of ballot notations also imply a concern for treating candidates fairly, without any special regard for the interests of voters.[100] The competitive view of electoral justice that underlies many of these arguments distorts the debate by making the contest between the candidates seem more important than the informational resources voters have to decide it. Proponents of this view no doubt assume that fair competition among the candidates serves the interests of voters, but they rarely consider the possibility that promoting competition may conflict with some of those interests. The emphasis on candidates, whether they be coerced or free, is misplaced.

Nevertheless, the conflict between the rights of individual candidates to choose their messages and the rights of individual voters to be informed is not the most important issue. The deeper conflict is between institutional concepts of representation—the mandatory and discretionary views of representation described in the previous chapter.[101] Ballot notations tend to support the former: representatives are "instructed" to support term limits. The Missouri law specifically lists eight ways representatives should act; for example, they should always second a proposed term limit amendment if it lacks one, reject any attempt to delay, table, or otherwise prevent a vote on the amendment, and decline to sponsor any competing amendments weaker than their own state's amendment.[102] Representatives are thus told not only how to vote but also what issues to concentrate on and what procedural actions to take.

It makes little difference whether the instructions are advisory or compulsory. Even if representatives are not coerced, the instructions do not give them as much scope as a more discretionary view of their role would allow. A ballot notation simpler than the Missouri scheme (for example, one that merely said "Supports Term Limits") would perhaps not limit a representative's discretion as much. But the aim of any such notation, especially if limited to only a few issues on which citizens had already voted, would still be more in the spirit of mandatory than discretionary representation.

Some critics of ballot notations recognize that competing conceptions of representation are at stake in this dispute. But they tend to put the point in historical terms: the framers would not have approved of such notations.[103] The critics are no doubt correct that most of the framers disliked instructed representation. Madison argued that a right to instruct—if it means more than the "people have a right to express and communicate their sentiments"—is "of a doubtful, if not of a dangerous nature."[104] If representatives are "obliged to conform to those instructions," then establishing this right runs "the risk of losing the whole system." Madison asked: Suppose a representative "is instructed to patronize certain measures, and from circumstances known to him, but not to his constituents, he is convinced that they will endanger the public good; is he obliged to sacrifice his own judgment to them?" Madison thought the answer obvious.

If today we are inclined to accept Madison's view of the role of the representative, it should not be simply because he held it, or even because our constitutional tradition favors it. We should accept the view only if we believe that it remains relevant despite the changes that have taken place in our political system. One reason to think that it does remain relevant is that the current system already tends to make representatives sufficiently—some say excessively—responsive to voters.[105] Under these conditions, preserving some discretion for representatives is especially important. Measures that diminish the discretion, as ballot notations do, require a compelling justification. Such a justification is not likely to be found. The kind of information notations provide—focused only on one or two issues—does little to inform voters, and may in fact distract them from other equally or more important issues about which they may care even more.

Whatever we conclude about ballot notations, we need to move beyond the dispute framed as a choice between more information or less coercion—between informative ballots or scarlet letters. In deciding this dispute, as in resolving other similar disagreements, we need to be guided by a principle of free choice that gives greater emphasis to the institutional dimension of the electoral process than is common in contemporary debates.

The Mischief of Exit Polls

During the final days of the 1980 presidential campaign, right up to the day before the election, the race was considered too close to call.[106] Most polls showed Ronald Reagan ahead of Jimmy Carter, but only by a few percentage points, with significant numbers of voters still undecided. On the night before the election, all three television networks featured major stories about the Iranian hostage crisis. They recapped accounts of the taking of the American embassy and its personnel, the failed rescue attempt, the stalled negotiations, and the growing criticism of Carter's management of the crisis. On the night of the election on the basis of exit polls, the network commentators indicated early in the evening that they expected a landslide. At 8:15 eastern standard time, while the polls were still open in at least twenty-two states, NBC predicted a Reagan victory.[107] When the returns were in, Reagan won overwhelmingly, with 51 to 41 percent of the vote. Many observers attributed the magnitude of Carter's defeat partly to the last-minute TV coverage of this foreign policy crisis. An experimental reconstruction of the campaign, carried out later by two political scientists, showed that the TV coverage "primed" voters to give more weight to this episode than other factors they might have considered in deciding how to vote.[108] The authors suggest that the TV coverage "dealt a devastating and fatal blow to the President's reelection chances, inducing many voters to conceive of the decision they confronted as a referendum on the Carter presidency's performance on foreign affairs."

The TV coverage had another important effect: the predictions of the Reagan victory significantly reduced turnout. According to the most systematic study of this general effect, the TV predictions on election night "decreased the likelihood of voting among those who had not already voted."[109] This information provided by the networks did not directly influence voters' opinion of the candidates, but it did evidently affect their inclination to go to the polls.

No one would suggest that the media should be prohibited from reporting on a major foreign policy crisis just before the election, or indeed even that they should be discouraged from doing so (though of course they should be expected to present balanced coverage). Any prohibitions on the content of programs would violate principles of free speech and free press. Even voluntary constraints would run the risk of denying voters critical information they need to exercise their free choice. But many people have urged that the media not report exit polls at all on election night. Congress has passed resolutions asking that broadcasters "voluntarily refrain from characterizing or projecting results of an election before all polls for the office have closed."[110] After the 2000 election most of the networks finally agreed that in the future they would not declare a winner in any state until all its polls had closed.[111] Some other countries have gone further. Canada prohibits reporting the results of public opinion surveys about the election seventy-two hours or less before the election.[112]

If a principle of free choice would not approve limits on the publication of information such as reports about a foreign policy crisis, why should it permit—let alone favor—constraints on predictions of election results? Proponents of such constraints might try to distinguish the two kinds of information in this way. Because the former kind is content-based, it cannot be regulated without exercising political judgment, which tends to be subjective and partisan. Because the latter is process-based, it can be restricted by invoking more objective considerations and is thus more likely to be impartial. Regulating the content of information would require making substantive judgments about what issues are relevant, and would therefore involve the state in favoring one candidate or party over another. Limiting information about exit polls and other predictions seems more neutral; it appears to affect only who votes, not whom they vote for, or why.

The difficulty with this distinction is that the effects of projections are not generally neutral.[113] Although the effects on turnout cannot always be known in advance, they often favor one party or one type of candidate (incumbent or challenger) over others. The decision to report the projections is therefore not likely to be perceived as impartial. Furthermore, that projections may be more objective compared to some content-based information counts more as a reason for than against reporting them. Some content-based information is merely the expression of prejudice or calumny, but electoral projections, though admittedly only estimates, are based on veri-fiable facts, such as the results of exit polls. Objective facts are just the kind of information voters ought to have.

But it might be suggested that this objectivity is illusory, and for that reason the projections should be treated differently than content-based in-formation. Projections purport to be accurate, and are presented as conclu-sions reached by scientific methods. Viewers sometimes even take them as definitive statements about the outcome of the election. Yet as witnesses in the hearings repeatedly emphasized, not only the projections but also the exit polls on which they are based are much less reliable than is generally believed.[114] The projections convey an aura of authority greater than they merit, and therefore may require greater regulation.

Certainly, projections can be wrong, as they were, spectacularly so, in the 2000 election. On election night before all the polls had closed in Florida, the networks called the state for Al Gore. (Florida's electoral votes were by that time seen as critical to victory.) Some four hours later, the networks changed their mind, and declared George Bush the winner. About two hours later, they retracted that call, but only after Gore had phoned Bush to con-cede. Whatever the effects on turnout, the projections continued to shape the opinion and events in the month-long controversy that followed. In the House hearings devoted to election night coverage, Democratic represen-tative Henry Waxman argued that Gore's "concession" caused by the net-works' projection of a Bush victory "set in motion a chain of events that were devastating to Al Gore's chances. And it immeasurably helped George Bush maintain the idea in people's minds that he was the man who won the election."[115] Republicans also complained that the earlier call for Gore caused some of their supporters in the western states to stay home.[116]

In the aftermath of this election, much of the criticism centered on the errors the networks made rather than the effects their projections had on turnout. In the House hearings, several network witnesses conceded that they had made errors and needed to change their methods, but said they doubted that projections affected turnout.[117] An outside group, commis-sioned by CNN to review election night coverage, presented a highly criti-cal assessment, and recommended major reforms. They proposed that the networks cease using exit polls to call elections, stop relying on one source to collect and collate data, and undertake organizational changes to ensure that accuracy in reporting takes priority over speed.[118] Some of the networks seemed inclined to make changes of this kind, but none wanted Congress to legislate in this area.[119] The president of the Associated Press heatedly objected that the act of holding these hearings was itself a threat to freedom of the press.[120] But clearly these and similar reforms, whether legislated or not, would be desirable. If the media are to make projections and report polls, it is important that they do so accurately. Misinforming voters is hardly a way to enhance their free choice.

But potential inaccuracy, even in reports that viewers tend to take as authoritative, cannot be a sufficient reason for denying voters access to information. That kind of justification would permit far too broad an intrusion into free choice. Moreover, this preoccupation with inaccuracy neglects the more general problem—the potential damage to the democratic process that results from reporting projections even when they are accurate. It is not simply inaccurate projections that we may wish to limit, but any projection that may affect how people vote while the election is in progress. We can begin to develop the justification for such a limit on information by examining a common argument against it.

Restricting election night projections, it is said, would deprive voters of the chance to vote on the basis of information some think they need to make a decision, and therefore would impair their free choice. A "true freedom to vote as one chooses" includes "the right to not vote at all or even to vote as everyone else does."[121] The assumption evidently is that free choice requires providing the option of deciding not to vote because other voters appear to have already determined the outcome, and the option of basing your vote on how others are voting. "Neither the networks, nor the lawmakers should be permitted to decide which information is useful to voters and which is not. . . . The choice must belong to the individual."

This argument is questionable in two respects. First, it misconceives the nature of elections in a system with the secret ballot. In principle, such a system provides a structure for simultaneous decision making. Although in practice citizens cast their ballot at different times, they are expected to act as if they were voting at the same time. They are supposed to vote without regard to how others have voted, and they are not permitted to change their vote after it is cast. In this respect, an election is quite different from voting in a legislative assembly, such as Congress, where members may change their votes after they see how others have voted and what the provisional totals are. In an election the candidates stop campaigning when the voting starts, and supporters are not permitted to demonstrate near the polling places. While the voting continues, politics temporarily ceases.

The simultaneous character of an election—the fact that voters are not supposed to adjust their votes in relation to how others have voted—is not an arbitrary or merely conventional procedural requirement. It has a normative rationale. If citizens vote at the same time (or have only information they would have if they were voting at the same time), then the value of each citizen's choice is no greater than that of any other citizen. All make their choices on the basis of the same information, and in this respect each enjoys the same experience. Election projections distort the experience of voting by giving some voters information that other voters lack. Western voters lose their chance to participate in an event that is still in progress rather than one that is already in the history books. Also, to the extent that election projections discourage efforts by parties and candidates to mobilize voters in the western states, some citizens who might have voted do not make a choice at all. When information is unevenly distributed, the election is less just. The problem is not that the competition among candidates is less fair, but that the value of choice for some voters is less than that of others.

The other questionable aspect of the argument for unrestricted reporting of projections is the claim that the "choice must belong to the individual." In a process in which projections are publicized, citizens may choose what information they wish to use, but they are denied some other kinds of choices. They cannot choose how information about their own choices and those of others is used. They do not have a choice of a system that better preserves the simultaneous character of elections, even if they believe that such a system is better for the democratic process. Free choice is not simply a matter of individual decision, but also of institutional structure, which only citizens together can choose.

Although restrictions on publicizing projections would limit free choice in some respects, they could enhance it in others. Citizens may reasonably decide that the choices they make in an election are more valuable if no one has information about how they voted until the polls have closed. When citizens decide to limit choice for the sake of improving the value of choice, they are choosing between different aspects of liberty, not between liberty and other values. Their decision may of course also take into account other values, such as the quality of the democratic process, but it is not correctly characterized as favoring a collective over individual choice.

Nor would the restrictions on projections be objectionably paternalistic. They are not imposed by a more competent authority on less competent subjects for their own good. Rather, they are imposed by a majority on itself.

If the restrictions constitute paternalism, it is a form of self-paternalism, like the Ulysses contract mentioned earlier. The majority restricts its own access to information for its own good. The restrictions that fall on a minority who may happen to want more information are side effects. They are justifiable if the majority has no other way to protect itself from the information and are narrowly tailored to serve that purpose.

Limiting information about projections thus can be justified by showing that it enhances the value of electoral choice. It does so by preserving the simultaneous character of elections and the fair distribution of information in the electoral process. But notice that the scope of this justification is quite circumscribed. It would not permit limiting information about campaign issues, such as reports on foreign policy crises. Such information obviously does not undermine the character of elections in the same way that projections do. On the contrary, it contributes to making citizens better informed.

The justification does not even go very far toward supporting the regulation of election predictions. It would not, for example, support a ban on reports of public opinion polls (as in Canadian elections), as long as the information is equally available to all voters before the election. A different argument would be required to suppress information of this kind. One such argument might emphasize the detrimental effects of conformity. Projections tempt voters merely to follow the opinions of others and to abdicate personal responsibility for exercising free choice. Another argument would point to the effects on the rhythm of the campaign. The act of voting marks the end of the campaign and provides necessary finality, but publicizing public opinion polls in advance of the election may in effect bring the election to a premature close. Citizens may decide that the outcome is a foregone conclusion when it is not, or when it would not be if the results of polls had not been known.

These broader restrictions merit serious consideration, but even if they are rejected, some significant regulation of projections on election day could still be justified. Even those who think that the government should not prohibit networks from making projections could still urge that they voluntarily adopt a policy of restraint. More generally, we should continue to seek ways to protect the simultaneous character of voting. A law mandating the closing of the polls at the same time throughout the nation is a prime example of a measure that would promote this goal. Such laws have been often proposed, but never adopted. They usually founder on the difficulty of setting a time convenient for citizens of all states in a nation in which time zones differ as much as six hours.[122] Also, in some forms, uniform poll closing could disproportionately affect turnout of lower status and less educated citizens.[123] Another alternative (mentioned in chapter 1) would be to declare election day a national holiday, and keep the polls open all day. This proposal would avoid the problem of different time zones, though it would not be without economic cost.

Some limitations on information may improve the quality of individual decision making and public deliberation, but at the same time impede the influence of independent and minor party candidates. In such cases, we confront another conflict between two elements of free choice: the demand for adequate information and the need for an acceptable range of alternatives on the ballot. Television producers, for example, may correctly decide that a political debate is likely to be more informative if limited to the major candidates. The producers might reasonably believe that viewers can better concentrate on the differences between candidates who have a serious chance of winning. Courts have permitted even public television networks to exclude candidates from debates they sponsored, provided that the decision was based not on the content of the candidates' views, but on their lack of "appreciable public interest."[124] If networks were required to invite all candidates, without regard to their electoral chances, they might decide to avoid the "prospect of cacophony" by televising no debates at all. Either way, voters would be less informed.

Yet exclusion could also deprive voters of having the benefit of a wider range of choices on the ballot. A candidate may generate appreciable public interest only after participating in televised debates. Running for governor as a third party candidate in Minnesota in 1998, Jesse Ventura was not considered a serious candidate until he began appearing in three-way televised debates.[125] He went on to win the election. Excluding him from the debates would have not only limited the range of voters' choice, but also denied a plurality of voters the opportunity to choose their preferred candidate.

If we have reason to believe that as a result of greater exposure a candidate would become a choice voters could take seriously, we should insist that the candidate be permitted to take part in any televised debates featuring the competition. But usually we cannot predict in advance whether participation in a debate will turn a marginal candidate into a serious contender. When in doubt, we should not demand that TV networks routinely open the debates to all or even most candidates. That could impair the quality of the debates, and thereby reduce the value of the information voters receive—

without increasing the range of serious alternatives they see on the ballot. Voters might be better served by a more extended series of debates, initially inclusive but increasingly exclusive. Candidates who failed to generate public interest after the early debates would drop out as the series proceeded, until only two (or three) candidates remained in the final encounters.

We cannot specify in general what the right balance between the elements of free choice should be. Nor can we stipulate in advance the extent to which information should be limited in order to promote free choice. But the problems we have seen in the use of ballot notations, publicized exit polls, and inclusive TV debates should encourage us to consider institutional changes that would limit the political information we receive. The principle of free choice that we use to assess these changes should not presume that more information is always preferable. Sometimes electoral choice is more valuable if citizens choose to restrict what they know when they vote.

FINANCING CAMPAIGNS

Selecting candidates and informing voters take place in a political environment where money talks as much as politicians. There is widespread agreement that the system of financing campaigns is seriously defective, but there is equally widespread disagreement about what should be done about it. Thoughtful critics disagree about what should be regulated (contributions to candidates, expenditures by candidates, or both), who should be regulated (wealthy individuals, advocacy groups, parties, unions, corporations, the media), and what should be targeted (inequity, corruption, quality of debate, lack of competitiveness, distortion of opinion, distraction of representatives from their legislative duties).[126]

It is therefore not surprising that reformers have rarely succeeded in making significant changes in the system of campaign finance. It takes a major scandal, such as the revelations of Watergate or the collapse of Enron, to persuade most politicians to take reform seriously. After Watergate, Congress acted to limit contributions and expenditures in the campaigns.[127] But before those reforms could be implemented, the Supreme Court struck down the expenditure limits. After a brief pause the amount of money spent on campaigns, as well as the criticism of how it is spent, continued to rise dramatically.[128] Much later, after the 2000 election, reformers mounted another major effort. Their main vehicle was the McCain–Feingold bill, which targeted soft-money contributions to political parties. [129] The bill passed in the Senate but initially failed in the House. After the Enron scandal, the bill gained new life, and was finally signed into law in March 2002.

But even its own sponsors acknowledge that this legislation represents only a modest step. It leaves many loopholes unclosed and many problems unaddressed. As Senator John McCain remarked during the Senate debate on the bill: "It isn't comprehensive reform. It is a modest beginning, and I hope in the future we can do much more to improve the way we finance campaigns." [130] Some reformers themselves doubt whether this modest beginning should be considered a beginning at all. The limits might stanch the flow of soft money to parties, but only by diverting it to independent advocacy groups, which are less accountable to the electorate. Although the prospects for further significant reform may be uncertain, the probability of persistent disagreement about it is not. The debate about the way campaigns are financed is certain to continue.

Liberty versus Equality

Although principles of democratic theory can hardly be expected to resolve this complex and contentious issue, they can help clarify some of the terms under which the arguments are conducted. Indeed, the debate so far has taken place to a remarkable degree within a framework defined by two principles—which in their most general form express the values of equality and liberty.

The proponents of greater regulation appeal chiefly to equality: just as each citizen has an equal right to vote, so each citizen should have an equal opportunity to support a candidate, and each candidate should have an equal opportunity to win support. To the extent that fund raising is not regulated, economic inequalities are translated into political inequalities. Some citizens and some candidates thereby gain unfair advantage over others. [131] Senator John Kerry offered a form of this argument when he opposed an amendment that would have raised the contribution limits in the McCain–Feingold bill. He objected that the amendment would increase "the clout of people with money, and [reduce] the influence and capacity of the average American to have an equal weight in our political process." [132]

Opponents of greater regulation appeal chiefly to liberty: just as citizens have the right to speak freely, so citizens should have the freedom to support candidates, and candidates the freedom to seek support, by using any resources at their disposal. Money is not speech, but it facilitates speech.

In this media age, money may be a necessary condition for effective speech even if it is not a necessary part of the right of free speech. In the debate on the McCain–Feingold bill, Senator Orrin Hatch insisted that the state must not "burden a person's right to expend money to ensure that his or her opinion reaches the broadest possible audience."[133] To the extent the fund raising is limited, the free choice of citizens and candidates is constrained.

The Supreme Court's decision in *Buckley v. Valeo*, upholding contribution limits and striking down expenditure limits, may be understood as splitting the difference between these two principles.[134] It respected the value of equality by treating political contributions as similar to voting, which may be regulated to equalize individual opportunities. It acknowledged the value of liberty by treating political expenditures as similar to speech, which may not be regulated to equalize individual opportunities. The Court held that unlike expenditures, contributions to candidates pose a risk of corruption (as wealthy contributors seek favors from legislators they support), and therefore can legitimately be regulated. The distinction has been widely criticized because direct contributions to candidates are not the only or even the most important source of corruption in politics.[135] But the critics (including some of the justices) are divided between those who would regulate both contributions and expenditures, and those who would regulate neither. The distinction has therefore survived, and the larger tension it presupposes between liberty and equality still shapes the debate.[136]

Philosophers usually choose the equality side of this tension in arguing for campaign finance reform. John Rawls appeals to a principle of "fair value of political liberty" to justify regulation of campaign contributions and expenditures.[137] Although the principle is intended to combine "liberty and equality into one coherent notion," the equality element does most of the work. Rawls's principle holds that "the worth of the political liberties to all citizens, whatever their social or economic position, must be approximately equal, or at least sufficiently equal in the sense that everyone has a fair opportunity to hold public office and to influence the outcome of political decisions."[138] This principle applies most clearly to voting, for which the opportunities can be equalized without infringing on other political liberties. But in the case of campaign finance, regulation may enhance the liberty of some at the cost of limiting the liberty of others. In the most frequently quoted statement in the opinion, the *Buckley* Court wrote: "The concept that the government may restrict the speech of some elements in our society in order to enhance the relative voice of others is wholly foreign to the First Amendment."[139]

Rawls is correct to criticize the Court's flat rejection of any attempt to make political liberties more nearly equal. Although free speech and fairness often conflict, neither the Court's precedents nor First Amendment principles rule out all legislation aimed at making the value of political liberties less unfair.[140] No satisfactory conception of democracy can tolerate extreme disparities in political liberties. Even if we were to reject the goal of making political opportunities equal, we should not wish to endorse the view of democracy as merely a "regulated rivalry between economic classes and interest groups in which the outcome should *properly* depend" on very unequal financial resources.[141] To the extent that extreme differences in wealth translate into differences in political power in elections, the justice of the electoral system is called into question. An equality principle should therefore have some role in assessing the system of campaign finance.

The controversy, however, should not be framed chiefly as a conflict between liberty and equality, or even as a conflict between more and less equal liberty. It can be more fully understood as a specific kind of conflict within the principle of liberty itself. Both the Court and Rawls write as if the dispute is only about whether some people's liberties can be restricted for the sake of other people's liberties.[142] But what is at stake is a trade-off not only between different people's liberties but also different kinds of liberties. In regulating campaign finance, the attempt to make one kind of liberty more equal is likely to make others less equal in the system as a whole. Regulating contributions in order to equalize one political liberty (the right to support a candidate) may also limit another political liberty (the ability of candidates to run an effective campaign).

The question of whether this kind of regulation is justified cannot be settled by invoking the priority of liberty, either in the form of free speech or the fair value of political liberty. The answer depends on how various political liberties should be balanced against one another. No simple affirmation of the value of liberty, whether based on the First Amendment or on a theory of justice, can determine that balance. An appeal to liberty in general cannot resolve the problem because what is at issue is the relative weight of particular liberties. The question of how to balance those particular liberties leaves considerable scope for reasonable disagreement, and therefore substantial opportunity for political deliberation as well as institutional experimentation.

Two Conflicts of Liberty

Once we recognize that the underlying conflict in the reform debate is not simply between liberty and equality, we can take more seriously the possibility that free choice may be enhanced as well as constrained by campaign finance regulation. The constraining effects are emphasized by those who regard spending money on political causes as an expression of free choice. Because money facilitates political speech, it enables some citizens to influence which candidates are nominated and what information voters receive. Any restriction on raising and spending money limits this influence and information. This kind of regulation directly impinges on voters' capacity to exercise free choice because it affects the alternatives they face, and the basis on which they choose among them.

Yet the absence of such restrictions can also seriously undermine free choice. The effects are less often recognized because they are more institutional than individual. But they can be no less detrimental. Political money can impair free choice in two ways. First, it can distort the information that voters receive and thereby make their choices less informed than they should be. The imbalance in political communication, the tilt toward the voices with more money, certainly contributes to this distortion. So do the financial pressures on the media, which dilute the quality of political communication. But distinct from the general problems of balance and quality is a further specific distortion; it results from voters' lacking access to certain kinds of critical information. In a system of unregulated contributions and expenditures, voters cannot easily discover who is funding the candidates and for what purposes. They vote knowing little about the major contributors to whom the candidates are indebted and even less about what those contributors will ask of the candidates if they win. They cannot have confidence that the person whom they are choosing as their representative will in fact be their representative. They cannot judge to what extent the candidate they vote for will represent their interests or will represent competing interests.

We do not have to assume that any candidates are corrupt in the sense they accept contributions in exchange for favors; we need to suppose only that if they win office, they are likely to grant major contributors greater access.[143] The objection is not that the access is unequal (though that is a problem too). It is rather that voters do not have adequate information about what is likely to take place when major contributors meet with their representatives. Some voters may not disapprove of the access that certain individuals or groups are granted, but if they do not even know about it, they are voting on the basis of less information than they ought to have. As Senator Bill Frist observed during the debate on the McCain–Feingold bill: "Most people in this body and most Americans understand the critical importance of increased disclosure today. What makes people mad is the fact that money is coming into a system and nobody knows from where it is coming. . . . It comes through the system and flows out, and nobody knows where it is going or who is buying the ads on television. How do you hold people accountable?"[144]

Why not simply require more disclosure? Public reporting of contributions and expenditures in various forms is the most common method of regulating campaign finance, and measures to improve the reporting are the most commonly proposed reforms. The popularity of disclosure as a reform suggests that nearly everyone recognizes the importance of information for securing free choice. Some politicians and candidates no doubt see it as a way to avoid more intrusive regulations. Many also view it as the best way to preserve free choice. Senator J. Bennett Johnston spoke for most of his colleagues and many other politicians and candidates when he declared: "We ought to disclose what we do, and let the voters decide."[145]

But disclosure is at best a partial answer to the problem. It tells voters only who has directly contributed to a candidate's campaign. Voters may try to infer from published reports which contributions to parties and other organizations go to support which candidates, but they will have considerable difficulty in tracing the connections. Open, direct contributions are not the only important kind of financial influence in politics. Many promises of political support and threats to withdraw it are only implicit. The countless financial transactions that sustain the promises and threats usually take place behind the scenes. The complexity and flexibility of modern financial institutions, with their manifold national and international connections, make it hard to follow the paper trail of shadowy transactions they permit and often impossible even to ask the questions that could prompt an investigation. Most of the time political money makes its rounds quietly, without raising any specific suspicions and without offering any openings for democratic accountability.

On the basis of what candidates typically disclose about the sources of their funds, voters cannot predict with any confidence how they will respond to the contributors' pressures to which they are likely to be subject if they win. Voters choose their representatives knowing little about what they owe to whom, and therefore little about why they legislate as they do. It is as if voters write their candidate a legislative blank check, and never find out how much it is cashed for. Even the disclosure requirements currently in effect in Congress, which are much more elaborate than any proposed to regulate campaigns, do not provide citizens with adequate information to judge their representatives.[146]

A further problem with disclosure exposes the second way in which free choice can be undermined in the existing system of campaign finance. The only citizens who in their voting decisions can use the information disclosed about a candidate are those in the candidate's district. As long as no laws are broken, they are the only ones who can hold the candidate accountable for the conduct of the campaign. While the electoral power of disclosure is confined within the boundaries of the district or state, the political influence of campaign contributions moves freely wherever its peddlers see profitable opportunities. Because the way campaigns are financed in each district affects the integrity of the electoral process in many other districts, voters properly take an interest not only in the practices of the candidates in their own district or state, but also in the financing system as a whole. They can contribute to the campaigns of candidates who, like John McCain or Russell Feingold, are committed to campaign finance reform.[147] But in the current system, they cannot through their votes control the conduct of campaigns beyond their own districts and states. As voters they cannot exercise much influence over the integrity of the system of campaign finance as a whole.

As a result, voters make their choices under conditions that in important respects are less free than they should be. Both the selection of candidates and the dissemination of information take place in a process pervasively influenced by political money. Voters can decide to join in the pecuniary competition, and contribute to their favorite candidates outside their district and state. They have a legitimate interest in whom the voters in other districts and other states choose. But they can express this interest now only through money, not votes. They have little choice about how the campaign finance system as a whole should operate. To the extent that voters lack control over fundraising practices, they are choosing among candidates, none of whom may be acceptable, because all were selected in a process that many voters find unacceptable. Informed choice also suffers in such a system. Voters choose mostly on the basis of information provided by a communication process similarly distorted by political money.

In these circumstances, the free choice of voters is impaired because the very conditions of choice are largely beyond their control. They do not have adequate opportunities to nominate an acceptable candidate because they may reasonably wish to reject all candidates selected in a process so pervasively driven by money. They do not have adequate information because they do not trust the communications produced in a system so dominated by money. Their predicament is worse than the dilemma faced by voters who do not like the positions of any candidates on the ballot and are forced to vote for someone they do not like, or no one at all. At least these voters have managed to acquire enough information to know that they do not like the candidates. If they object to the positions of the candidates rather than to the campaign finance system, they have the opportunity to work with others to nominate a different candidate next time.

The Root of Some Evil

Contrary to some critics of the system, political money is not inherently corrupting.[148] As Senator Fred Thompson insisted in the debate on the McCain–Feingold bill, such "money is not evil in and of itself."[149] Spending private money to win public office does not seem as objectionable as (for example) paying for a baby or buying a kidney. Like creative work and professional practice, politics is an activity in which the influence of money should be limited but not excluded. As in other activities that have noneconomic purposes, politics can be degraded or dignified by money depending on the conditions of its use. That is why some political theorists hostile to political corruption favor the sale of offices. Under certain conditions, money can serve as a check on political corruption. The Baron de Montesquieu and Jeremy Bentham, both staunch opponents of corruption, argued in favor of giving money a greater role in politics. They saw the aristocracy and monarchy as the most dangerous sources of corruption in their societies, and believed that the sale of offices would combat this traditional corruption by opening up politics to the rising commercial classes.[150]

Although their particular problem is not ours, their general approach is still relevant. We should not try to eliminate the use of money in politics but instead modify the way it is used. We should use it to counter undesirable tendencies in the democratic process—corruption in the broader sense of the deformation of political institutions. As Montesquieu and Bentham called on commercial energies to break down class barriers to public office, so we can seek ways to use money to open the paths of nomination and communication. (Even soft money can serve worthy democratic purposes if it is used to strengthen responsible party government, as it was originally intended to do.) An approach that uses money to combat the mischief of money implies, first, that more money should be directed toward persons and practices that could help clear those paths, and second, that some of the other influences of money should be moderated.

If we took the first implication seriously, we would put more effort into ensuring that credible challengers have adequate funding. Despite the "many cries of 'too much' " from both voters and candidates who complain that the cost of campaigns has become exorbitant,[151] the United States is probably not spending more than is appropriate for such a publicly important activity as choosing our representatives. In an age of mass media, an informative and competitive campaign is expensive, and even larger amounts of money than are now spent—if deployed effectively and fairly—could enhance the democratic process. The problem is not that too much is spent on campaigns but that too little is spent by challengers compared to what is spent by incumbents.[152]

Adopting an approach that uses money to check money, we would look more favorably on public funding for campaigns. Although some limits on expenditures may eventually be required, the first priority would be to increase contributions from public sources. Building floors would be more important than imposing ceilings. Any system of public funding would have to strike a balance between allocating funds to candidates and parties with established electoral reputations and newcomers with some proven popular support.[153] But that is a constraint on the design of the system, not a reason against its establishment. Another important reform would open the paths to office and communication. Television and radio outlets, especially national networks, would be required to provide significant free time. The objections to such reforms are more practical than principled, though they have so far proved fatal.[154]

The second implication of the theorists' approach is that we should directly constrain the use of political money so that it does not dominate the electoral process as much as it does now. From this perspective, the problem with political money is not that its influences are so evil, but that its pressures are so pervasive. Free choice is impaired when one factor systematically dominates other relevant factors in decision making. Voters' choice is therefore less free insofar as the influence of money in the electoral process overwhelms other legitimate influences, such as the effects of volunteer activity and political ability.[155]

To be sure, money is not the only problematic influence in campaigns. The media can distort the political process in equally harmful ways, and its power might increase if the candidates and parties were subject to extensive regulation. But political money is the single most potent influence in the electoral process today, and most other influences depend on it. Party volunteers, for example, may be free, but they are more effective the more funds a party has for mobilizing them. To moderate the influence of money, we may need to place greater restrictions not only on contributions but also on the kinds of activities and communications for which campaign funds may be spent.

Moderating the influence of money would begin to restore a balance in the process so that other resources—political talent, skill, and experience—could be deployed more regularly and more effectively. Encouraging politicians to raise funds may be justified as a way of demonstrating that they have substantial political support. But requiring them to rely so heavily on campaign contributions, and permitting their relative success in fundraising to determine so decisively their political success, is inimical to free choice. A campaign finance system more friendly to free choice would promote a pluralism of influence, rather than the plutocracy of influence that prevails now.

The Scope of Free Choice

A standard that prescribes a pluralism of influence cannot be applied generally to all political activity in the same way. If the principle of free choice were to require a balance of influences in politics generally, it would justify constant intervention by the government in nearly all aspects of the political process. Intervention on this scale would be excessively intrusive, leaving scarcely any sphere of political liberty beyond the scrutiny of the state. As a justification for regulation, then, the principle of free choice should be limited to the electoral process. Yet it is by no means obvious how to justify that limitation, and how to draw the line between electoral and other kinds of politics.[156] (Notice that some distinction between the electoral process and the rest of the political process is necessary even for defending minimal reforms such as disclosure; presumably we would not want to require everyone who takes part in ordinary political activity to reveal his or her sources of financial support.) [157]

The electoral process is in principle distinguishable from ordinary politics in two respects, which together justify subjecting it to stronger or at least different standards. [158] First, unlike ordinary political activity outside government, elections (including the campaigns that precede them) result in decisions that are binding on all citizens. All therefore have an interest in the integrity of the process, and a claim to participate in setting the standards that govern it. Second, again unlike ordinary political activity, campaigns come to a definite and foreseeable conclusion; an election takes place at a particular moment, which until the next election marks an end to the process of deciding who will hold office. Because of these distinctive characteristics, elections and the campaigns leading up to them may be considered more a part of government than a part of politics that influences government. The standards that control the conduct of elections should therefore be determined more by collective decision than by individual choice. Voters together should set the standards for the process that determines who will make and execute the laws by which they are to be bound.

But can electoral politics be separated from other kinds in practice? Any line is arbitrary, but that is not an argument against drawing one. (The temporal boundaries between days and the spatial boundaries between states are arbitrary in this sense, but nonetheless significant.) It may be desirable to shorten the length of campaigns, as some European countries have done, but in any case some temporal limits on what communications may be regulated should be set. Sixty days before the election, the favored period in current legislation, is as sensible as any.

More difficult to establish but no less essential is a distinction *within* the temporal boundaries of a campaign, however they are defined. The distinction is between types of advocacy: financial support for advocating the election of candidates (which should be regulated), and support for advocating a particular policy or general program (which should be left unregulated). [159] Candidate advocacy is obviously part of a campaign, and is only partially protected under the First Amendment. Issue advocacy is clearly part of ordinary political debate, and is fully protected under the Amendment. But the line between the two kinds of advocacy is anything but clear in practice. The problem of drawing the line goes beyond the disputes about the differences between contributions and expenditures, the distinctions between money and other kinds of influences, and the controversies about private and public financing. The problem is not resolved by any reform proposed so far. It would remain even if *Buckley* were overturned.

A line dividing the electoral process from the rest of political life is not to be discovered by undertaking further explorations in the political world, as if one were setting out to look for some natural boundary like a river. It will have to be constructed, one case at a time, as citizens and their representatives decide how expansive an electoral process they wish to encourage, and how broad a concept of free choice they want to support.

Some critics may object to the concept of free choice proposed here even if the electoral process to which it is applied is well defined and clearly limited. The concept would justify regulation that goes beyond what some citizens would accept because they take a quite different view of what free choice requires. They hold a conception of democracy in which individuals are free to use whatever resources they can mobilize to support candidates and communicate information at any time in any part of the political process. On this view regulation is justified only to prevent bribery, extortion, and other acts that are already illegal outside of politics. Any further regulation would have to be based on a substantive political ideal, which some citizens may reasonably reject.[160] Such regulation is objectionable because it involves imposing on all citizens a contestable theory of democracy that only some accept. Regulation of campaign finance is not justified, these critics argue, if it is directed toward such substantive goals as improving the quality of political debate, advancing the pursuit of the common good, correcting for the civic incompetence of voters, promoting more extensive political participation, and encouraging representatives to act as trustees rather than delegates. Protecting electoral choice against excessive pecuniary influences would on this view count as merely another unjustifiable goal of regulation.

The objection that regulation to protect free choice is unacceptable because it imposes a particular theory of democracy is not compelling. To be sure, many of the goals of campaign finance reform appeal to substantive political ideals, and some presuppose contestable conceptions of democracy. The principle of free choice developed here, especially as applied to campaign finance, is not purely procedural. It carries substantive implications. It is more friendly toward conceptions of democracy that expand the range of influences on citizens and candidates, and toward conceptions that support self-reflective choice among an acceptable range of electoral alternatives. But the critics who raise this objection also unavoidably presuppose a concept of free choice that favors some conceptions of democracy over others. They assume, for example, that the prevailing pattern of influences produced in society is less constraining than the pattern likely to be created by the state. That may be a defensible view, but it is neither value free nor historically privileged. It too must be justified to the citizens who are to be bound by the results of the electoral process it prescribes.

The decision not to regulate is as much a substantive conclusion as the decision to regulate. An unregulated campaign finance system does not represent a default position, a state of affairs that should prevail in the absence of a strong reason for change. The electoral process is not, like some state of nature, a pristine condition any departure from which requires a compelling justification. It is, like the rest of the democratic process, a set of politically constructed institutions, defined by rules that citizens and their representatives have within their power to change. We have already taken note of the numerous normative choices implicated in the institutional design of other parts of the electoral process, even some that seem purely procedural. The design of the system of campaign finance is no different. Citizens cannot avoid making institutional choices about the character of the system that significantly affects their individual choices and the information they have to make those choices.

How can citizens freely choose among campaign finance systems if they must make their choices in a system in which money dominates? They could do so if the conditions under which they choose electoral practices are less dominated by money than the conditions under which they currently choose their candidates. For example, they could make the rules on fundraising for popular initiatives that propose campaign finance reform stricter than the rules the reform itself would establish. If the conditions under which electoral institutions are chosen provided a more balanced set of influences than those found in current campaigns, citizens and their representatives could decide, free of domination by any particular influence, which system they prefer. They could even choose a system, like the current one, in which money plays a prominent role. At least such a system would have been freely chosen in a way that the present system has not.

To make an informed choice among systems, citizens need to be aware of a wider range of alternatives than have been presented in the past. The various financing schemes with which some states are now experimenting in their own elections can help serve this purpose. The scheme put into effect in Maine in the 2000 election illustrates both the problems and opportunities the states confront. Impatient with the inaction of their representatives,

Maine voters passed their own initiative to reform the state's system, the Clean Election Act.[161] In the new system, qualified candidates for state legislative and gubernatorial office who agree to limit their expenditures and accept no contributions receive full public funding for their campaigns in both the primary and general elections. If candidates who decline to participate exceed the spending ceiling of their participating opponents, the opponents automatically receive more public funds.

The reform immediately expanded the range of choice. It increased the number of candidates seeking seats in the legislature from 305 in 1998 to 352 in 2000. Almost a third of those running in the 2000 election participated in the public financing scheme.[162] One of the new recruits, Deborah Simpson of Auburn, explained her decision to run for office: "With Clean Elections, it seemed less daunting a task to run. I could do what I can do, which is talk to people, as opposed to raising money, which in my life, I didn't have any experience in."[163] In this respect, the scheme reduces the influence of money and further enhances free choice.

However, the aim of the proponents of "Clean Elections" is to remove all private money from politics. To the extent that they succeed, they would limit the free choice of those who wish to contribute their own money to campaigns. A principle of free choice should call for moderating the role that money currently plays without eliminating it entirely. During the legislative debate before the scheme was adopted, members pointed to provisions that they claimed unduly limit the liberty of candidates. One opponent objected: "You are limited in your freedom of expression in spending your own money towards your own campaign."[164] Proponents replied that candidates cannot complain that this freedom has been denied, because they can choose to ignore the limits if they decline public funds. But the critics still argue that this choice is not fully free; it is constrained by the threat to increase the funding of an opponent if a candidate exceeds the spending limits. So far the courts have found the scheme sufficiently voluntary to pass constitutional muster, and several other states have acted on similar measures.[165] But the ultimate justification for this approach depends on how citizens wish to interpret the conditions of free choice in the financing of campaigns.

CONCLUSION

In the land of the free, even the brave may shrink from defining the meaning of freedom once and for all. Deciding what free choice means in elections is only slightly less daunting. Even matters as seemingly mundane as how candidates' names appear on the ballot raise issues of principle and create conflicts among fundamental values. We began by considering a straight-forward principle of free choice: the more alternatives, information, and independence from external pressures voters have, the more valuable their free choice in elections. But exploring the institutional dimensions of electoral choice revealed a more complex picture, with several different interpretations of each of these elements of choice contending for recognition. In all three, the free choice of individuals can sometimes be enhanced by institutional constraints that in other ways limit their choice. In choice as in art, less is sometimes more.

Neither the number of alternatives on the ballot nor the difference between them is as important as the way they are selected and presented to voters. What the ballot in a general election expresses about the nomination process is therefore critical in assessing the value of electoral choice. Should a candidate be permitted to be listed as a nominee for more than one party (as in fusion candidacies)? Should voters be allowed to choose nominees for any party in a primary election (as in blanket primaries)? The answers to such questions cannot be decided by considering only the perspective of individual voters. The answers depend on institutional issues such as the value of the two-party system. But how we should think about such issues is not so obvious. From an institutional perspective the case for a fusion ban seems stronger if it is treated as just another limitation, like the winner-take-all rule, designed to preserve the two-party system. But proponents of fusion can distinguish the ban from other constraints on third parties. The fusion ban is a greater interference with free choice because it regulates not merely whom the parties can nominate but the reasons they have for nominating them.

Some critics may challenge the value of the two-party system itself, or at least urge that alternative systems such as PR be seriously considered. But whatever the merits of alternative systems, it is a mistake even in institutional analysis to think that the only important questions are differences among institutions rather than differences within them. Even if we have to accept the two-party system, we can make it more or less friendly to free choice. Permitting fusion candidacies and closed primaries arguably contribute to that end.

Focusing on institutions does not completely avoid distortions of an individualist perspective. In arguments about political parties, individualist categories often misleadingly intrude. Maintaining the two-party system should not be assumed to require preserving any particular party in its current form, because parties should not have rights just like those of individuals. Restraining the liberty of parties for their own good should not be regarded as paternalism, because parties do not have the moral status of individuals. Surveying the opinions of individual members of a party should not be treated as equivalent to determining the view of the party, because the parties have procedures that define what counts as their collective decisions.

These and similar caveats serve as reminders that in evaluating particular electoral practices we need to consider their interrelationships and the consequences for the electoral system as a whole. To determine whether blanket primaries promote free choice, for example, we need to decide what kind of process of representation we want. Do we prefer one that settles disagreements at earlier stages and produces more centrist candidates (as blanket primaries tend to do)? Or do we want one that continues disagreements into later stages and produces more divergent candidates (as closed primaries tend to do)? Free choice probably thrives more in the latter than the former, an answer that strengthens the case for closed primaries. But apart from any conclusion we may reach about primaries, the principle of free choice makes institutional considerations such as these a critical part of any deliberation we conduct about electoral practices, and a central part of the meaning that we give to the principle itself.

The meaning of the second element of free choice similarly depends on broader institutional consequences. When we take them into account, we see that more information does not always enhance free choice. Voters may not need more information if they use shortcuts well, but whether they rely on shortcuts, they may make better choices if they deny themselves certain kinds of information. Although we may no longer favor the two-stage elections that Tocqueville commended, we can seek other ways to insulate ourselves from certain information and thereby improve the quality of our decision making, as he urged.

Ballot notations certainly give voters more information, but they encourage voters to focus on only a few preselected issues. They are objectionable not because they coerce candidates or confuse voters, but because they drive the electoral process further toward a mandatory form of representation with a limited range of issues. Television networks give voters information when they report election projections, but they do not necessarily enhance free choice. The usual arguments for (and against) regulating this information are incomplete because they focus on individual voters: the projections mislead voters, or the regulations deny citizens the right not to vote. The more fundamental objection is that they undermine an important institutional feature of elections. An election should be a simultaneous decision-making process: no citizen should have information about how others have voted until all have voted. The simultaneity helps ensure that no citizen's range of realistic alternatives and quality of electoral experience is greater in this respect than that of any other.

Denying voters information need not be paternalistic. It is not like opposing fusion candidacies on the grounds that some voters might find the ballot confusing. Any justifiable limit on information must be applied to all voters equally and adopted democratically. The majority may impose restrictions on its own information for its own good, but not merely for the good of the minority. Nor are restrictions of this kind likely to lead to less overall information in the electoral process. In most campaigns, the pressures all favor publicity much more than secrecy. The greater challenge is not to preserve freedom of information but to improve its quality.

The ideal of the independent-minded voter, casting a ballot in a process free from external pressure, is enticing. But even as an ideal it is misleading. Intimidation at the polls, bribery in the primaries, and other corrupt influences are of course not acceptable, but some pressures on voters and candidates are not only permissible but desirable. Promises, bargains, even some threats are perfectly legitimate, part of the robust give-and-take on which democracy depends. Rather than seeking to reduce legitimate influences, we would do better to multiply them. Choice is sometimes more free when the pressures are more numerous. The aim should be to prevent the dominance of one by promoting a competition of many—a pluralism of pressures on choice. Extending Madison's approach to electoral competition, we would adopt a variation of the "policy of supplying, by opposite and rival interests, the defect of better motives."[166]

The problem of political money illustrates the advantage of such an approach. The solution to this problem should not be to eliminate the influence of money in the electoral process even if it were possible to do so. Freeing candidates completely from financial pressures would have the effect of restricting the liberty of citizens who want to spend their own money to run for office or support others who run. It could also discourage the dissemination of useful information in the campaign, and thereby impair the free choice of all voters. Yet a financing system as unrestrained as the current one makes money too dominant a factor in decision making at every point in the process. A more balanced set of influences would be better for free choice. But that balance is not likely to be achieved through the unregulated decisions of uncoordinated individuals, however visible or invisible their hands may be.

The problem of political money underscores a general implication of the principle of free choice. Individual voters, acting together only in their own state or district, cannot choose to make their decisions in an environment less dominated by money. Political money does not respect political borders. Its influence spreads without regard to electoral constituencies. As citizens must act together across these boundaries if they are to reduce the dominance of money in politics, so they must act together if they are to enhance the conditions of choice in any aspect of the electoral process—the institutions in which candidates are selected, information disseminated, and pecuniary influence exercised.

THREE

Popular Sovereignty
Who Decides What Votes Count

Now that the votes are counted, it is time for the votes to count.
GEORGE W. BUSH, NOVEMBER 26, 2000

In a democratic election, the people speak—but they do not themselves always determine what is said. Their voice is filtered through an electoral process governed by rules mostly made by legislatures and interpreted by courts. Because the rules are neither neutral nor noncontroversial, the procedures and results of elections are often disputed. Whether "it is time for the votes to count" depends on whether these disputes have been justly resolved. Disputes may arise about any phase of the electoral process—from drawing the districts to counting the votes. The principle of popular sovereignty addresses the question of authority: Who should finally settle such disagreements, and on what basis?

In a democracy, the people in their collective capacity have the strongest claim to decide such questions. To be sure, Americans live in a representative, not a pure democracy, and one constrained by a constitution. In the language of the framers, this government is a republic, distinguished from what they understood as a democracy by "the total exclusion of the people, in their collective capacity, from any share" in governing.[1] Yet even those framers who most firmly insisted on the republican character of the new government affirmed the importance of popular control of the governors. As James Madison explained, the essential feature of a republic is that the government "derives all its powers directly or indirectly from the great body of the people, and is administered by persons holding their offices during pleasure, for a limited period, or during good behavior."[2]

The voice of the people expressed through the electoral process thus enjoys a special status in any democracy, even the limited Madisonian kind. Elections provide the ultimate check on representatives and finally on officials in all branches of government. To preserve the power to choose their representatives, the people must be able to decide how representatives are chosen. If it were generally true that elections were a process "in which the representatives have selected the people," rather than one "in which the people select their representatives," we should doubt that elections were truly democratic.[3] If elections are to realize rule by the people, the people should be able to decide what kind of elections they want. The authority to govern elections is the authority to decide finally when the votes count—to determine ultimately what the people say. If that authority were vested entirely in courts or legislatures, it would make the electoral process less closely connected to the people than the idea of a democratic control implies. Popular sovereignty would turn out to be not so popular after all.

From these considerations, we draw this principle of popular sovereignty: citizens should have adequate opportunities to determine the procedures that govern elections. In its unqualified form, the principle implies that a majority of citizens should decide disagreements about electoral justice. (The principle also implies that a majority should decide what counts as a majority for this purpose, and at what point to call a halt to the otherwise indefinite regress of majorities' deciding what a majority is.) Even unqualified, majority rule is not an arbitrary principle. Like equal respect and free choice, it rests on fundamental moral values. In the face of political disagreement, it offers a decision-making procedure that under the right conditions respects citizens as free and equal persons. It gives the vote of each the greatest possible weight compatible with equal weight for the votes of all.[4]

The principle of popular sovereignty, with its majoritarian cast, cannot be absolute. One reason it must be qualified is that it is not the only principle of electoral justice. The principles of equal respect and free choice also have independent roles to play. Majorities form and work within a framework of rights such as free speech and equal protection. In the American constitutional tradition, nonmajoritarian institutions such as courts are properly granted some authority to protect these values. But if the potential conflict with these other principles were the only constraint on the principle, it would still have considerable scope. The majority would still exercise more authority over electoral justice than is often assumed. As we saw in previous chapters, the meaning of equal respect and free choice requires interpretation, which courts are not always well suited to provide. In some cases, more popularly based institutions may be better placed to decide disputes about these principles. Which institution is most likely to develop and defend a justifiable interpretation of the principles depends on the particular issue in question and the context in which it arises. Majoritarian institutions may sometimes qualify. The people in their collective capacity thus have some claim to authority even in the application of the principles of equal respect and free choice.

The principle of popular sovereignty must be qualified for another reason, one that imposes more subversive limits on majority rule. This challenge to the principle comes from within—from the value of popular sovereignty itself. Even if no values other than majority rule were at stake, the principle cannot give any particular majority final authority. Why the principle needs to be qualified in this respect may seem puzzling. As long as a dispute does not involve conflicts with equal respect or free choice, majoritarian institutions would seem to be the most suitable site for determining the procedures of elections, which after all are intended to express the will of the majority. Insofar as the question concerns only what counts as the majority, the only appropriate authority, it would seem, is the majority itself.

But which majority? The identity of the majority is problematic in two dimensions. First, spatially: there is reasonable disagreement about which unit—local, state, national—should be taken as the proper locus of the majority. The way that majorities are constituted at one level may adversely affect the way they function at another level. Second, temporally: there is reasonable disagreement about whether earlier or later majorities should have precedence. Some continuity is necessary to sustain a constitutional democracy. It is also necessary to confirm that the expression of majority will at any particular time is genuine, not the product of temporary impulses or manipulated desires. But too much continuity—too much deference to past majorities—prevents desirable change. It also gradually undermines popular sovereignty itself as new majorities find themselves increasingly constrained by the dead hand of past majorities.

The conflicts between majorities across time and space constitute what may be called the problem of many majorities. Because the meaning of the majority will is problematic for these reasons, the principle of popular sovereignty does not once and for all grant the majority at any particular level or any particular time final authority over the rules and results of elections. We can understand more fully how the problem of many majorities arises, and how it affects the meaning of the principle of popular sovereignty, by considering three different ways in which the people can govern the procedures of the electoral process. The people in their collective capacity—the majority however defined—can exercise authority over the electoral process directly through popular initiative and indirectly through legislative representation and delegation to independent bodies.

As we consider these modes of authority, we shall see that the principle must be significantly qualified, and the majoritarian institutions that it initially favors substantially modified. Two provisos, inspired by Madison and Alexander Hamilton respectively, make the principle less majoritarian than it at first may appear. The first limits majorities that would control membership in their own institutions in the future, and the second constrains majorities that would undermine a conception of national representation.

TAKING INITIATIVES

Embraced by several of the states at the turn of the last century, the initiative was a child of the Progressive movement. More recently it has been adopted by a wide variety of reformers in the service of many different causes.[5] Twenty-four states, the District of Columbia, and hundreds of local governments now permit citizens to enact laws by some form of initiative.[6] In the past several decades, the number of statewide initiatives has risen steadily. Since 1990 more than three hundred statewide initiatives have appeared on the ballot, about half of which passed. Although many have dealt with public policies such as taxation, the environment, housing, and transportation, an increasing number of initiatives—nearly one hundred in the last decade—have sought changes in the electoral process. By far the largest number of those have dealt with issues rarely submitted to voters in earlier years—campaign finance and term limits. Examining one initiative typical of the recent wave of term limit propositions and one state's abortive attempt to regulate initiatives can illuminate the limits of the exercise of direct popular authority over elections. To respect these limits, we shall see that we need to attach provisos to the principle of popular sovereignty.

The Terms of the Term Limit Debate

By the time of the 1992 elections, the national movement for term limits had gained enough support to place the issue on the ballot in nearly a dozen states. In Arkansas, proponents of term limits for state and congressional candidates had cleverly crafted a proposition that avoided barring anyone from running for office. The proposition, known as Amendment 73, enforced the limits simply by denying a place on the ballot to any candidates who had served more than the specified number of terms.[7] Veteran legislators could still run as write-in candidates. This stratagem did not ultimately convince the courts that congressional term limits were not a "qualification" for office (which under the Constitution the states have no power to change), but it did enable proponents of the law to argue that the term limits did not interfere with anyone's free choice of candidates.[8]

The proponents had another trick up their legislative sleeve. They inserted a "severability" clause in the law so that if the congressional limits were declared unconstitutional, as many thought likely, the limits on state legislators would survive. Some critics charged that this was "dishonest and unfair." It amounted to "misleading political packaging" because the two types of term limits were "packaged and sold together" before the election, even though only one was expected to be enacted after the election.[9] Severability had another awkward implication. By distinguishing so clearly between the two types, it highlighted the comparative weakness of the state's claim to sovereignty over congressional terms.

The public debate then turned to the merits of term limits. The arguments the proponents made in favor of term limits were familiar: "[E]lected officials who remain in office too long become preoccupied with reelection and ignore their duties as representatives of the people." Such "entrenched incumbency" reduces voter participation, and "has led to an electoral system that is less free, less competitive, and less representative" than it should be.[10] Opponents argued that term limits reduce voters' choice by eliminating candidates from the ballot for whom voters have shown a clear preference, produce legislatures with less experienced members, increase the power of unelected staffers and lobbyists, and make legislators less accountable in their last term in office.[11] Like majorities in many other states, the voters of Arkansas found the arguments in favor of term limits to be more compelling. Amendment 73 won 60 percent of the vote statewide and a majority in every congressional district.

A group of opponents, led by the League of Women Voters and joined by a U.S. congressman, immediately mounted a legal challenge. Before the vote, the antagonists had debated important issues of free choice, including institutional questions about representation itself. But the legal challenge set aside the question of the merits of term limits, and focused instead on the question of authority: Who has the right to impose term limits?

The Arkansas Supreme Court upheld the limits on state legislators, but struck down the congressional term limits on the grounds they violated the federal Constitution. The judges held that no state on its own may add to the qualifications for Congress stated in the Constitution.[12] A 5–4 majority of the U.S. Supreme Court agreed, thereby invalidating not only the Arkansas congressional limits, but all those previously adopted by other states.[13] The Court did not accept the proponents' claim that the law merely denies access to the ballot and therefore does not impose a qualification for office. The indirect effect is the same as if it prohibited someone from running at all, the Court said, because write-in candidates rarely win. The proponents' other stratagem—severing the state and congressional provisions—did serve its purpose, however: the term limits on state representatives survived.

For the purposes of a principle of sovereignty, the key issue in this episode is the question of authority: Who should decide what qualifications are required for elected office in a democracy? The question goes beyond the constitutional issues posed in the case, but because the argument in the court case was conducted without reference to the substantive merits of term limits, it provides a suitable frame for exploring the extent to which the question of authority can be answered independently of the underlying substantive issue that prompted it. Is there any basis on which we can determine whether states should have the authority to set electoral qualifications without deciding whether term limits are a desirable policy? Neither constitutional history nor democratic theory, as presented by the Court, provides such a basis; but as will become clear later in this chapter, the provisos inspired by Madison and Hamilton can serve that purpose.

Both the majority and minority opinions of the Court looked to history—the original meaning of the Constitution and the past practices of the states.[14] They produced a remarkable pair of historical essays, definitely instructive about the early debates in the Constitutional Convention and the ratification process, but ultimately inconclusive on the question in dispute. Thoughtful commentators declared the essay contest a "draw."[15] The contest took many turns, but the exchanges for and against what may be called the "minimal qualifications view" gives an indication of its flavor. On this view no qualifications beyond those listed in the Constitution should be required for serving in Congress, and therefore no term limits should be imposed.

The majority pointed out that Madison successfully argued against proposals that would have given Congress the authority to add qualifications for serving in the House or the Senate. Such authority would be "improper and dangerous," Madison warned. If the legislature could regulate "qualifications of electors and elected," it could "by degrees subvert the Constitution," turning a republic into an aristocracy or oligarchy.[16] He reminded his colleagues of the "abuse" the British parliament had made of this power. Another delegate, Hugh Williamson, warned that if the legislature could set the qualifications, they might try to reproduce their own kind. He imagined the worst: What if the majority were lawyers?[17]

The dissenters on the Court doubted that the framers intended to limit the power to set additional qualifications. They pointed out that the delegates to the Convention had rejected a proposal that would have limited the qualifications to those expressly listed in the Constitution. If age, citizenship, and residency were meant to be the only qualifications, the framers would have said so. The minority's most powerful point did not depend on determining the authority of Congress but rather that of the states: the "fact that the Framers did not grant a qualification-setting power to Congress does not imply that they wanted to bar its exercise at the state level."[18] Neither the state legislators nor the citizens of the states would face the same conflict of interest in setting qualifications as would members of Congress. Furthermore, the states originally selected senators, and soon acquired other powers over federal elections, such as the right to draw congressional districts. These other powers affected the composition of Congress as much as setting qualifications for its members.[19]

The Undemocratic Face of Elections

Evidently recognizing that the historical arguments were not sufficient, both sides turned to democratic theory and appealed to what they called the "fundamental principle of our representative democracy": that "the people should choose whom they please to govern them."[20] They assumed that this principle could determine who should have the authority to decide who could run for office. If the assumption were correct, this principle could support a principle of popular sovereignty that would give a definite answer to at least part of the question of authority—namely, who should have the power to set qualifications for office.

For the proponents of the minimal qualifications view, the "fundamental principle" meant that no official or institution should have the authority to impose additional qualifications. During oral argument, justices who favored this view tried to show that the implications of assuming that such authority exists are implausible. They managed to get the Arkansas attorney general to concede that his position implied that "Congress could pass a statute saying every Senator must be at least 50 years old."[21] The states might even decide, one justice worried, that no one over age seventy should appear on the ballot.[22] At the same time, the opponents of the minimal qualifications view were also pressed to accept some awkward implications of their view—for example, that "a State could bar a felon from voting but not for running for office."[23]

Despite the exaggerations, these exchanges proved illuminating. They reveal an ambiguity in the "fundamental principle," and expose an important tension in the concept of democratic elections. By their nature, elections combine what traditional political theorists considered democratic and aristocratic modes of governing.[24] Elections are democratic insofar as any citizen may vote, and aristocratic insofar as only certain types of citizens are likely to be elected. Aristotle and later Rousseau and Montesquieu regarded elections as primarily aristocratic institutions. Elections select the few who are distinguished from the many by having to a greater degree certain qualities that a particular society values (such as courage, intelligence, wealth, or possession of property).[25] The theorists considered the only truly democratic institution to be selection by lot, which gives everyone an equal chance not only to be a candidate but also to be chosen for office. By the time of the drafting of the American Constitution, lot was not taken seriously, and election had become the most democratic of the methods available for choosing representatives.[26] But the tension between the democratic and aristocratic elements in the institution of election remained because most people assumed that the political if not the social qualities of the elected would continue to differ significantly from those of the electors.

This tension plays out in an ironic way in the debate on qualifications. The minimal qualifications view seems at first more democratic (and more consistent with the principle of popular sovereignty) because it excludes few candidates. Almost anyone can run, and win office. Madison's ringing endorsement of the view is often quoted by the proponents of minimal qualifications: "Who are to be the objects of popular choice? Every citizen whose merit may recommend him to the esteem and confidence of his country."[27] But in this early form the appeal to minimal qualifications had another purpose. Madison's argument was directed not only—or even mainly—against those who favored a more aristocratic constitution. It was also directed against the Anti-Federalists, who wanted a more democratic one. They favored institutions (such as larger legislatures) that would increase the chances that representatives would be more "like" ordinary citizens. Madison had no use for representation by "likeness," and fully expected that even if anyone could run for office, voters would be more likely to choose men of the "most wisdom" and "most virtue."[28] He turned the tables on the Anti-Federalists by turning their anti-aristocratic objection against them.[29] He used the democratic principle to achieve an aristocratic result.

In a similar way, many of the opponents of term limits in our time use the "fundamental principle" to defend the minimal qualifications view. They do not of course want to recreate a social aristocracy, even the moderate kind that the framers knew. On the contrary, they assume that candidates of higher social status, or at least more comfortable financial circumstances, can more easily adapt to a system with term limits. But the opponents can be viewed as trying to maintain a kind of political aristocracy, a class of leaders distinguished from ordinary citizens, if not by their wisdom and virtue, then by their knowledge and experience. In the absence of term limits, a political profession, composed of individuals who make a career of politics, is more likely to develop and endure because incumbents are more likely to be reelected.[30] Under these conditions, representatives are likely to be more experienced and more knowledgeable about government. By requiring only minimal qualifications, the system can in this way produce more qualified representatives.

Proponents of term limits do not see much virtue in this kind of experience and knowledge. Like the Anti-Federalists, they believe that representatives should be "closer" to the people. Legislators who remain in office for a long time, they assume, tend to care more about preserving their own influence and status than promoting the interests of their constituents. If so, a requirement that a candidate must not have served more than a certain number of terms may be more democratic than permitting all incumbents to run. It gives the people more control over the electoral process because over time it opens the process to more candidates who are less under the sway of the political class.

According to the advocates of minimal qualifications, the "fundamental principle" implies that the "right to choose representatives belongs not to the States, but to the people." The opponents reply: "[T]here is only one State whose people have the right to 'choose whom they please' to represent Arkansas in Congress."[31] This appeal to individual rights made by both sides plainly does not resolve the dispute because it does not answer the institutional question: Who are "the people" who should have the right to set qualifications for office? The people in each state, their representatives in the state legislatures, the people in the nation voting together, the people in the nation voting state by state, the people's representatives in Congress— a combination of some or all of these? The possibilities are numerous. To choose among them, we need to consider the institutional consequences of allocating electoral authority to one or another set of the "people."

The "fundamental principle" that the people should choose whomever they please to govern them thus does not settle the question of what qualifications should be necessary to run for office. It provides no default position that would justify minimal qualifications independently of the substantive merits of the case against term limits. Nor does it support a default position that would justify adding qualifications merely because the people voted for them. The "fundamental principle" does not settle the dispute about term limits because it leaves open the institutional questions of what kind of representatives and elections citizens wish to encourage. Do they prefer, for example, that their representatives be more experienced or more responsive? Do they want their elections to be more stable or more competitive? These institutional questions are critical in any interpretation of the still more fundamental principle of popular sovereignty.

Two Provisos of Sovereignty

Both the majority and minority on the Court in the term limits case recognized that institutional issues were at stake, but they framed them almost entirely as a dispute about the constitutional status of federalism. Do the states, as the majority held, have no authority over the federal government unless the Constitution expressly grants it? Or do they, as the minority concluded, have reserved powers over the federal government unless the Constitution withdraws them? As a leading commentator observed, the opinions turned into a display of "dueling sovereignties."[32]

As important as the question of federalism is, it does not address the critical institutional issues in determining who should have the authority to govern elections. Focusing on federalism gives the impression that we have to choose definitively between state or federal sovereignty. In practice, this division, at least in the regulation of the electoral process, has never been so sharp, and probably could never be made so. State and federal authorities are inevitably involved in many important aspects of the electoral process at both levels of government. States draw districts for congressional elections. Federal authorities require state elections to meet the standard of equal protection.

Where authority should be located to enable citizens to control the electoral process depends on which part of the electoral process is in question. We should not expect to find one answer that fits all parts of a process that ranges from drawing districts to counting ballots. And we certainly should not expect that one "fundamental principle" about voters' rights or one formal position on federalism can yield a definite answer to contestable questions such as the desirability of term limits. But there are two sets of considerations that can guide the deliberation concerning who should have the final authority about qualifications and similar electoral rules. Both can be accepted independently of one's views about the substantive merits of those rules, although both presuppose substantive views about the nature of democratic representation. Both place limits on the principle of popular sovereignty.

The first set of considerations flows from Madison's admonition about the dangers of letting representatives decide their own privileges. We can trust the normal process of representation, he said, provided that the issue under consideration is one in which representatives share a common interest with their constituents, not one in which they "have a personal interest distinct from that of their constituents."[33] This may be called the Madisonian proviso. When representatives decide questions that affect their own status or that of their party, they will tend to preserve the privileges and more generally perpetuate the practices of the institution, regardless of what their constituents may desire or need. On such issues, we should be "jealous" of assigning the representative body final authority.

We may no longer worry, as Madison did, that legislators who control the qualifications of their successors may turn the republic into an aristocracy or an oligarchy. But we may be concerned that they would favor rules that protect incumbents and discourage challengers. Whether they pursue their individual political self-preservation, they are likely to engage in institutional self-perpetuation. Whatever differences the parties in the legislature may have, they share a common interest in minimizing challenge from outside. They are likely to join in opposing term limits and campaign finance regulation, which reduce the influence of incumbency. They are likely to work together to discourage fusion candidacies, which help third party challengers.[34] It is no accident that Congress and most state legislatures rejected all the term limits laws that they considered, and that all but one of the term limit measures that have passed were adopted by popular initiative in the states.

Even if one favors such measures as term limits and fusion bans, one could still agree that they would be more justified if they were rejected by a body less contaminated by this institutional conflict of interest. Institutional self-preservation is more likely to be justifiable if the institution being preserved is not the final judge. The measures are more likely to receive consideration on their merits if those who are deciding whether to adopt them are not the same as those whose electoral future they would determine.

The point may be generalized beyond legislatures: no democratic institution should have the final authority to determine the rules or settle the disputes about its own membership. This is another way of stating the Madisonian proviso, and it should be part of the meaning of any adequate principle of popular sovereignty. Whether it should be extended to the democratic nation itself may be uncertain, but that it should apply to institutions within the nation should be clear. It implies that a legislature should not make decisions about term limits or other electoral rules when the decision determines who will become its members. It also implies that judges should not choose their own colleagues, as some critics believe that the U.S. Supreme Court indirectly did in intervening in the 2000 presidential election.[35] (Later in this chapter we return to this particular hazard of judicial intervention.)

A second set of considerations, though not unknown to the framers, is more familiar today in the form of collective action problems. The problems arise because each individual (whether a voter or a state) may favor a particular rule if all others adopt it, but any individual who alone adopts the rule will be disadvantaged. Citizens in many states wanted term limits, but they could see that any state that put this rule into effect on its own would suffer relative to other states in the competition for funds and influence in Congress. Without term limits, incumbents might be less responsive to constituent opinion over time (exhibiting "ideological slack"), but they would be better positioned because of seniority and experience to deliver benefits to their constituency (bringing home conventional "pork"). This point about collective action has been used to argue that term limits are not undemocratic. If they were adopted by most states, more citizens would be able to effect their true preferences, which (it is assumed) are for less ideological slack and more pork in their own state. In the absence of term limits in most states, their only alternatives are to vote for incumbents or lose in the competition for government benefits.[36]

There are institutional factors that point in the opposite direction, however. Less experienced legislators with shorter time horizons (the probable profile of term-limited members) may be less likely to cooperate with their colleagues, less likely to support legislation with high long-term benefits but high short-term costs, and more likely to rely on lobbyists and special interest groups for information and support.[37] The quality of deliberation in the national legislature suffers in these ways even if only some states adopt term limits. The citizens of other states who (for these or other reasons) reject term limits nevertheless must suffer the consequences of the decisions of the states that adopt them. The external costs of decisions made by only some fall on all. The possibility of these externalities suggests that decisions about electoral rules should be made not by some but by all who are eligible to vote for the members of the institution whose membership the rules govern. The qualifications of all members of Congress, and also (as we shall see later) the method by which all members are elected, are questions in which all citizens justly take an interest.

For the principle of popular sovereignty, the significance of these institutional factors does not depend on whether they determine that term limits are more or less democratic, or more or less desirable as public policy. That these factors do not yield a definite conclusion on this question underscores the more general point that most of the issues of authority over electoral rules are not resolvable at an individual level (whether the individual be the voter or the state). Rather they require finding the right institutional level at which the decision should be made.

This point can be generalized to formulate a second limitation on popular sovereignty, which may be called the Hamiltonian proviso. It grants localities and states electoral authority provided they do not impair the justice of representation at the national level. The collective action problems we have noticed are one important way in which delegation of authority can undermine national representation. By extending Hamilton's observations, we can recognize other more general ways in which national representation may be threatened.

Hamilton accepted that the states should retain the primary authority to regulate the mode of election for Congress and the presidency. The Constitution is right to assign "the regulation of elections for the federal government, in the first instance, to the local administrations; which, in ordinary cases, and when no improper views prevail, may be both more convenient and more satisfactory."[38] But he immediately added that we must reserve "to the national authority a right to interpose, whenever extraordinary circumstances might render that interposition necessary to its safety. Nothing can be more evident than that an exclusive power of regulating elections for the national government, in the hands of the State legislatures, would leave the existence of the Union entirely at their mercy."

In Hamilton's view the limit on state authority set by the proviso followed from the general proposition that "every government ought to contain in itself the means of its own preservation."[39] We can extend the proviso beyond the extreme cases he mentioned (a state's refusing to send any representatives to Congress), and interpret it as requiring the preservation of not only the Union and the federal government, but also a just form of representation in the national legislature and in the selection of the executive. Although just representation must also satisfy the principles of equal respect and free choice, the chief focus of the proviso is popular sovereignty. The proviso requires that forms of representation used by the states in federal elections support a coherent expression of the view of a national majority in the Congress and the election of the president. Variations in modes of election in the states should not be permitted to undermine the conception of representation that identifies and justifies the national majority in the legislature and in the executive. This requirement does not mean that the conception of representation must be exactly the same in all states, at least not in election of members of Congress, but it does imply that the final authority for judging whether and to what extent variations are permitted must rest at the national level.

In the term limits case, the Court majority came to the right conclusion for the wrong reasons. They concluded that term limits for members of Congress could not be imposed by individual states but could be instituted only by a constitutional amendment.[40] The conclusion in effect preserved a coherent national conception of representation by preventing states from imposing different qualifications for representatives in Congress. But the justification for the conclusion should not be simply that the Constitution prohibits additional qualifications, or that it requires uniform qualifications for members of Congress. Even if the Constitution and its history were not as inconclusive on these points as most commentators believe it to be, we should still use the process of constitutional amendment to make major changes in the authority for setting legislative qualifications. The Court may have employed the best constitutional reasons it could find, but the best general reasons lie outside the Constitution in conceptions of popular sovereignty and democratic representation. The two provisos of sovereignty constrain the possible solutions to any problem of finding the right institutional site for the authority to set legislative qualifications. Because of the first (the dangers of institutional self-perpetuation), we cannot rely on the national legislature. Because of the second (the problems of collective action), we cannot rely on the actions of individual states, whether by their legislatures or their initiatives. Constitutional amendment seems to be the only legitimate hope.

For proponents of term limits, this conclusion cannot be welcome. Indeed, it is not an agreeable result for proponents of any major electoral reform that requires uniform national action. Constitutional amendment is a notoriously difficult route to political change.[41] The only method that has ever been successful requires a proposal to go through both houses of Congress, a procedure that in the case of legislative qualifications runs counter to the self-perpetuation proviso. Even worse, a proposal with substantial majority support may still fail; any proposal can be blocked by either thirty-four senators or 146 members of the House, or during ratification if only thirteen states fail to act.[42] Although the amending process has been used more often for changes in the electoral procedures than any other single constitutional revision, it has produced only six election-related amendments in the past century.[43] At the state level, the constitutional convention is a feasible alternative. More than two hundred constitutional conventions have been held in the states. In recent years, however, few have been called and even fewer have succeeded in making major changes to their states' constitutions.[44]

The more challenging objection to the difficulty of constitutional revision is not the bias it creates against change as such (though that is certainly a concern). The more fundamental objection is that it gives past majorities excessive authority over present (and future) majorities. This problem was of deep concern to Thomas Jefferson, who urged that we "consider each generation as a distinct nation, with a right, by the will of its majority, to bind themselves, but none to bind the succeeding generation, more than the inhabitants of another country."[45] He suggested that "a solemn opportunity of [revising the Constitution] every nineteen or twenty years should be provided . . . so that it may be handed on with periodical repairs from generation to generation."[46]

We have not followed Jefferson's advice—perhaps because we think that he struck the balance too much in favor of current majorities. But if we do not look for some ways to give the current majority greater voice in the control of the electoral process, we risk sacrificing an important part of the value of popular sovereignty. The current majority (and minority) will continue to be bound by laws enacted in a system some key elements of which they have not approved and cannot change. Some critics have suggested calling a new constitutional convention, and others have advised modifying or reinterpreting the amending procedure.[47] These proposals are worthy of serious attention, but more instructive for our purposes are two institutions that already exist in some states. One—the popular initiative—is problematic, while the other—the independent commission—has more potential.

Rules for Initiatives

The case for granting federal courts the authority to overrule state initiatives on term limits is strong, but not necessarily generalizable to other kinds of initiatives. Federal courts are well placed to consider the claims of majorities beyond state borders, and therefore to challenge the legitimacy of initiatives that seek to regulate national representation. What about initiatives that deal with the rules by which states regulate their own initiatives on subjects clearly within their authority? It would seem that if the principle of popular sovereignty is to give a majority any power at all over electoral processes, it should give a state majority the authority to regulate its own initiatives. The majority should not be permitted to violate the rights of minorities or other basic liberties, and should not be able to prevent future majorities from revising the rules. But when the aim is to ensure that initiatives more accurately record the will of the majority within the state, the principle of popular sovereignty should let the states decide how to conduct their initiatives.

This implication of popular sovereignty should be distinguished from the broader claim that initiatives are the most authentic expression of the people's will and should take precedence over legislation. The broader claim, though often asserted, is hard to justify even in terms of popular sovereignty.[48] An initiative reflects only the views of those voters who happen to be interested in the issue it poses. Unlike legislators, initiative voters have almost complete discretion about whether to vote on a particular issue at all. Furthermore, an initiative records views that express only individual preferences because, unlike legislators, initiative voters do not represent anyone but themselves. They are not expected to try to balance the claims of many different constituents. Even when combined their votes are therefore likely to represent a narrower range of interests than that manifested in legislation. Also, because initiatives present issues one at a time (and are legitimately required by most states to do so), they do not permit voters to express their views on combinations of proposals; they preclude the forging of compromises that voters might prefer to proposals adopted sequentially.

As initiatives have been more widely used, their weaknesses have been more clearly exposed. Critics object that the complexity of the procedures and the difficulty of the content of the propositions discourage many citizens from voting at all. The process is in this way also biased against the less educated.[49] Public discussion about the issues on the initiatives, critics also claim, is less enlightening and more subject to manipulation than the debates in ordinary political campaigns. Instead of the instrument of the popular sovereignty that the populists envisioned, the initiative has become the tool of special interests, employed by mostly white, affluent groups, backed by large, well-financed organizations. The critics are especially concerned about what some see as bands of "election gypsies"—petition circulators traveling from state to state paid by the number of signatures they gather for proposals sponsored by their national organizations.[50] In light of these criticisms, states began placing restrictions on the initiative process to try to ensure that it would more accurately express the will of the majority of citizens of the state, not the will of special interests and outside organizations.

After the Supreme Court struck down laws that prohibited payments to petition circulators, several states began looking for other ways to regulate the initiative process.[51] Colorado citizens had earlier amended their constitution to require that petition circulators be registered voters, and in 1993, the state's general assembly added additional requirements. One stipulated that circulators wear badges identifying themselves and their sponsoring organization; another specified that initiative proponents publicly report the names and addresses of all paid circulators and the amounts each received.[52] Several individuals and organizations active in initiative drives in the state mounted a legal challenge, objecting that the requirements infringed on their First Amendment right to petition.[53]

An 8–1 majority of the Supreme Court agreed that the badge requirement threatened core political speech because it deterred potential circulators from participating in the petition process.[54] The state could require petition circulators to identify themselves on an affidavit after they collected the signatures, but not during the process. Circulators had a right to anonymity while they gathered signatures so that they would be protected from the "risk of 'heat of the moment' harassment."[55] Six members of the Court extended this protection beyond the "moment," and struck down the requirement that petition sponsors report monthly how much they paid to each circulator. We might question whether much political speech actually takes place in the process of gathering signatures, and whether the anonymity of the speakers who come to our door is more important than our right to know who they are.[56] But the badge requirement and at least part of the disclosure requirement raise a genuine First Amendment issue, one on which the courts may reasonably claim some authority.

More questionable is the Court's overruling the other requirement—that circulators be registered voters. The majority argued that the requirement excessively burdened political expression because it limited "the number of voices who will convey [the initiative proponents'] message" and consequently cut down "the size of the audience [proponents] can reach."[57] This argument is too general. Almost any requirement reduces the pool of circulators. Other requirements that the Court tacitly accepted, such as the rule that circulators be residents of the state, reduce the pool even more than does the registration requirement.

On the other side, the state based its case largely on administrative convenience. State officials claimed that as they work to prevent fraud in the signature-gathering process, they find it easier to confirm that a signatory is a registered voter than to verify that he or she is a state resident.[58] It was understandable that the state would rely on this kind of argument because legal precedents give states considerable latitude in regulating elections for the purpose of preventing fraud and corruption. But standing against an appeal to the value of political expression, the state's defense seemed pallid.

The more significant and potentially more evenly matched dispute turns on a larger question of democratic citizenship, specifically on who should be encouraged to participate in the initiative process. This is not simply a question of who has a right to circulate petitions, but whether participants in this kind of political activity should have to meet the same standards that voters must satisfy. Paul Grant, one of the leading opponents of the requirement, testified: "Trying to circulate an initiative petition, you're drawing on people who are not involved in normal partisan politics for the most part. [L]arge numbers of these people, our natural support, are not registered voters."[59] The initiative offers political opportunities to citizens who do not think that their views are represented by the candidates in regular elections, or who generally feel alienated from the regular political process. On this view, requiring less of circulators than voters is a modest way of enlarging the community of political participants, and multiplying the paths of political representation.

The defenders of the requirement doubted that most citizens who fail to register to vote are trying to make a political statement. They pointed out that Jack Hawkins, another petition organizer who had testified against the requirement, acknowledged that the reasons for not registering are probably not always noble: many do not register because "they're under a misconception that they won't be called for jury duty if they're not registered to vote, and they're really concerned about being a jurist."[60] Such an attitude, the requirement's defenders could say, does not reflect a commitment to fulfilling one's common responsibilities as a citizen.

Whatever the motives of those who do not register, the purpose of the registration requirement is respectable. The requirement may be justifiable as a duty of citizenship. It is a reasonable demand not mainly because registration is relatively easy. The dissenters in this case emphasized the ease of registration, but the main justification should focus on the rationale for the requirement, not the effort to meet it.[61] The demand is reasonable because it expresses a norm of mutual obligation that democratic citizens should be prepared to accept. If you ask fellow citizens to support your cause, you should be willing to follow the same rules you expect them to follow. If petition signers must be registered voters, then petition circulators should be willing to assume the same obligation. Accepting the same obligations as your fellow citizens whose support you are seeking is an expression of respect, a recognition that you are prepared to take on the same responsibilities that they have assumed.[62] You owe them this respect all the more because you are asking them to act on your behalf—in effect to serve as a representative for your cause.

The petition circulators—at least those who refuse to register on principle—could reply that they are only asking their fellow citizens to help put an issue on the ballot, and that if their effort is successful, they will then register to vote. They are accepting their common obligations of citizenship conditionally, but the conditions should be agreeable to anyone who supports their cause. Nevertheless, their fellow citizens should find this conditional acceptance insufficient. Anyone who plays an official role in the electoral process (as circulators arguably do) should accept the obligation to register to vote, without making it a condition that one's cause succeed. Participating in an electoral process always involves the risk of defeat. To use that risk as a reason to make one's obligations conditional is to refuse to participate on the same terms as one's fellow citizens, and in that respect to stand outside the political community that will be voting on the initiative. Similarly, those who are not eligible to register because they are not residents or because they are too young (like one of the parties in this suit) should not expect to participate as full members of the community. They have not yet taken on the full obligations of citizenship of that community.

The argument for the registration requirement fits better with the principle of popular sovereignty than does the argument against the requirement. The principle implies that, insofar as possible, the majorities that make the rules should be the same as the majority that is subject to them. The aim is to reduce the temporal discontinuity and thereby mitigate the problem of many majorities. In pursuit of this aim, a majority could even decide to limit its own authority by instituting multistage initiatives, a process in which a measure is adopted only if majorities in several sequential votes support it. Such a process could help make a majority more authentic by increasing the chances that an initiative expresses a stable view, that it is not the product of fleeting or extraneous influences. But if the whole process were allowed to extend too long, it would reinstate the temporal discontinuity.

In a lonely dissent upholding all the Colorado restrictions, the chief justice came close to making the argument for preserving the identity of a majority. The registration requirement, he wrote, is "intended to ensure that the people involved in getting a measure placed on the ballot are the same people who will ultimately vote on that measure."[63] He then went on to overplay the importance of easy registration and to exaggerate the consequences of loosening the job requirements for petition circulators (states will be constitutionally forced to let convicted drug dealers circulate petitions). But his exaggerations should not detract from the validity of the basic idea of a common electoral community.

Citizens who wish to put a measure to a vote of their fellow citizens should be part of the body who will vote on the measure. They would in that sense be part of the same electoral community, and would therefore accept the same terms for membership in that community. Thus if a majority imposes restrictions on the initiative process in order to protect the integrity of this electoral community—to protect it from not only those who fail to register to vote but also those who are under the control of outside interests—they are acting in accord with the principle of popular sovereignty. The restrictions are consistent with the Hamiltonian proviso. They do not undermine the basis of representation in the nation as a whole, and they may well strengthen the shared norms of representation within a state.

Another general lesson of this case is that the judicial process is not the most suitable forum to resolve questions of authority of this kind. In legal proceedings, the parties are likely to pose the issue, as they did in this case, as a dispute between an individual right and the state's interest in an honest and efficient electoral process. Larger institutional questions such as which majority should prevail are difficult to debate in this setting, partly because no one has standing to raise them, and partly because respect for precedent inclines the courts to favor past over current majorities. When the issue involves basic liberties (as the badge requirement presumably did), the courts have a legitimate role to play. But when the issue involves competing conceptions of citizenship and representation (as the registration requirement evidently did), the majority of citizens in the state deserve more deference, especially when expressing their will through the state constitution (as they did in this case). Whether majorities deserve comparable deference when they express their will through the state legislature is a different and more complicated question.

DEFERRING TO STATE LEGISLATURES

Tocqueville was surprised, and thought many of his compatriots would be offended, by the degree of decentralization he found in the United States. "There decentralization has been carried to a degree that no European nation would tolerate," he wrote. In general, he himself approved of it. State and local authorities know better their own particular circumstances and can therefore fashion laws more appropriate to their specific needs. Even more significant, when citizens have more direct control over their government, they are more likely to "care about each of their country's interests as if it were their own." But in at least one respect even Tocqueville thought that this decentralization had been carried too far: "the legislature of each state is faced by no power capable of resisting it. Nothing can check its progress . . . for it represents the majority, which claims to be the unique organ of reason."[64] As a result, these legislatures are "constantly absorbing various remnants of governmental powers."

Because the federal government has expanded its role in so many areas of policy over the years, the states did not succeed in absorbing as many powers as Tocqueville expected. But they did keep their power over at least one important area—the electoral process. As Tocqueville was surprised to find how decentralized American politics in general was, a European observer today would be no less surprised to see how decentralized our electoral system is. Indeed, many Americans would also be surprised to find just how much authority over federal elections has been left to the states. As they have begun to recognize the extent of electoral decentralization—dramatically illuminated by the events in Florida after the 2000 presidential election— many have begun to become concerned, in the spirit of Tocqueville, that decentralization in the electoral sphere has been "carried too far." When it is carried too far, it violates the Hamiltonian proviso, the second limit the principle of popular sovereignty must recognize. When states begin to subvert the justice of national representation, they go too far.

From the early days of the Republic, the states have enjoyed remarkably wide authority over the electoral process. The justifications today continue to be Toquevillean: states know their own circumstances best, and citizens are likely to take more interest if they have more direct control.[65] The power of states is of course not unlimited. They cannot discriminate against minorities or violate free speech. The principles of equal respect and free choice (expressed in various ways through the Constitution) limit their discretion. But the states have almost unlimited authority to determine who counts as the majority—not only in the elections for state offices but also for Congress and the presidency. With few exceptions, the states can adopt any practices they like, and can delegate to cities and counties the same discretion. From drawing the districts to recounting the ballots, the states write the rules. They have nearly complete control over the appearance of the ballot, the voting technology, and the procedures for counting votes and contesting elections. Some of these may have seemed routine matters, but after the Florida controversy in the 2000 election their larger significance cannot be doubted.

To what extent should a principle of popular sovereignty grant so much power to the states? We have already considered a federal power, the authority to set qualifications of members of Congress, on which the states have allegedly encroached by adopting term limits. We can further clarify the meaning of the principle by examining two cases in which the authority of state legislatures over the electoral process has been challenged in the name of the majority itself. In one case, the dispute is about one of the few powers that the states do not now possess but should (the authority to create multimember congressional districts). In the other case, it is about a power that states enjoy but should not, at least in its current form (the right to choose presidential electors).

Multimember Districts and Cumulative Voting

Neither Congress nor any state legislature has devoted much time to considering alternative electoral systems. They have been content with the familiar single-member district and winner-take-all systems that have prevailed in national and most statewide elections for most of our history. Legislators have not considered alternatives partly because they have seen no need to change the system that elected them, and partly because until recently their constituents have shown no great interest in the electoral process. As one congressman remarked during the hearings on alternative systems: "[If] citizens in my district were asked to rank the top 1,000 issues, this would not be among them. This is, utterly, just an academic exercise in terms of the work that is important to my constituents."[66]

But several factors are prompting politicians to pay more attention to proposals for major electoral reform: the increasing complexity of redistricting, the growing support of third parties in some states, and the mounting criticism of electoral procedures provoked by the 2000 election. The increased attention has so far produced more talk than action, but some states have moved closer to making major changes, such as adopting an instant runoff voting.[67] No member of Congress has yet seriously proposed implementing an alternative voting scheme at the national level, but several members have introduced bills that would give states greater discretion to experiment with different methods if they wished. The most frequent target of the bills is one of the few limits on state authority in this area: the 1967 federal statute that requires states to maintain single-member districts for congressional elections.[68]

In 1999, the House Subcommittee on the Constitution held hearings on a bill that would amend this statute and permit states to establish multimember districts for congressional elections.[69] Multimember districts give states more flexibility in drawing boundaries, making it easier to satisfy the equal-population requirements for redistricting plans while also maintaining some balance among the major parties. But for many proponents the main advantage of these districts is that they would enable states to replace winner-take-all systems with some form of proportional voting. Congressman Tom Campbell argued strongly in favor of the bill because it would permit cumulative voting.[70] In this system (mentioned in chapter 1) voters are given as many votes to cast as there are seats to be filled.[71] They can distribute their votes among the candidates as they choose, giving all their votes to a single candidate if they wish. The feature of this system that especially attracted Campbell is that "it allows a self-defined minority to achieve representation."

The most vigorous objections to the bill were directed against this and other "controversial" voting systems that multimember districts would encourage. The subcommittee chair Charles Canady summarized the arguments: cumulative voting would "undermine majority rule," be "detrimental to the two-party system," and increase "ethnic division and separatism."[72] Another witness added: "[C]umulative voting changes more than the method of election. Because it provides for 'interest group' representation, it also changes that which is represented."[73] Some opponents also worried that multimember districts might be used, as they had been in the past, to discriminate against minorities (for example, by submerging blacks in white-dominated districts).[74]

For the purposes of the principle of popular sovereignty, the argument about the merits of multimember districts and the alternative voting schemes they enable is less important than the dispute about who should decide the question. The critical issue is whether the states or Congress should decide. By giving states discretion, rather than imposing a specific system on them, this bill created a dilemma for those who opposed the reforms but favored giving states more power. This tension comes out clearly in the testimony of one of the witnesses at the hearings: "My first reaction . . . was a favorable one . . . this is giving more flexibility to the States, and I am a conservative, so that sounds like a good thing. [I]sn't this consistent with federalism principles?"[75]

But then he answered his own question negatively, and in the spirit of the Hamiltonian proviso suggested that even friends of states rights should not try to carry decentralization too far: "[T]here is a limit on the amount of deference that Congress should give to the States. In the proper composition of Congress, the national legislature has a real responsibility to . . . make its own considered judgment on what the most appropriate system is."[76]

Why should Congress deny states authority over this aspect of voting when it gives them authority over most of the rest of the electoral process?

Some opponents mentioned the possibility that the states would abuse this additional authority. But if they can be trusted with redistricting, why should they not be trusted with choosing between single- and multimember districts? In any case, the courts as well as Congress could quash any schemes that violated constitutional rights. Granting the states final authority to constitute electoral majorities does not entail granting them final authority to interpret the principles of equal respect and free choice.

The Hamiltonian proviso suggests an institutional objection against allowing states to choose their own voting system. Dispersing authority in this way could undermine the possibility of a coherent conception of legislative representation by creating a Congress in which some members are elected by one system and others by another system. Even those who favor cumulative voting may object to mixing the modes of representation in this way.[77] Some members would stand in a completely different relationship to their constituents than would others. Those elected by cumulative voting in multimember districts would represent interest or identity groups, while those elected by a winner-take-all procedure in a single-member district would represent groups defined only by their place of residence.[78] Opponents of mixed systems are right to doubt whether "such an important decision as a change in the basis of representation in the Nation's legislature should be left to the states."[79]

A mixed system complicates relationships within the legislature. Some members may feel more bound to act on behalf of interest groups, and less free to change positions and make compromises. They might be more likely to seek committee assignments to pursue predetermined special interests. Other members would be less constrained, and could either pursue the general interest more readily or their own district interests more assiduously. These and other consequences could make collegial cooperation more difficult, create confusion about the responsibilities of members, and weaken public confidence in the legislature.

To cooperate to achieve their individual and collective goals, members must recognize that despite their differences, each has equal standing as a representative. No member can claim greater representational authority on the ground that his or her mode of election is more just than that of other colleagues. The greater the differences in the ways in which members are elected, the more difficult it may be to sustain this sense of mutual respect. Although members may acknowledge one another's authority even if differently elected, they would have less reason to do so when some are elected by methods that are claimed to be, and actually may be, more just than the methods by which others are elected.

Even in the relatively unmixed system that now prevails in the United States, considerable variation already exists. Some representatives speak for groups based on interest or identity because the groups dominate their geographical constituencies, make substantial campaign contributions, or share the racial, ethnic, or gender identity of the representatives. The methods by which members are elected, and the nature of the districts from which they come, also vary significantly. House members from Vermont or the Dakotas represent whole states (as if they were senators), while some members from New York or California represent only sections of large cities. The procedures for regulating primaries, recounts, and other election practices differ from state to state. This diversity creates differences in the political relationships between members and their constituents, and among members within the legislature. Moreover, legislatures in some other democracies (for example, the German Bundestag, whose members are elected by mixture of single-member districts and party-list systems) have even greater variation in modes of representation, without seeming to experience any breakdown in collegial cooperation.

In light of the variations that already exist, it is difficult to argue that cumulative voting and multimember districts would by their nature undermine the possibility of a coherent conception of representation at the national level. Those systems probably fall within the range of acceptable variation; they do not seem to prevent a national majority from coherently expressing its will. But neither can it be denied that voting systems may have an effect on the functioning of national representation. We cannot rule out in advance the possibility that some versions of these systems, or other systems that may be proposed, could have the detrimental effects that critics of mixed systems worry about. To decide how serious these consequences are, and how much they should weigh against the benefits that a mixed system could provide, we would need more empirical evidence than is currently available. But the issue is also normative: we would need to make judgments about the relative justice of various forms of representation and the extent to which they are consistent with one another. The key question, therefore, is who should make these empirical and normative judgments. Who should decide how much variation is permitted in modes of election and which should be prohibited because they undermine the justice of national representation?

The Hamiltonian proviso locates the authority to answer such questions at the national level. It does not demand uniformity in modes of election, but it does insist on a unity of authority over the modes. It disapproves of dispersed authority less because of the effects on relations among members of the legislature than because of the implications for the relation of citizens to the legislature. Citizens are equally bound by the laws that representatives make, and the representatives who make them should serve equally on the basis of a conception of representation that each can acknowledge as just. Citizens have reason to object if some representatives, whether or not their own, are less justly elected than others. Ideally, all members should be elected by the most just method, but practically, once an acceptable level of justice has been reached, it is more important that modes of election be equally than maximally just. A true legislature therefore cannot leave the choice of the mode of representation, which affects the fate of the whole body, to the mercy of a few members and their constituents. The modes may vary, but how much they may vary should not be determined by individual states.

The objection to granting discretion for this kind of decision, then, is not that the present system of single-district winner-take-all elections is preferable to the alternatives. Nor is it that a mixed system that includes cumulative voting and multimember districts necessarily undermines national representation. It is that granting such discretion ignores the interdependence of systems—the problems of collective action described earlier, the potential legislative effects of variation, and, most important, the mutual dependence of citizens on the legislature as a whole. The interdependence consists in more than simply the fact that the effects of the actions of one state often extend beyond its borders. When a state adopts a divergent policy for law enforcement or the environment, its actions may have significant consequences for other states. But the state's decision does not actually change the nature of the authority of the institutions that make the policies in the other states—the conception of representation on which that authority rests. Yet that is exactly what variations in modes of election to the national legislature can do.

To be sure, even if the actions of all members in the national legislature affect all citizens, members still owe special allegiance to their constituents. The constituents in one state may reasonably decide on different modes of election than constituents in other states choose. A completely uniform conception of representation evidently is not necessary for just elections.

But granting citizens of one district exclusive authority over the mode of election of their representative creates a national assembly that is more like a meeting of delegates from different nations than a legislature of members representing citizens of the same nation. Dispersed authority of this kind may be appropriate for a transient convention—what Edmund Burke called a "congress of ambassadors from different and hostile interests."[80] It is not fitting for a permanent legislature—a congress of members who may have different interests but who act for a whole nation and should have the right to judge the process by which their colleagues win their seats. All together are entitled to question the title to legislative authority that each alone may claim.

The Hamiltonian proviso does not preclude states from experimenting with different modes of representation for their own legislatures. Nor does it prevent city councils and other local bodies from adopting different systems. Indeed, to the extent that the principle is realized, and the modes of representation in the national legislature are standardized, encouraging electoral diversity in the states becomes more important. The more the national legislature adopts a common conception of representation, the more the political system as a whole needs to maintain a wide range of options from which to choose. To make these options real, states must be able to experiment, to serve as laboratories for the nation, testing various practices and keeping at least some of them alive as alternatives that could challenge the one that happens to prevail at any time in the national system.[81]

The principle of popular sovereignty thus holds that for any practices that imply different conceptions of majoritarian representation, a national body should retain the final authority to decide how much and what kind of variation in the practices should be permitted. State legislatures and other local bodies should not be allowed to undermine the representational coherence of national majorities in Congress. The principle does not specify which national body should exercise this ultimate authority. The Madisonian proviso reminds us that Congress may not be the most reliable judge of questions that affect its own membership over time. Members may be unduly attached to the current system of single-member districts and winner-take-all elections by which they won their seats. To bring about any significant change in the current system, citizens may have to turn to other institutions, such as courts, independent commissions, or the process of constitutional amendment. In any case, the Hamiltonian proviso does not rely on only one institution for its realization.

Although its use in protecting a national majority has been emphasized here, the proviso has implications that go beyond the concerns of majoritarian representation. In a more general application, it can work together with other principles of justice, such as equal respect and free choice. Variations in voting machines, for example, may not involve different conceptions of majoritarian representation, but they may give rise to violations of the principle of equal respect. If a common standard for voting machines is necessary to provide equal opportunities in voting, then the proviso should limit the discretion of states to decide what kind of machines they should buy. Similarly, if fundraising practices in one state threaten to impair the free choice of voters in another state, the authority of individual states over such practices cannot be sovereign. Popular sovereignty does not entail state sovereignty.

Florida's Presidential Electors

Among the major institutions that played a role during the climactic days of the 2000 presidential election, the Florida House of Representatives can claim the distinction of taking the least consequential action. Fearing that the courts or Congress would challenge the legitimacy of the state's electors to the electoral college, the Republican-led House resolved on December 12 to appoint its own slate of electors, all reliably committed to George W. Bush. After the U.S. Supreme Court had stopped the recounts, Gore had conceded, and the Florida Senate had adjourned without taking action on the election, the House resolution died stillborn, scarcely three days after its adoption. Inconsequential though its action turned out to be, the consequences it threatened were of great moment, and the debate it stimulated of considerable import. While the nation's attention was fixed on the presidential candidates and the courts, the Florida legislature was considering an action that would have not only decided this election but also changed the locus of authority for future elections. Examining the arguments the legislators used and those they should have used during this episode reveals another important limit on the authority of states to control national elections.

Both sides in this debate claimed that they were acting in the name of the people—specifically, the voters of Florida. The proponents of the resolution believed it was necessary to ensure that Florida's twenty-five electoral votes would be counted when the electoral college met on December 18. The continuing recounts and court challenges had cast doubt on the validity of the electors' authority. Republican representative Gaston Cantens posed this question to his colleagues: "[I]f Congress rejects the certified slate [of electors] . . . would you rather . . . go back and tell your constituents . . . that Florida didn't count and Florida's 25 electoral votes were not counted when the Electoral College met? Or, that we, the Florida Legislature, chose those 25 electors?" [82] Representative Mike Fasano had no doubt what the answer should be: "It is simply unconscionable that we could leave here today without absolutely and finally guaranteeing that Florida's 15 million people are represented on December 18th." [83] By this time, everyone recognized that Florida's votes would decide the election for Bush, but the proponents maintained that they were not attempting to secure Bush's victory: they were only trying to make sure that Florida's electoral votes were counted. [84]

The opponents of the resolution also insisted that they only wanted the votes to count, but they meant the votes that were cast in the election but still in dispute. Some used the occasion to repeat complaints about the "disenfranchisement" of their constituents. [85] But most simply urged that the legislature stand aside and let the ongoing legal process resolve the disputes about the recounts. All the opponents believed that legislative intervention at this stage would actually deny the rights of the voters of Florida. Democratic representative Timothy Ryan captured the general spirit of the objections: "The foundation of our democracy is based upon the premise that all power is derived from the people. . . . The Legislature is not empowered to substitute its will for the will of the people." [86] Another Democratic representative, Sally Heyman of Miami Beach, pointed out that the resolution itself stated that voters had failed to make a choice of electors, and that by passing the resolution the legislature was therefore contributing to, and perhaps even creating, the problem it was supposedly trying to resolve. "How ironic," she observed, "that the legislative cure to a counting crisis will create now what is a nonexisting constitutional crisis." [87]

A difficulty that the resolution's opponents had to overcome is that the Constitution seems to empower state legislatures to select presidential electors, or at least to determine the method of their selection. [88] The framers probably had no clear theoretical principle of democratic authority in mind when they adopted this constitutional provision. They assumed that most states would select electors district by district (following the practice of the election of legislative representatives). But to accommodate a minority at the convention, they left open the possibility that some states would prefer a different method. [89]

By the 1830s nearly all state legislatures had ceased to choose delegates, but most continued to assert their constitutional authority over the process. A representative from New York in the early nineteenth century believed that a state legislature could, if it so wished, vest the power to select presidential electors "in a board of Bank directors—a turnpike corporation—or a synagogue."[90] Fortunately, no state did so. All but two eventually adopted the practice of automatically appointing electors pledged to support the candidate who won the majority of the state's popular vote. In one of the few cases in which the state's authority was challenged, the Supreme Court reaffirmed the right of the legislature to intervene, while also suggesting that the right was not absolute. Several later decisions imposed some limits on that right.[91] Yet by the time of the 2000 election, enough vestiges of the states' authority remained that state legislators could make a plausible, if problematic, case that they are permitted to intervene in the process of selecting delegates.

Why did the legislative leaders in Florida believe they were not only permitted but obligated to act? They interpreted the constitutional provision that says that each state "shall appoint" electors as creating a duty to make sure that Florida would be represented in the electoral college.[92] But whose duty? The provision grants the legislature the power to decide the "manner" of appointment, but this seems to refer to determining the method of selection in advance (in this instance simply an election). In any case, the power is not mandatory: the provision says "as the Legislature thereof *may* direct." The key provision on which the legislative leaders relied is a federal statute that specifies that if a state has "failed to make a choice" on election day, the legislature may choose the electors.[93] Because the election results were still in dispute, the state, they argued, had "failed" in the relevant sense. Some authority had to choose, or the constitutional requirement to send electors would be violated. This statute seemed to give the responsibility to the legislature.[94]

The Democrats denied that there had been any failure. "What do my colleagues point to," Representative Dan Gelber asked, "to show there has been a failure to make a choice?"[95] After all, Florida had voted, and the secretary of state had certified the results.[96] Yes, "there is a contest of the election, there are all these lawsuits . . . it's a close race." But the existence of disputes surely should not count as the "failure to make a choice," which under this law is necessary to activate the legislature's power to choose electors on its own. If "merely the presence of litigation allows the legislature to hijack an election . . . the state with a legislative majority whose candidate of choice appears to have lost simply needs . . . any partisan or just anyone [to] file a lawsuit about something."[97] An "interpretation like that would turn the rule on its head," Gelber said.

Gelber's point has force beyond the interpretative use to which he put it. Quite apart from what the law says and how it should be applied in this case, his point underscores the importance of paying attention to institutional incentives when allocating authority. A principle of authority that grants the legislature the power to choose electors if the voters fail to do so seems sensible enough on its face. But if the criterion of failure is the mere existence of a dispute, then the principle creates an incentive for the dominant party in the legislature to contest elections. They could register a protest in order to be able to select their own electors, regardless of the result of the popular vote.

Could a more stringent criterion for "failure" avoid this problem? At the joint hearings prior to the House session, the Republicans' expert witness was asked if he was suggesting that, even if there were time for the courts to resolve the disputes, the "Legislature simply could step in and act just because somebody contested the election?"[98] The witness replied: "Not merely because somebody contested it. [T]he legislature would have to conclude there was a deviation from preexisting rules." In this case, the Republicans firmly believed that the Florida Supreme Court's decision extending the deadline for certification amounted to such a deviation—"changing the rules of the game after it was played."[99]

This claim was vigorously challenged by the Democrats, who argued that the extension was necessary to comply with a more important rule, the provision of the law that requires recounts to be completed.[100] Although this dispute was central in some of the judicial proceedings about the election, it was never finally resolved, not even by the Supreme Court.[101] As a criterion for failure, "deviation from preexisting rules" may be more stringent than the mere existence of a contest, but it still leaves the process open to a wide range of challenges, and thus does not eliminate the incentive for "legislative hijacking."

This institutional problem of adverse incentives underscores the importance of dividing authority in this area. The authority to determine the method of election, resolve disputes, and to decide when a dispute needs to be resolved should not necessarily be lodged in the same institution. If the state legislature is the right authority to decide how the electors should be chosen, it may not be the right one to decide when there has been a failure to choose electors, or if there has, how it should be corrected. To see why not, and what authority would be appropriate, we need to step back from the Florida case and ask why state legislators should have any authority over presidential electors at all.

Madison's comments in *The Federalist* are often cited as support for giving states authority over presidential elections.[102] But he uses the states' power to select electors simply as an example, one of several, to reassure critics that the Constitution does not make the federal government too powerful. Aside from the general view that some important powers should be reserved to the states, the framers did not provide any justification for this specific power. Madison later explained that the mode of presidential election was not carefully considered by the Convention, and that it was a compromise arrived at late in the deliberations when the delegates were rushing to finish.[103] Once it was decided that representation in the electoral college would be by state, it must have seemed natural to assign authority for choosing presidential electors to the state legislatures.

The strongest justification for lodging this authority in the state legislatures is that, except for the election itself, they come closest to expressing the will of the people in each state who voted for president.[104] Compared to courts, even those in which the judges are elected, these state legislatures seem to have the stronger claim to speak for the people when the people cannot speak for themselves. Legislators themselves are chosen in a process that is more conventionally political than a judicial election. If disputes about presidential electors should be considered a "political question," as many commentators support, the courts, as a matter of constitutional jurisprudence, should leave it to the political branches.[105]

Three considerations, however, tell against the claim of state legislators to represent the popular will in disagreements about the electoral process. (Two express the provisos already described, and the third relies on a norm presented in the last chapter, which should also be part of the meaning of the principle of popular sovereignty.)

First, the views of state legislatures, individually or collectively, do not necessarily express the will of a national majority. Even if the legislatures are the most accurate expression of the majority will in a particular state, they may not represent the majority will in the nation. If the legislatures adopt different modes of selection, or apply different standards to resolve disputes, their collective conclusion expresses different, and potentially conflicting, conceptions of representation. This variation could violate the Hamiltonian proviso if the different standards weaken the basis of national representation.[106] The state legislatures should not be the final judge of whether it does. They should not have the ultimate authority in disputes about the mode of selection of the president.

In the 1820s the states that used district-based elections to select presidential electors switched to the at-large system that were in effect in other states. Nearly every state now allocates all its electoral votes to the candidate who wins a majority of the popular vote in the state. Two states—Maine and Nebraska—follow a different rule. They assign electoral votes to the winner of the popular vote in each of their separate congressional districts and in the state as a whole. Their rule may be preferable, but their electors represent the state on a somewhat different basis than do the electors from other states. If a large number of states were to adopt substantially different modes of selection, the sense that the presidency rests on a common conception of representation could begin to erode, and along with it any shared basis for recognizing the authority of the electors and the president they select. The greater the variation among the methods that the states use, the greater the chance that citizens in some states will object to the methods adopted in other states. Extensive variation, unless approved by all the states, could undermine the legitimacy of all the electors and ultimately the president. Maintaining a uniform conception of representation is more important in selecting presidents than members of Congress. The case for insisting on a common method is stronger when the office is one that exclusively represents all citizens. The president represents the nation, and how he is selected should be determined by national authority.

The second reason that state legislatures should not have this final authority invokes the Madisonian proviso. Even if we were to grant that they represent the will of the relevant majority at the time their members were elected, they may not represent it at the time of the presidential election. The terms of legislators do not always coincide with presidential elections, and the partisan majority in a state legislature often does not correspond to the partisan division of the vote in the presidential election. These divergences give rise to the temporal discrepancy highlighted by the problem of many majorities—the conflict between past and present majorities. Of all regular decision-making institutions, elections are most distinctly designed to express the will of the current majority (appropriately modified to protect disadvantaged minorities and to guard against impetuous action). To the extent that a legislative majority, selected at one time, is permitted to determine the outcome of an election at a later time, the will of the current majority is thwarted, and the spirit of the Madisonian proviso, violated. The problem is of course not purely temporal. The proviso is not violated simply because today's majority does not or cannot overrule yesterday's majority. The problem arises only when the views of a current majority depart substantially from those of past majorities on questions of major political significance for the democratic process.

Our current constitutional solution for resolving disputes about electors does not escape this problem even at the national level because it assigns the final authority to Congress, an institution whose members are not all elected at the same time.[107] But the solution partially responds to the problem by establishing a distinct process for resolution of these disputes. The body created for this purpose is unique: a joint session of both the Senate and the House, convened only for resolving a single dispute, and governed by special procedures. This institutional design sends the message that the legislators should adopt a different perspective when deliberating and voting on the dispute. Legislators are in effect told to assume a different role, one in which they see themselves not as delegates of their constituents but as trustees of the current majority. They are told to respect the electoral will as best they can determine it.

This national perspective still leaves room for partisanship. But it is a partisanship constrained by the aim of reaching an accurate judgment about the results of the election. Some of the particular procedures (such as voting by state in the House) may discourage members from taking a national perspective. But the design as a whole conveys the sense that the decision is of national moment, and that a national perspective is called for. Members of Congress may not always rise to the demands of this special responsibility. But they are more likely to do so than are members of state legislatures. The deliberations of Congress are not obscurely dispersed among fifty separate legislatures conducting politics as usual, but are visibly concentrated in one body convened for a specific national purpose.

Temporal discrepancies cannot be completely avoided. The rules governing an election have to be made in advance, and therefore established by officials whose authority depends on an earlier election or previous appointment. The officials who resolve disputes must be similarly designated ahead of time. Some institutions, however, are more likely than others to mitigate the temporal problem. Disputes about the outcome of an election could be handled by an independent body specifically charged with making a good faith effort to interpret the intention of the current majority as expressed in the election. Unlike legislators, the members of such a body would not be bound to represent the will of the majority who elected them, or the majority whose support they expect to seek at the time of reelection. (The last section of this chapter explores further the merits of independent commissions.)

A third reason to qualify the authority of state legislatures applies specifically to the resolution of disputes—the right to resolve disputes and the right to decide when that authority should be exercised. The institutional competence of legislatures lies in making rules, not interpreting them. If asked to interpret rules at issue in an election dispute, legislators may be tempted to select the interpretation that favors their preferred political outcome.

But since the outcome is supposed to be the product of a political process, why should that be considered unjust? One objection raises again the problem of many majorities: the legislative majority may not represent the same will as the electoral majority. The objection is not that the resolution is political but that it is the product of a politics of a different period. Suppose, however, that the divergence is not great because the legislative majority tracks the electoral majority reasonably closely. Some critics might still object that the procedure is unfair: a judgment posing as an interpretation could actually constitute a change of rules. In the Florida case, Republican legislators charged that the Florida Supreme Court, dominated by Democrats, changed the rules after the election, and claimed that the state legislature should intervene to reverse the change.[108] Democratic legislators replied that even if the court had changed the rules, the legislative intervention was a further wrong, and "two wrongs don't make a right."[109]

What is wrong with changing the rules in the middle of a process? Generally, we assume that rules established in advance are more likely to be fair than rules adjusted after more is known about how they will affect the outcome. We assume that changing the rules serves only the interests of those who prefer the outcome the change favors. But this assumption does not always hold. As one Florida representative observed, legislatures themselves often modify their procedures as circumstances change.[110] Changing the rules of a process may be necessary to avoid an unintended consequence, or to clarify an ambiguity or fill a gap. The change may be justified if it does not otherwise make the process less fair, even if it also affects who wins the election. In this respect (as in others previously mentioned), the political process is not like a game. The competitive view of elections, which often underlies the objection against changing the rules, is misleading here because it focuses on the rights of the candidates and their supporters rather than the character of the electoral process. Changing the rules affects voters too, but not merely as spectators who want to see a fair fight between competitors. It affects them as citizens who want the democratic process in which they participate to be just.

Another reason the objection against changing the rules is usually misplaced, as it was in this case, is that most electoral disputes are about what should be done after the election has taken place. The disputes center on the recounts—whether they should be held, and by what standards they should be conducted. The game is over, and the dispute is only about how we should decide who won. The closer analogy is not to changing the rules in the middle of a race, but to arguing about the accuracy of the methods used to determine who crossed the finish line first. In oral argument in one of the 2000 election cases, the attorney representing the Gore campaign commented: "[A]lthough it is part of the popular culture to talk about how unfair it is to change the rules of the game, I think that misses the point when the game is over." He suggested that the manual recount is like "looking more closely at the film of a photo finish," not like "suddenly moving Heartbreak Hill or adding a mile or subtracting a mile." [111]

The objection to changing the rules of the game must be both more specific and more institutional than the form in which it is usually presented. In the typical election dispute, the adjudicators do not simply change the rules and let the process proceed, but they actually decide the outcome of the election. In the Florida case, the House selected its own slate of presidential electors. Had the Senate followed suit, the legislature would have decided who won the national election. The problem is not that legislators are acting as partisans. Indeed, it could be argued that this is exactly how they should act because they were elected on the basis of their party affiliation. [112] The problem is rather that legislators are deciding the election in light of how other voters have cast their ballot (including information about the vote totals in other states, and the totals and margins of the candidates). Deciding the outcome under such conditions undermines the simultaneous character of the election, and thus violates the norm that voters are not supposed to adjust their votes in relation to how others have voted. As we saw in the previous chapter, this norm is an important element of the principle of free choice. It should also be respected by the principle of popular sovereignty.

Insofar as possible, authority should be allocated in a way that preserves the simultaneous character of elections.[113]

To be sure, anyone who adjudicates an election dispute is likely to know the provisional totals, and the political implications of resolving it one way rather than another. There are only two methods of resolving a dispute without letting this knowledge influence the judgment: sequester the adjudicators in advance of the election, or rerun the election itself. Understandably, no jurisdiction has attempted to sequester the adjudicators. Occasionally, new elections have been ordered, but only in specific districts or localities, never in whole states or in a presidential election.[114] In the 2000 presidential election some partisans proposed that the contest be rerun in several counties in Florida, but almost no one took the proposal seriously. Even if a rerun had been practical, it would have violated the simultaneity norm. The Palm Beach county voters would have been voting with the knowledge that the election was very close. Many would have probably voted differently (shifting their votes from Nader to Gore, for example).

Although no adjudicators of an electoral dispute can operate in complete ignorance of how people in other districts and states have voted, legislators are more likely than most officials to use their knowledge to strategic advantage, and thus to the systematic disadvantage of voters who have already voted. Legislators are inclined to vote according to the wishes of their party or their constituents, which in itself is often perfectly proper. But under the circumstances of a postelection dispute, their voting can unfairly disadvantage other citizens. Partisanship or constituency loyalty, often acceptable and sometimes obligatory, become objectionable when combined with the opportunity to vote strategically after others have voted. Although no institution can avoid this problem entirely, legislatures are less likely to mitigate it than are more independent bodies such as commissions or courts. An institution in which members have fewer obligations to party and constituency provides a more favorable setting for judging disputes about elections independently of knowledge about how the judgment will affect their outcome.

State legislators, subject to elections and often living and work in their districts, have a more substantial claim to represent the will of the people than do less accountable officials. Yet they are not justified in exercising as much authority as they have claimed, or as the Constitution and current law arguably assigns to them. Their authority to control national elections should be limited by constraints that would preserve a coherent national conception of representation, reduce the temporal divergence between majority wills, and maintain the simultaneous character of voting. To respect these constraints, we should allocate authority for resolving electoral disputes to more independent and specialized bodies.

Judicial Intervention

Courts typically enjoy the independence required to resolve electoral disputes justly. Although the courtroom may not always be the most suitable forum in which to debate how the rules of elections should be framed, courts are often the most reliable authority to decide when the rules have been followed. Judges are practiced in applying rules, and detecting when others misapply them. Even when appointed or elected by partisans, they are more inclined by temperament and training than are legislators to render impartial judgments. Even if they prefer some candidates to others, they usually care less about the political outcome than their reputation for judicial integrity. For these reasons, majorities—at least those unsure of their permanence—may reasonably place their trust in courts instead of legislatures. In the United States, citizens have relied on courts to decide when a new election should be ordered, an upcoming election enjoined, vote totals adjusted, damages awarded, or criminal sanctions imposed on election officials.[115] Courts sometimes even decide to count the votes themselves. In a primary election in a congressional district in Massachusetts in 1996, the state supreme court recounted all of the 956 disputed ballots itself (even though they had already been reviewed by the district court), and reversed the outcome of the election.[116]

Yet courts are not always the appropriate body to deal with disputed elections. The most striking illustration of the perils of judicial intervention in an electoral dispute is the U.S. Supreme Court's decision to halt a statewide recount of presidential votes in Florida in 2000. Objecting to the Florida Supreme Court's order to conduct the recount, the U.S. Court suspended the process. The effect of the decision was to let the current totals stand, and to decide the national election in favor Bush. In chapter 1 we saw that the Court majority's justification for the intervention—equal protection of the laws—is dubious. But the more sophisticated defenders of the Court believe that the intervention can be justified on other grounds. Essentially, they argue that its judicial intervention was justified to counter the unjustifiable judicial intervention by the Florida Supreme Court.[117] Their argument consists of two parts, one primarily legal and the other principally political.

The legal part of the argument emphasizes the authority of the state legislature. On this view, the U.S. Supreme Court was simply reaffirming the state legislature's authority over the selection of the state's presidential electors.[118] The constitutional basis for this authority is Article II, which specifies that state legislatures determine the "manner" of appointing electors. By overruling the secretary of state and extending the deadline beyond the date that Florida law stipulated, the Florida Supreme Court had usurped the legislature's authority.

Much of the legal argument turned on the interpretation of Florida statutes, which were in some respects contradictory. One section stated, for example, that returns filed after the deadline "shall be ignored," while another said that the secretary of state "may ignore" late returns.[119] Defenders of intervention by the U.S. Supreme Court pointed to other provisions that suggested that the state court had ignored the will of the state legislature. They maintained that state law, which allows for recounting only ballots that are damaged or defective rather than those spoiled by voter error, gives the secretary of state and canvassing boards wide discretion in applying and interpreting election laws, and makes little provision for judicial review of the decisions of the secretary and the boards.[120] Some defenders of the intervention also claimed that the "intent of the voter" standard adopted by the Florida court had not been used before in a recount, and that the legislature could not have intended that the partisan canvassing boards be trusted to use such a subjective standard.[121]

Critics of the Supreme Court questioned whether it should have intervened at all on a question that had been traditionally left to the states.[122] Even if that Court does have the authority, it did not have adequate grounds in this case for concluding that the Florida court had disregarded the will of the legislature.[123] The critics pointed to precedents establishing that ballots that could not be read by machines, for whatever reason, may be recounted. They also cited legislative history and statutory language to show that the legislature did not rule out state judicial review of the decisions of the secretary of state and canvassing boards. The reason that the "intent of the voter" standard had not been used earlier is that demands for recounts on any standard had rarely been granted. In 1999 the Florida legislature itself had changed the law, making challenges to election results easier; the change encouraged more recounts and a more tolerant standard for validating ballots. Even before the change, state courts had usually declined to reject ballots except in cases of widespread fraud. Finally, the critics argued that the recount process was no more partisan than many other aspects of the electoral process, including the count itself. If the legislature had intended to purge the process of partisanship, it would have created an independent nonpartisan commission.

The critics of the U.S. Supreme Court's intervention present the stronger legal argument. Given the ambiguity of the statutes, the primary purpose of the electoral system should have determined the conclusion. As the Florida Supreme Court had earlier declared, the fundamental goal of the election law is to preserve the "right to vote [which] is more importantly the right to be heard."[124] Despite claims to the contrary, the recount probably would not have prevented Florida from having its electoral votes counted.[125] But stopping the recount certainly denied many voters the chance to have their individual votes counted and clearly frustrated their "right to be heard." The people of Florida—expressing their will through their constitution and the actions of previous legislatures—had evidently declared that counting votes accurately has a higher priority than reporting the totals promptly. In these circumstances, equal respect and popular sovereignty combine to support the continuation of the recount.

This conclusion does not depend on accepting the view that state legislatures and constitutions should always prevail in electoral disputes. Popular sovereignty does not require that state law have the final authority for governing disputes about presidential electors. The debate about Florida's electors understandably focused on how to apply the law current at the time, which granted substantial authority to the state legislature. But the larger question of electoral justice does not turn on whether the Florida Supreme Court was deferring to the state legislature, as Article II seems to require, or usurping its authority, as the concurring justices on the U.S. Supreme Court evidently believed. Deferring to state legislatures on this question is only one possible way to allocate electoral authority. It is not unjust provided the authority is exercised consistently with equal respect and free choice.

A more just arrangement would give more weight to the Hamiltonian proviso: states should have authority to control national elections provided they do not undermine a national conception of representation. If the Florida legislature had decided, without regard to any popular vote in the state, to appoint its own delegation of presidential electors, other authorities including the U.S. Supreme Court would have been completely justified in intervening. To preserve a national basis for representation, the principle of popular sovereignty permits substantial constraints on state legislatures in their role in choosing presidents.

Some defenders of the Supreme Court acknowledge that the constitutional argument for deferring to the state legislature in this case is not compelling. The most that an appeal to Article II can show is that the Court is permitted to intervene, not that it is required to do so. They therefore turn to the second, more political line of reasoning—the so-called pragmatic argument.[126] In the absence of a compelling legal case against intervention, the potential political consequences, they suggest, provide a strong political argument in its favor. If the Court had not intervened, constitutional confusion and political turmoil might have ensued. Neither Bush nor Gore would have been able to take office in a timely manner. Whoever finally became president would have lacked the legitimacy necessary to lead the country effectively. Even some commentators who think the Court erred on legal grounds believe that its intervention may have saved the country from a political crisis.[127]

On the most commonly mentioned scenario, the recount would have continued, Gore would have won, and Florida would have sent two competing slates of electors to Congress, both certified by the governor.[128] The Bush slate had already been certified (and would have been endorsed by the state legislature). The Gore slate would have been imposed on the governor by the Florida Supreme Court. Under the Electoral Count Act (adopted in 1887 after the disputed Hayes–Tilden election), Congress would then have faced the question of which slate to accept. But Congress itself was divided. The Republican-controlled House would have chosen the Bush slate, and the Senate, split 50–50, would have gone for Gore, after he exercised his right as the presiding officer to cast the deciding vote.[129] The law provides no clear guidance to a Congress faced with two competing slates certified by a state's governor.[130] In those circumstances, defenders of the Supreme Court's intervention argue that "whatever Congress did would have been regarded as the product of raw politics with no tincture of justice." Whoever had been chosen "would have been deprived of a transition period in which to organize his Administration and would have taken office against a background of unprecedented bitterness."[131]

Most commentators not only doubt that a constitutional crisis of this kind would have occurred, but also question whether any officials should have reasonably believed at the time that it was likely to occur.[132] This deadlock scenario, like most others, depends on the assumption that Florida's governor, George Bush's brother, would have certified the Gore slate of electors. He certainly would not have done so on his own. It is doubtful that the Florida courts would have ordered him to do so, or that he would have complied with any such order. To be sure, if only the Bush slate went forward to Congress, it still might have been challenged. A partisan battle still might have erupted, and the final resolution of the election could have been delayed. But at this stage in this dispute the Constitution, supplemented by the Electoral Count Act, would have provided an acceptable, if imperfect, method for resolving the controversy.

That an acceptable method was in place in the 2000 presidential election and should have been followed does not imply that it should not be revised now. The process could be substantially improved. Some of the familiar reform proposals revived after the controversy about the 2000 election deserve serious consideration.[133] For example, the Twelfth Amendment's complicated method for deciding the winner when no candidate has received a majority of the electoral votes should be simplified, and its one-state, one-vote system in the House eliminated. Proposals to abolish the electoral college, fitfully considered in the past, should receive more careful attention in Congress and more sustained debate by the public.[134] Neither equal respect nor popular sovereignty categorically rules out choosing presidents in a system that gives more weight to votes in some states than in others. But the principles raise substantial doubts about such a system, and expose the need for justifications that are more responsive to contemporary conditions than most of the justifications offered in the past. Even if the electoral college is preserved, the appointment of actual electors should be discontinued so that a few maverick electors could not on their own decide the result in a close election.

The existing constitutional and statutory provisions do not remove politics—not even partisan politics—from the process that resolves disputes about presidential electors. But they create conditions that can mitigate the abuses of partisanship. By establishing a distinct procedure and bringing the deliberation into the open, they signal that the resolution of electoral disputes is an extraordinary question that deserves special attention and calls for a heightened sense of responsibility. The procedures create a distinct constitutional moment, an occasion standing apart from normal politics. The aim is not to eliminate political passion but to channel it into political actions that serve electoral justice. If some members mistakenly see the special circumstances as an excuse for even more zealous partisanship, they will be held accountable at the next election. The "lesson is we do not need to be saved *from* politics; instead the constitutional structure augmented by statutory procedures allows us to be saved *by* politics."[135]

The deeper difficulty with the "pragmatic" argument is not that it over-estimates the risks of a constitutional crisis. The argument begs the question of who should have the authority to judge those risks—who should finally decide when the intervention is necessary. Even if we believe that avoiding a constitutional crisis warrants judicial intervention, we might still doubt that judges—state or federal—should have the final authority to assess the risks of intervening or failing to intervene.

The principle of popular sovereignty reinforces the case for letting Congress rather than the Court deal with disputes about presidential elections. Even if the Constitution and other relevant laws did not require that conclusion, electoral justice would recommend it. Not only is Congress more accountable to the democratic majority that the principle pays heed to, it is also less vulnerable to the institutional bias that Madison warned against. That bias comes clearly into play when the Supreme Court decides a presidential election. But it also affects the pragmatic reasoning itself—the assessment of the likelihood of a constitutional crisis and the need for judicial intervention to prevent it. The Court's own judgment about whether its intervention is necessary is conspicuously questionable when its own future is at stake.

In the 2000 presidential contest, the Supreme Court justices had a direct institutional interest in the result. The next president would appoint their new colleagues. Given the closeness of the ideological divisions on the Court, new appointees would significantly influence the future work of the Court and undoubtedly determine the outcome of many its cases. Who the candidates would nominate to the Court was a question prominently debated during the campaign. The justices knew the kind of appointees Gore and Bush favored, and many voters also knew they knew. If the Court decides in favor of one candidate, as it did in this episode, its intervention is bound to be suspect.[136] The Court's majority appeared to be trying to perpetuate its control of the institution because its decision improved the chances that new members would share their views.

Members of Congress also have an institutional interest in who becomes president. The chances of passing their favored proposals, winning appointments for their preferred nominees, and raising funds for their next campaign are greater if their candidate becomes president. But the specific interest in the composition of the institution itself is less direct. If Congress were to decide the outcome of a presidential election, any effects on the membership of the body would show themselves only in the next election. The president that Congress selected could not change the membership of that Congress, and could only indirectly influence the membership of future Congresses. Another difference between Congress and the Court in this respect is that in any particular dispute no single member of Congress and no small coalition of its members is as likely to be decisive as a single justice or small group of justices on the Court. Furthermore, the next election provides a check on Congress' institutional interest. The members are accountable in a way that the justices are not.

To recognize the institutional bias in judicial interventions of this kind does not imply that individual justices act out of political partisanship or that they vote on a judicial case as if they are voting in an election. Some critics of *Bush v. Gore* were too quick to attribute partisan motives of these kinds to the majority.[137] They failed to consider other possible explanations for the decision. Apart from a sincere belief that the decision was correct on the merits, the justices may have been motivated by a conviction that the recount in Florida had become so chaotic that the man who had actually lost the vote would be named president. They may have been driven by a strong dislike of the judicial activism of the Florida court, a deep distrust of Congress' capacity to resolve the dispute fairly, a genuine fear of a constitutional crisis, or a general "cultural orientation to democracy" that abhors political "disorder."[138] The motives of individual justices are probably manifold and in any case difficult if not impossible to establish with any degree of confidence.

The institutional bias that the Madisonian proviso is intended to guard against does not depend on the assumption that judges act as partisans. To acknowledge that bias, we need only presume that judges are likely to act in what they see as the best interest of the court. Like the conscientious members of other institutions, judges presumably believe that the good of their institution is best served if newly appointed members share their view of what is good for the institution. Whatever their motives, judges—especially conscientious ones—should recognize that their decision in a dispute about a presidential election affects the future membership of the institution. If they ignore the effects on membership, they fail to take into account an important factor affecting the good of the institution as they see it. But if they take those effects into account in making their decisions, they perpetuate their control of the institution. They thereby undercut the authority of present and future sovereign majorities, and in effect place a lock on the membership for several generations. Whether they ignore or exploit the effects on membership, they do not serve electoral justice well. The principle of popular sovereignty therefore does not favor granting a court whose members are appointed by the president the authority to decide presidential elections. Because it seeks to keep institutions open and memberships fluid, the principle warns us to be skeptical of any institutional process that permits current members to choose their successors.

EMPOWERING COMMISSIONS

Initiatives are often dominated by special interests and tend to focus on a few salient issues, not necessarily the most important for the justice of the electoral process. Legislatures are prone to the vice of institutional self-perpetuation and the pressure of political fundraising. Except for the Supreme Court when it is dealing with disputes about presidential electors, courts usually can be more independent. But they generally concentrate on the rights of individuals rather than the needs of the democratic process. Consequently, a relatively new institution, the constitutional revision commission, which can consider these broader needs, merits more serious attention. It should play a more prominent role in effecting electoral change.[139]

These commissions take many different forms. Some meet regularly, others only once for a specific task; some are substitutes for conventions, others supplements to them; and some are creatures of the legislature or executive, others are more independent.[140] But none has the authority to make constitutional change on its own. Their proposals must be approved by the people of the state, and in most cases also by the legislature.[141] They are usually not as permanent as independent agencies of government, such as regulatory bodies, which often develop cozy relationships with the groups or industries they are supposed to control, and bureaucratic interests of their own. Constitutional revision commissions offer a better way to secure some greater popular control over the electoral process without sacrificing the need for deliberation and expertise.

But their democratic legitimacy has often been challenged. This excerpt from a debate in the New York state constitutional convention, which was considering establishing such a commission, captures the essence of both the challenge and the response:

> *Mr. [J. Irwin] Shapiro:* [I]t would be a very dangerous practice to have a commission not elected by the people and over whom they had no control to propose amendments and then necessarily have those go on the ballot to be voted upon by the people without any choice by anybody.
>
> *Mr. [Burton S.] Cooper:* [Y]ou ought to be aware that the people who would be responsible for the commission would be the elected public officials. [They] would be charged with the responsibility and would be answerable to the people that they selected to this commission, and in the final analysis, nothing that the commission would have done would have been without approval of the people finally when it came to ratifying the work of this commission. [142]

Delegate Shapiro points to the democratic elements that a commission lacks: the people have no voice in deciding whether to create a commission, what its agenda will be, who will serve on it, and what propositions will finally be submitted for a vote. Because of these missing elements, critics object that commissions are less democratic than initiatives or conventions. It is true that the people may have less control over these parts of the process than they might have with initiatives or conventions. But as was noted earlier, initiatives are not as democratic as they seem. A relatively small minority of the voters can place an issue on the ballot, and most citizens have no chance to determine what the initiative actually says. Furthermore, initiatives do not usually provide an opportunity to consider a coherent package of proposals. Citizens who would prefer to vote on a set of propositions arrived at by deliberation have no effective voice in this process.

In theory, conventions offer more possibilities, but in practice they provoke opposition from many different interest groups, who fear that an unrestrained convention will take away their hard-won exemptions and privileges. [143] In any case, conventions tend to focus more on issues of policy than on matters of procedure, which are generally less salient. When they take up procedural matters, they rarely challenge the existing structures of power. Four-year terms for governors have been easily adopted, but limitations on legislative influence, such as terms limits or unicameralism, are rarely even proposed. [144] Compared to the leading alternatives, then, the commission does not lack democratic authority. Moreover, as Delegate

Cooper emphasized, both the officials who appoint the commissioners and the proposals the commission produces are subject to electoral approval.

Neither delegate mentioned the most important element that could make a commission democratically accountable, and thus more consistent with the principle of popular sovereignty: the opportunity to approve the design of the commission itself. When commissions are created by executives or legislatures without any prior authorization—the most common method—the people are denied this opportunity. A commission established in this way is also likely to reproduce the partisan battles that it is supposed to overcome. The commission that Congress created to resolve the dispute about the Hayes–Tilden election of 1876 is a classic case of this kind of failure.[145] But if a constitution provides for the creation of a commission and the constitution itself is subject to periodic review by the people, the people in effect have the opportunity to approve the commission. If the commission further has the power to take its recommendations directly to the people without legislative intervention, then it is about as popular as it can be without being directly elected. Only one institution in the United States now fits this description: the commission in the state which, appropriately enough, attracted the most attention in the 2000 election—Florida.

Florida's Uncommon Commission

Created in 1968 in response to the reapportionment decisions that forced all states to revise their electoral processes, the Florida Constitution Revision Commission has broad authority to propose constitutional amendments to the people on virtually any subject.[146] It comes into being automatically at regular intervals, and remains in session for one year. Its members are variously appointed by the governor, the speaker of the house, the president of the senate and the chief justice of the supreme court. Proponents hoped that the commission would give the people more direct authority over their constitution. Its first efforts in 1978 came to nothing. All of its proposals were rejected by voters, including its plan to establish an independent reapportionment commission. According to most observers, the failure was not the fault of the commission but rather the result of the presence on the ballot of a highly controversial measure on casino gambling, and a pervasive public skepticism about proposals from any official government body.[147]

The 1997 commission fared better: eight of the nine revisions it proposed—nearly thirty separate amendments—were adopted.[148] The package of electoral reforms included protections for independent and minor party candidates, provisions for a semi-open primary, and public financing of campaigns.[149] This commission enjoyed greater success in large measure because it combined in its own institutional practices two different modes of governing—the aristocratic and democratic elements mentioned earlier. Before the commission was appointed, a highly professional and experienced steering committee prepared the agenda and rules of procedure. The commission sponsored an extensive series of town meetings and held public hearings in sixteen different parts of the state. In addition, it adopted a rule that required a supermajority to place a revision on the ballot, which had the effect of encouraging consensus.[150]

Defenders of the Florida commission appealed to standards that might seem to follow from the principle of popular sovereignty. As the state considered the proposal to establish the commission, one Florida legislator declared: "Neither the Legislature nor the Executive should be allowed in the future to block constitutional amendment or constitutional revision. The people must be the repository of power to change the constitution."[151] These declarations imply that a commission should become a super legislature. They go beyond what a principle of popular sovereignty over the electoral process should require. That principle does not justify such a broad scope for the commission. It would extend the commission's authority only to the parts of the constitution that, for reasons emphasized by the Madisonian proviso, should not be entrusted to the legislature.

The Florida commission itself went further. Many of the revisions—such as gun control and promotion of conservation and education—look more like ordinary legislation than constitutional amendments.[152] Removing such issues from the regular political agenda could weaken democratic authority. Ordinary politics allows for more interplay among the various interests in the society and in a legislature, which is more directly accountable than any commission. Substantively, the debate on some of these issues could just as well have taken place in the normal course of legislative politics. This can be seen in the commission's public meetings by comparing a typical debate on a policy issue—gun control—and a debate on an electoral process issue—public financing.

When the commissioners considered a modest gun control measure that would grant local communities the option of imposing longer waiting periods and stricter background checks, they sounded like legislators using the standard arguments from the ongoing public debate. The sponsor of the amendment, Commissioner Katherine Rundle, argued: "Let's talk a little bit about the gun crisis, the gun emergency . . . we have . . . in all urban areas throughout the state."[153] She then proceeded to cite the statistics on violent crimes, concluding: "Now are guns the only problem that contribute to violent crime? No, but they are a major contributing factor." The opponents appealed to arguments so familiar by this point in the debate that they could use shorthand references to some of the claims. Commissioner Kenneth Connor asserted: "[T]here are lots and lots of people out there who cherish the rights that have been accorded them under the Second Amendment to keep and bear arms. So I'm not going to address the issue on the turkey hunter exception or the duck hunter or the deer hunter."[154]

The debates on the proposals to change the electoral process were significantly different in an important respect. The commissioners argued frequently not only about whether a particular matter was appropriate for a constitution, but also specifically about whether it was best left to the legislature. They were very much concerned with the allocation of authority. Consider this exchange during the discussion of the public financing bill:

> *Commissioner [Richard] Langley:* [T]he Legislature created [the trust fund for public financing] and the Legislature could have continued to breathe life in it if they, being the people most responsible to the citizens of this state, thought that was the right thing to do. [A]ren't we really trespassing into the Legislature's grounds again?
>
> *Commissioner [Dexter] Douglass:* [T]he only way . . . that the public can be ensured that there will be public financing to have a level playing field is to put this into the Constitution. [W]e're trying . . . to prevent any political party [that] happens to get control over everything . . . turn around and make it possible and probable for large money to control our statewide elections. [T]he public does not trust the Legislature enough [and] if they do, they can respond to your argument and vote this down.[155]

That the legislature cannot be trusted is not a sentiment often expressed in legislative deliberations in Florida and other states or in the U.S. Congress. Representative democracies have no alternative but to entrust legislatures with most of the authority for ordinary legislation; they are after all more accountable than commissions or courts. But with respect to the electoral process, the Madisonian proviso (stressing the need to prevent institutional self-perpetuation), provides a compelling reason to look for alternatives like the Florida commission, which are not creatures of any existing branch of government. It is true that when the citizens of Florida approved the creation of the commission, they did not limit its authority to the electoral process. Had they explicitly decided not to do so, the expansive authority might have been justifiable, if ill-advised. But they were never asked whether they wished to impose such a limitation. Had they done so, their action would have been quite consistent with the principle of popular sovereignty.

From the perspective of this principle, one of the failings of the Florida commission is that it never took up several electoral issues in which the public had shown considerable interest. In particular, the commission never seriously considered the proposals that would have facilitated initiatives and referenda, or those that would have created single-member districts in certain elections. Most significant, the commission completely ignored the proposal to establish an independent commission to take over redistricting from the legislature. It is understandable that the idea of a redistricting commission was not pursued: the first constitutional commission put forward just such an idea, and it was rejected by the voters. But the logic of the justification for having a constitutional commission itself strongly argues in favor of a redistricting commission. If legislators should not regulate the elections that determine their reelection, they should not, it would seem, control the design of the districts from which they are elected.

Redistricting by Commission

Traditionally, state legislatures have carried out the revision of state and congressional districts after each decennial census, and today most still do. But in the wake of the new demands placed on the process by the Supreme Court's reapportionment decisions in the early 1960s, some states began to turn over the redistricting responsibility to independent commissions. Six states now authorize such commissions to redraw their own legislative districts, and eight more states use commissions to revise congressional as well as legislative districts.[156] The most recent state to join this movement is Arizona, whose voters in the 2000 election approved an initiative "creating an independent commission of balanced appointments to oversee the mapping of fair and competitive congressional and legislative districts."[157] The controversy that this proposition provoked illustrates the kinds of issues that arise in any debate about the authority of such commissions.[158]

In Arizona, the most prominent argument against the idea of such a commission was that the members would not be accountable for their decisions.

Congressman Bob Stump of Tolleson objected: "Accountability . . . is what you expect from your elected officials at all levels of government. [T]he Commission lacks any accountability."[159] Neither would those who nominated the members of the commission be accountable. Another commission (on appellate court appointments), which critics described as "a small, powerful group of activist lawyers," would choose a slate of twenty-five nominees. (The party leaders in the legislature would select four members, who would in turn select the fifth.) The result, Stump and his colleagues complained, would be to "make the redistricting process more secretive, more 'backroom' and more political."

The critics are right that the members of this commission, like those of most commissions, are not accountable for their actions in the way that elected officials are. Conceivably, we could create an elected commission, but then we would need a commission to determine what the procedures of their election should be. The quasi-political appointment process seems a reasonable place to stop this potential regress. It maintains an element of democratic sovereignty in the process. The more serious problem with the critics' argument is not in their attack on the commission but in their defense of the current system, the preservation of legislative control over the redistricting process. The defense begs the question. The critics contrast the unaccountable commission with the accountable legislature. This contrast would make a sound point in favor of the legislature if the issue were ordinary legislation. But in this case what is at issue is the electoral process itself, the procedures by which the members are selected, and by direct implication the validity of their claim to be accountable. If the districts are improperly drawn to ensure that the legislators who draw them are less subject to electoral sanction, those legislators can hardly be said to be accountable to the voters. Recall the apt admonition: democratic elections should not be a process "in which the representatives have selected the people," rather than one "in which the people select their representatives."[160]

In the Arizona debate, the arguments in favor of the commission won more support, but they were not without their flaws. The most common argument sounds like an appeal to the Madisonian proviso: legislators should not write the rules that affect the election of the members of the legislature. Nearly all of the submissions in the "arguments for" section of the secretary of state's official ballot pamphlet criticized the current system for granting incumbents too much power over the redistricting.[161] The state's attorney general, Janet Napolitano, argued: "This initiative takes redistricting out of the hands of incumbents who too often draw district lines to protect their seats rather than to create fair competitive legislative and congressional districts." Proponents cited other advantages, such as the greater likelihood that district boundaries would correspond to communities of common interest, and that the negotiations and compromises necessary to arrive at a new redistricting plan would be more open. But the most persistent point was the inherent conflict in the current system. In a public debate before the election, Susan Gerard, a Republican state representative, summarized the objection: "Letting legislators draw the lines is the ultimate in conflict of interest."[162]

Although the arguments favoring the commission resemble the Madisonian proviso, they make a broader and less plausible claim because they run together several different kinds of conflicts. To refine further the meaning of the principle of popular sovereignty, we should distinguish the different conflicts. Specifically we need to clarify the reasons that legislators should not have final authority over the electoral process. The reasons are usually stated in terms of the self-interest of individuals. But the individuals in question are not only legislators but also parties. Individual legislators may manipulate the districts to attempt to ensure their own reelection, but so may individual parties maneuver to try to preserve their dominance in the legislature. Furthermore, the major parties may work together to protect all incumbents, or to preserve a partisan balance against third party challengers. The critics tend to classify all these goals as forms of self-interest, and then contrast them with more admirable goals such as competitiveness, responsiveness, and lack of partisan bias—all of which are assumed to be in the general interest.

This way of putting the criticism obscures some significant conflicts. In the first place, the goals expressing self-interest conflict with one another, and some may promote the general interest more than others (or at least not impair it as much). To protect partisan balance, for example, the leaders may have to draw districts that put some individual members of their party at greater risk of defeat. Partisan balance may sometimes be better for the system than incumbency protection. Consider another choice leaders may confront: both parties may prefer to protect their incumbents rather than to increase their share of seats in the next election. Incumbency protection may sometimes be better for the democratic process than partisan dominance. In making choices such as these, politicians are probably better informed than commissioners would be about the relevant political circumstances, and therefore better placed to discover outcomes that could serve both their own interest and the general interest. Furthermore, even in the present system, because of these conflicting goals and the considerable uncertainty about the effects of any redistricting plan, politicians usually produce plans with districts that are more competitive than those that existed prior to redistricting.[163]

In the second place, we should not presume that the conflicts between the interests of politicians and those of the system always represent a choice between self-interest and the general interest. Incumbency protection is not always undesirable, and may under some conditions promote electoral justice even while serving the incumbents. Many voters want to reelect their own representatives, who have a known track record, familiarity with the constituency, and greater legislative experience. These voters would have good reason to favor redistricting plans that generally increase the chances of incumbents. In the debate with Arizona representative Gerard, former state senator Stan Barnes (a fellow Republican) asserted: "I don't believe that incumbency is somehow a bad thing. [I]ncumbents matter, because they have been elected by the people, and they have standing."[164]

Finally, electoral competition is not an end itself, but a means of allowing change that voters may want. It may also be a necessary means of discovering whether voters want change, or helping them recognize that they want it. But even as an instrumental goal, electoral competition can be misleading if it is conceived, as it often is, on the model of economic competition.[165] It neglects forms of contestation that do not readily fit within the categories assumed by market analogies. It gives more attention to the interplay of interests and preferences than to the interaction of principles and ideas. Furthermore, its preoccupation with making electoral contests more competitive distracts attention from other equally worthy goals, specifically making electoral reform more cooperative. More generally, concentrating too much on promoting competition may distract citizens and legislators from attending to the business of government. From an institutional perspective the goal should be to find the optimal level of competition, not to maximize it.

Nevertheless, whatever the optimal level may be, it probably requires more competition than exists in state and congressional districts in the current system. In Arizona, since 1992 (the first election after the decennial redistricting) more than 90 percent of incumbents seeking reelection in legislative races have won.[166] In the last two elections, more than one-third of the incumbents in the legislature faced no opposition at all in their races. Similar patterns show up in other states, both in the legislatures and in congressional elections.[167] The high rates of reelection may indicate that voters are satisfied with their incumbents, or it may show that incumbents have discouraged challenges in other less creditable ways. Whatever the causes of the lack of competition, granting complete control over the redistricting process to incumbents does not seem the most effective way to achieve an optimal level. That is the important core of truth in the charge of conflict of interest that the proponents of commissions bring against legislative control. A commission is a better instrument for preserving popular control over redistricting than the legislature because it is more likely to keep the process open to change. The chief concern should be not self-dealing but self-perpetuation, where the "self" is not only individuals or even parties but also the legislature—its structure, composition, and patterns of representation.

These Madisonian considerations also apply to the process of counting votes and adjudicating disputes about the counting. Foreign observers are astonished to learn that the political parties operate the polling stations in most elections in the United States. In most European democracies, the management of elections is entrusted to officials, often career civil servants, who are completely independent of the political parties and the political leadership.[168] But in U.S. elections, the political parties usually design the ballots, schedule the voting, provide the poll watchers, recruit the aides in the precincts, and oversee the actual count. The members of canvassing boards and other bodies that initially hear claims regarding recounts are appointed by the political parties or have recognized party affiliations.

Some of the unfortunate effects of these practices were strikingly apparent during the disputes about recounts in Florida in the 2000 election. In Palm Beach County, a critical site in the recount battle, the members of the canvassing board worked openly as agents for their own party.[169] The judge who chaired the board was more circumspect, but as a result was suspected by both parties of acting out of partisan motives. Unable to resolve the dispute, the board sought a ruling from state officials, and then found itself caught between contradictory orders, one issued by the Republican secretary of state and the other by the Democratic attorney general. Although a less partisan and more independent process could not have completely avoided the rancorous controversy that occurred in this election, it could have provided greater assurance that the counting and recounting had been conducted legitimately and justly. A system more respectful of the Madisonian proviso would reduce the influence of political parties in the supervision of elections and in the resolution of disputes about them. In the spirit of the proviso, we should encourage the nascent efforts to develop election administration as a profession, with distinct norms of impartiality and fairness, and definite paths of professional advancement separate from the regular political process.

The implications of this case for commissions are more limited than might at first seem. The argument casts doubt only on letting the legislature have final control, not on allowing politics to influence the composition of commissions or their proposals. Redistricting is an unavoidably political process. As we have seen, it involves making choices among a complex set of values, which cannot be readily sorted into those that promote the self-interest of politicians and parties and those that serve the general interest of the democratic process. There is no objective or neutral standard that can determine these choices. The criteria now stipulated in the Arizona constitution are typical of those used by many states: equal population, compactness, contiguity, community of interest, geographical saliency.[170] Plainly, the criteria can yield conflicting results, and choosing among them requires deciding which should weigh more or less heavily. Interpreting and applying the criteria, as well as making the other choices between the various goals we have canvassed, calls for political judgment.[171]

The futile quest for a politically neutral judgment persists in the provision in the Arizona law stipulating that "party registration and voting history data shall be excluded from the initial phase of the mapping process."[172] This veil of ignorance is lifted, as it necessarily must be, when it comes time to "test maps for compliance with the above stated goals" (the criteria listed above). Commissions would be better advised to recognize openly the political nature of their task and explain publicly their use of the available political information. Most states, including Arizona, acknowledge the unavoidably political nature of redistricting decisions by permitting former politicians to serve on their commissions (though like Arizona most bar current and recent office holders). Politics also often intrudes into the appointment process: legislative leaders typically appoint the majority of the commission members, sometimes from a restricted pool of candidates (as in Arizona, where they are selected by a judicial committee).

Commissions thus offer a potentially valuable way for the people to exercise indirect control over the electoral process. Granting more authority to commissions to regulate the electoral process does not presuppose a vision of politics as rational and disinterested decision making. Not only do the structures they create allow robust political competition, their own deliberations inevitably lead members to take strong political positions and make hard political bargains. Commissions are not above politics, but their politics need not be purely partisan. To the extent they are partisan, the partisanship does not need to be the same as that found in other bodies, such as legislatures, which would otherwise control the process. Commissions do not give citizens unmediated authority, as initiatives do. But the mediation they introduce provides opportunities for deliberation, in which members can consider the welfare of not only current but also future majorities. The principle of popular sovereignty requires that we attend to the electoral claims of future as well as present citizens.

CONCLUSION

If as Hamilton declared "the people should choose whom they please to govern them," should they not also choose the procedures that govern whom they choose? The principle of popular sovereignty says they should, but then immediately adds two qualifications. Both point to institutional considerations that go beyond the individual rights of voters and candidates. They provide reasons that bear on where we assign authority for deciding questions about electoral procedures, whatever our views about the merits of those procedures may be.

The first qualification is the Madisonian proviso: authority for governing procedures may be assigned to an institution only if the procedures in question do not grant the institution final authority over the rules that determine its membership. The basis of this proviso is not merely the commonly cited concern about individual conflict of interest—the suspicion that legislators will write the rules to ensure their own reelection. The deeper institutional reason addresses the temporal aspect of the problem of many majorities: the majority of the present should not unduly constrain the majorities of the future. The mischief is not self-dealing, but self-perpetuation. The democratic process becomes less open to change, and future majorities have less authority than they are entitled to. Control over membership is a particularly potent tool of present majorities. It need not be exercised intentionally to be effective in perpetuating the parties, policies, and practices of a current majority.

The proviso applies most obviously to legislatures. It casts doubt on granting them final authority to draw districts and to reject term limits. But the problem of self-perpetuation also arises in the direct exercise of authority by the sovereign majority itself. Initiatives are problematic in part because they express the will of the majority of the moment, without regard to the claims of future majorities. It is, after all, a future majority whose will is to be expressed in the elections for which a present majority is writing the rules. Ideally, initiatives should be conducted in stages over time, so that they are more likely to express a durable majority will.

The second qualification to the principle of popular sovereignty is the Hamiltonian proviso. It is a response to the spatial dimension of the problem of many majorities—the potential conflicts among different levels and jurisdictions of authority. Although Hamilton was prepared to grant some power to the states, he insisted that, like any government, the federal government must retain control over the means of its own preservation. If we understand preservation to include maintaining a just form of representation in the national legislature and in the selection of the executive, then state legislatures should not have final authority over the process of election of members of Congress and the president.

Spatial variation can frustrate electoral justice in various ways. As we saw in chapter 1, some variation within states, such as differences in voting technologies, may be objectionable because they violate the principle of equal respect. Variation can also contravene popular sovereignty by undermining the idea of national representation. A representative process characterized by wide variation is more like a congress of ambassadors than an assembly of legislators. Because the parts of any system of representation are interdependent, too much—or the wrong kind of—variation among the parts can disturb the system as a whole. All citizens may have less reason to accept laws enacted by legislators who act on the basis of a form of representation that only some citizens have approved, especially if some regard it as less just than it should be.

Neglecting this interdependence of the representational system has practical consequences. It leads to disregarding problems of collective action. When a state adopts term limits on its own, for example, it is disadvantaged in the national legislature because its representatives are likely to be less influential than the legislators from other states. When a state controls the mode of selection of presidential electors, it can dilute the national conception of representation that gives the president legitimacy. In general, the authority to decide how much variation in electoral practices is just should be lodged not necessarily in the same institutions but at the same institutional level of the bodies that legislate and execute the laws to which those who vote in the relevant elections are bound.

Although these implications tend to favor the centralization of electoral authority over national elections, the principle of popular sovereignty, suitably qualified, does not preclude—indeed invites—variation in the procedures that govern elections for state and local offices. States act as laboratories for electoral experimentation, the results of which may be used by other states and by the nation to improve the process as a whole. States should be able to experiment with multimember districts or cumulative voting, though their experiments should be reviewed at the national level to ensure they do not have adverse consequences for national representation. The principle would also give states more authority than the Supreme Court currently allows to regulate their own initiatives for the purpose of seeking a more accurate and durable expression of the will of the majority of their citizens.

By exposing the limitations of initiatives and legislatures, the principle of popular sovereignty together with its provisos encourages consideration of other institutions that could enable the people more effectively to exercise authority over the electoral process. The principle favors institutions that more satisfactorily deal with the problem of many majorities. Such institutions, by virtue of their composition and structure, encourage their members to take a disinterested view of the claims of various majorities, temporal and spatial, and to make rules and resolve disputes with due regard to the claims of each.

More specifically, this conclusion implies that those who make the rules and resolve the disputes should not be the same—and should not have the same electoral interests—as those whose election the rules and resolutions decide. Popular sovereignty over the electoral process would in this way enjoy more security because the officials to whom the authority is delegated are independent of the officials who are subject to the elections. At least some of the institutions in which rules are made and disputes resolved should therefore be distinct from the ordinary political process. The institutions should stand independently so that the members are not practically or morally bound to one kind of majority rather than another, and are not inclined systematically to favor one type of candidate or party over another. Insofar as the institutions to which the people delegate authority are independent in this way, they are more likely to express the will of the appropriate majorities—whether past or present, local or national—as they make the rules for and resolve the disputes about the electoral process.

The requirement that the authority for governing elections should have some independence from the ordinary political processes might suggest that courts would be the most appropriate institution to assume this responsibility. Courts certainly have an important role to play in regulating the electoral process. They are well suited to protecting individual rights, notably the constitutional requirements of equal protection and free speech. That is why judicial deliberations figured in the analysis of the principles of equal respect and free choice in earlier chapters. That is why the Court was probably right to strike down Colorado's requirement that petition circulators should wear badges identifying themselves. It may also partly explain why the Supreme Court in *Bush v. Gore* strained to find a violation of equal protection (which implicates individual rights) instead of a violation of the guaranty clause (which involves the form of government).[173] But questions about the authority of majorities—which majority to prefer—raise issues that are less about individual voters than about institutional structures and the nature of representation itself. The conflicting demands of democratic majorities neither state legal claims that individuals usually have standing to bring, nor permit remedies that courts usually have competence to apply. Furthermore, courts are expected to respect precedents, and therefore are bound, more than other institutions, to the will of past majorities and to the decisions of supermajorities in constitutional ratification.

Compared to these alternatives, a relatively less familiar institution, the independent commission, looks more promising as a way to exercise popular authority over the electoral process. Less responsive but more deliberative than the initiative, less accountable but more disinterested than legislatures, such commissions can provide a partial solution to the problem of many majorities. They are generally not self-perpetuating, and they are usually not beholden to a majority representing any particular level of government. They have the further virtue of exemplifying in their own institutional design the structure of the institution they are governing. Like the institution of the election itself, an independent commission combines accountability and selectivity—recalling the classical mixture of democratic and aristocratic modes of governing.

We can maintain the democratic authority of commissions in various ways: by ensuring that voters have an opportunity to approve its constitutional role (its scope of authority and general procedures), the nature of its membership (the qualifications of members and their method of selection), and its substantive conclusions (the content and form of its preliminary and final proposals). The aristocratic element is supplied by appointing members who have expertise in dealing with elections including that gained from holding political office. Commissions are properly political creatures, but they can cultivate a politics different from the ordinary kind. They need not serve entrenched majorities of any time or place. Their aristocratic character can also be seen in the deliberative mode of decision making to which they aspire. Like Aristotle's ideal aristocrats (rather than like the more familiar social ones), members of commissions can view their role not as registering preferences of constituents, or even acting on their own conscience and convictions, but as working together to identify and express the will of the appropriate majority.

Commissions are most justifiable when, like the Florida Constitution Revision Commission, they serve as the means for revising a constitution. But the scope of the Florida commission, like that of many others, is broader than it needs to be—broader than the Madisonian proviso would require. By taking up a wide range of issues unrelated to elections, the Florida commission goes beyond what the principle of popular sovereignty prescribes, and encroaches on the democratic authority of the legislature. Although the Florida commission may be an apt model for determining the status that such bodies should have, it is not necessarily the most suitable guide for specifying their scope. For that purpose, redistricting commissions are a better model, because their power is limited to a specific task—redrawing the district boundaries for state and congressional races after every decennial census.

Given its foundation in majoritarian values, the principle of popular sovereignty favors institutions that are less majoritarian than might be expected. The principle does not completely deny the authority of initiatives or legislatures to govern elections, but it clearly affirms a role for independent commissions. This institutional implication reflects a more general conclusion about principles, like popular sovereignty, that would allocate electoral authority. Any principle that maintains that the people should control their own elections does not express a single set of values. Even if "the people" refers only to a majority, we still need to know which majority should have what authority. The provisos that are part of the principle of popular sovereignty developed here provide some guidance. They tell us to look with disfavor on majorities that would perpetuate themselves and majorities that would subvert national representation.

No principle of sovereignty can completely settle the question of authority in advance of democratic deliberation. The people themselves must decide who, for the purposes of governing elections, the people are. The paradox cannot be completely avoided. Who should have the authority to make the rules and resolve the disputes about elections is a complex question with more than one answer. We are more likely to find satisfactory answers if we recognize, as the principle of popular sovereignty emphasizes, that questions of authority require us to make choices among fundamental values and competing conceptions of democratic representation. If we fail to make those choices deliberately, we cannot justly declare, after any particular election, that it is time for the votes to count.

Electoral Deliberation

What we are talking about is having laws of sufficient specificity and sta-
bility that people can rely on them in advance and not have them
changed after the fact.
JUSTICE ANTHONY KENNEDY, DECEMBER 2000

Democratic politics is a site of persistent disagreement. Citizens and their representatives disagree about who should rule and how they should rule. Pursuing their disagreements, they organize, mobilize, protest, campaign, litigate, and even deliberate. Periodically they vote. The election does not resolve most of the disagreements, but it decides, for the moment, the question of who should rule. Citizens have more or less reason to accept that decision the more or less justly the election is conducted.

Electoral justice would be a simple matter if citizens could agree in advance on specific and stable procedures to govern elections, and accept whatever results the procedures produced. However deep their disagreements about the justice of the laws their representatives enact, they could at least agree that the process by which their representatives are elected is just. That is the aspiration of procedural justice—to establish a process that citizens can regard as just regardless of whether they accept all its results as just. That is also presumably the motivation of those who seek to base electoral justice on principles that are less contestable and more constant than those of other kinds of justice. Individual rights and fair competition are attractive foundations because they seem relatively familiar and readily acceptable in American democratic culture. But neither provides a way to escape the conflicts among fundamental values that electoral justice poses. Both yield approaches that fail not only to resolve those conflicts but also even to recognize some of them.

Some electoral disagreements are driven by personal and partisan prejudices, and some are fueled by people indifferent to the values of democratic process. Others are created by politicians and their supporters trying to manipulate the procedures to produce their favored outcomes. We certainly want laws to be specific and stable enough to check such abuses, and we generally can secure relatively durable agreements on relatively impartial rules to prohibit them. No one should object to rules against stealing votes or stuffing ballot boxes, and no one would defend, at least openly, violations of regulations for tabulating and recording votes. But even when the laws seem specific and stable, disputes may break out about whether they have actually been followed. The charge that the rules were changed during the process was at the center of the controversy that erupted in the wake of the 2000 presidential election. Some accused the Florida Supreme Court of changing the procedures the legislature had established before the election. Others accused the U.S. Supreme Court of changing settled law when they halted the recount ordered by the Florida court.

Many disagreements about the electoral process, even some motivated by parochial interests, express deep conflicts in the fundamental values of our democracy. Even disputes about whether the laws have changed may spring from differences about how specific and stable laws should be; they may reflect divergent views about how constrained by rules political conflict should be. Other procedural disputes ultimately turn on substantive values, such as liberty and equality. We fail to appreciate the depth of those conflicts if we assume that electoral justice mainly requires that we make sure in advance that electoral laws are specific and stable.

Disagreements about electoral justice are no less deep and no less difficult than disagreements about other kinds of justice. Electoral procedures give rise to fundamental disagreements about justice because the principles of electoral justice rest on the same foundations as do other principles of justice. Like justice in general, electoral justice expresses terms of cooperation that could be affirmed by free and equal persons. Like many political practices in a democracy, elections embody principles by which citizens seek to cooperate to pursue their collective projects. Elections and their principles express the shared meanings of citizenship in democracy.

Sometimes the meanings that electoral procedures express are not attractive, as when they imply that some citizens should be excluded because of their race. Sometimes the meanings are inspiring, as when they affirm that all citizens should have the chance to participate on the same day in the same way in a common act of citizenship. Sometimes the meanings are inchoate, as when they assert that the people should control elections without defining who the people are. Most of the time, disagreements are not only probable but also desirable. Even though the disagreements must be temporarily suspended at the moment of the election, they are necessarily and properly the subjects of continuing deliberation.

In the United States as in most modern democracies, voting is as much an act of will as of reason. Voters no doubt have their reasons for voting as they do, and political scientists devote much effort to trying to discern them. But voters do not need to give any reasons for their decisions. They do not have to explain themselves to anyone. Individually they simply mark their ballot, and collectively they express the popular will. The willful character of elections makes justifying the process by which the will is expressed all the more important. If an expression of will is to be accepted as a just basis for choosing rulers, the process by which they are chosen must be subjected to examination by reason. Citizens and their representatives must be prepared to give mutually acceptable reasons for the procedures they seek to impose on one another. They give those reasons in an ongoing process of democratic deliberation.

JUSTICE AND REPRESENTATION

The principles of electoral justice provide both the framework and the content for that deliberation. The principles identify the moral conflicts that need to be addressed and distinguish the good from the bad reasons that may be given to resolve or at least tolerate the conflicts. None of the values that the principles express—equal respect, free choice, and popular sovereignty—has only one simple meaning. They all call for interpretation and require choices among competing understandings, no one of which can claim to be uniquely reasonable. The choices among the meanings depend on the various institutional considerations canvassed in previous chapters—most fundamentally on conceptions of democratic representation.

Consider the principle of equal respect, which permits unequal treatment if respectful reasons can be given for it. What counts as a respectful reason plainly leaves room for reasonable disagreement. A striking instance of unequal treatment is racial districting. Whether it is justifiable depends on how we understand its meaning. If it expresses racial separation, it is not justified; if it promotes greater racial equality, it may be. Which of these meanings it conveys further depends on what kind of representation it fosters—the kind that builds unified support in the constituency or the kind that encourages coalition building in the legislature. Either kind can support (or undermine) the legitimate claims of disadvantaged groups under certain conditions. The effects of each kind must therefore be taken into account in deciding the meaning of equal respect.

The principle of free choice similarly implicates conceptions of representation. Free choice implies informed choice, but that does not necessarily mean that citizens should always receive more information. Noting on the ballot that a candidate has refused to support term limits is useful information if one holds a mandatory conception of representation and if one believes that imposing term limits is an issue of overriding importance. But a more discretionary role for representatives would justify giving that kind of information less prominence in the electoral process.

Popular sovereignty says that the majority should decide disagreements about electoral procedures. But which majority? A current majority has the most obvious claim, but if the current majority imposes severe constraints on future majorities, the claim is self-defeating over time as each future majority becomes a current majority. If current majorities assert too much control over the future, democratic representation becomes less fluid and less responsive to change than it should be. Representatives in the current majority perpetuate themselves and their parties without due regard to the views of succeeding majorities.

Similarly, popular sovereignty poses but does not answer the question of whether local or national majorities should have final authority over electoral justice. As Tocqueville stressed, local majorities may be closer to the people and should have control at least over the process of the election of their own representative. But as Tocqueville also recognized and the Hamiltonian proviso emphasizes, local control can go too far. The composition and character of the national legislature affect all citizens. All citizens therefore have a legitimate interest in the procedures by which all the representatives are selected, not only their own.

If the people themselves must decide who, for the purposes of governing elections, the people are, we encounter a potential paradox of authority. It seems that we need to know what counts as a majority before we can conduct a vote to decide what counts as a majority. The majority votes to decide who the majority is. This difficulty is not limited to defining a majority. If the officials who make decisions about any electoral procedures are to be accountable, they must be subject directly or indirectly to elections, and some democratic authority must make decisions about the procedures of those elections. It seems we face the prospect of an endless cycle of elections. In practice, we avoid the paradox by temporal sequencing. Today's electorate decides on the procedures for tomorrow's elections (or chooses the representatives who will decide on them). But that solution does not escape—indeed it reproduces—the temporal dimension of the problem of many majorities. The majority of the present controls the identity of the majority of the future.

Although we cannot completely escape the temporal aspect of the problem of many majorities, we can mitigate its most troublesome effects. Those come from entrusting the procedures for running the elections to the same people who are running *in* them. This practice violates the Madisonian proviso. Politicians and their supporters should not completely control the means of access to the institutions of which they are members. This institutional conflict of interest can be avoided by more sharply separating the institutions that govern elections from the institutions that elect the governors. A body that deals with only electoral rules and procedures is for this reason preferable to a body that deals with the whole range of law and policy. A distinct division of organizational labor is more likely to produce a just distribution of electoral labor. Divided authority does not resolve the temporal problem, but it reduces the opportunities for exploiting it.

FROM PRINCIPLES TO INSTITUTIONS

The principles of electoral justice accommodate a range of meanings, but they are not completely open-ended. They point to some definite conclusions about electoral institutions. The conclusions are still open to challenge in the deliberative process, but to the extent that the arguments in the preceding chapters are accepted, they may be regarded as fixed points in the deliberations, relative to claims that have been shown to be subject to reasonable disagreement.

Equal respect may not finally resolve the question of racial districting. But it forbids denying any citizen the right to vote and placing obstacles in the way of exercising that right. It further supports positive measures such as easing registration requirements and improving facilities at the polls. We may not be required to place optical scanners in every district, but we should seek an equitable distribution of resources among districts so that votes of no citizen or group of citizens count less than those of others. Voters who need assistance should be able to get it in whatever district they happen to live.

Free choice does not entail the elimination of money in the electoral process, but it does require the moderation of its influence. If voters' choice is freer to the extent that they are exposed to a reasonable balance of types of influences, then the present system, dominated by the pressures of money, needs to be substantially reformed. It can be shown to be deficient on grounds that it weakens liberty, the same value invoked to defend the extensive use of political money. The principle of free choice points toward reforms that promote a pluralism of influences rather than the plutocracy of pressures that currently reigns in the electoral process.

Like those of the other principles, popular sovereignty's prescriptions depend significantly on the context of electoral politics at a particular time. In the current circumstances, the principle of popular sovereignty takes a critical view of many of the institutions that claim title to the authority to decide electoral disagreements. Initiatives at first look like the best friend of majorities, but they are often captured by special interests. They deal with only a few issues, not necessarily the ones that enduring majorities would select. Legislatures have broader agendas, but they enable certain majorities to endure for too long. Entrenched in the legislature, the representatives of any current majority are prone to the vice of self-perpetuation that Madison warned against.

In light of the deficiencies of initiatives and legislatures, we should look with more favor on a less familiar institution, the independent commission. Such an institution may not at first seem the most natural expression of popular sovereignty. Usually composed of recognized experts or prominent citizens, commissions are in some respects less democratic than initiatives, legislatures, and even some courts. Yet they are already performing democratic service for majorities in several states. They can be designed to be more accountable and less self-perpetuating. In any case, the institution of election itself is not purely democratic in conception. It is selective: the many choose from only the few. In that respect commissions mirror the institution they regulate. The difference lies in the basis of the selectivity. Commission members can be more reliably chosen for their knowledge and experience. Moreover, if commissions were to regulate elections, they would mitigate the problem of self-perpetuation. They offer an institutional strategy that divides the power to decide who is elected from the power to decide the procedures by which they are elected.

The institutional implications of the principles of electoral justice depend on social and political circumstances, which in a healthy democracy are continually changing. Judgments about institutions need to take account of such changes, and thus need to be made in a continuing process of deliberation. Even more important than the institutional designs the principles imply, therefore, are the deliberative prescriptions they suggest.

NORMS OF ELECTORAL DELIBERATION

In the course of examining actual deliberations about electoral practices, we have taken note of some lines of argument that are commendable, some that are misconceived or mistaken, and many that are incomplete. To try to recapitulate all the lessons that might be learned from such an examination would be to miss part of its point; much of its value lies in the details. But several general conclusions are worth restating as guides for the public discussion of electoral practices. They may be regarded as norms of deliberation about electoral justice.

The first and most basic norm is that electoral practices must be justified to the people who are bound by their results. The practices must be defended with reasons that could be mutually accepted by citizens considered as free and equal persons. The reasons must be clearly accessible and appropriately respectful. They must satisfy the requirements of public reason that should apply to deliberation about the justice of any law. Voting may be an expression of will, but in this respect the process of voting should be a manifestation of reason. If the election is to be just for all citizens, its procedures must be justified to all citizens.

Justification is required not only when change is proposed, but also when it is resisted. Like much of the rest of the democratic process, the electoral system is a set of politically constructed institutions, defined by rules that citizens and their representatives can alter. There is no default position, no electoral state of nature that must be presumed to prevail in the absence of compelling reasons to abandon it. Declining to regulate campaign finance is no less a choice, no less in need of justification, than deciding to regulate it. Continuing to accept the rights of states to control congressional elections is no less a decision, even if supported by the Constitution, than transferring more control to national authorities. The Constitution of course makes some changes more difficult than others and properly carries considerable weight in any deliberation. But most of its provisions require interpretation, and some invite revision of the document itself.

That a practice has survived without widespread challenge counts in its favor. This is so especially if the alternative is a significantly different system that has not been tested in the relevant circumstances and is likely to have substantial effects on other parts of the political process. In the United States, the two-party system warrants respect on these grounds. But even if that system can be justified and is recognized as a sensible starting point in any discussion about our electoral process, we need not accept it in exactly its current form. A defense of the two-party system should not be confused with a defense of the two parties that happen to exist at any particular time.

The second norm recommends that we situate deliberation in the midrange of political argument—between abstract theory and concrete practice, where principles and institutions meet. It counsels theoretical modesty: concentrate on institutional meanings rather than philosophical doctrines. The most fruitful arguments rarely turn on choices between grand theoretical alternatives—liberalism or conservatism, libertarianism or egalitarianism, and other competing isms. Many of the debates about electoral practices evoke elements of these theories, and are easily turned into battles between ideologies or comprehensive philosophies. But deliberation is more likely to be productive in the midrange of controversy, where more citizens can express their disagreements and accommodate their differences without abandoning their comprehensive conceptions of morality and politics.

This norm also implies that we should not try to order the principles of electoral justice or assign priority to one principle over the others. The norm seeks to ensure that none of the values expressed by the principles is neglected. No priority rule is likely to be satisfactory for all or most cases in which values conflict in the electoral process. We cannot determine in advance that equal respect, for example, should take precedence over free choice in all circumstances. We might suppose that at least we could say that equal respect and free choice take precedence over popular sovereignty. After all, we want to prohibit majority tyranny. But the principles of equal respect and free choice both need to be interpreted, and a sovereign majority is sometimes the proper authority to carry out that task. The sovereign majority might even decide that in certain kinds of disputes equal respect should trump majority rule, but because the authority for making that decision in that case derives from popular sovereignty, the decision could hardly be said to establish the general priority of equal respect.

In any case, before we try to resolve conflicts between principles, we need to attend to the conflicts within each. An apparent conflict between principles often turns out to be not as severe as it first appears. It may even disappear or at least diminish if we successfully resolve the conflict within one of the principles. The issue of automatic registration, for example, is not constructively posed as a conflict between equality and liberty—between making the exercise of the right to vote more equal, and preserving the choice not to register. Instead, by analyzing the nature of free choice more carefully in an institutional context, we can see that under certain conditions free choice itself may justify automatic registration. Preserving the opportunity to choose not to register to vote could reasonably be regarded as less important than enhancing the opportunity to choose whom to vote for.

Neither is the controversy about campaign finance adequately portrayed as a conflict between equality and liberty—between the equal opportunity of citizens to participate in the process, and the liberty of candidates and their supporters to use their own resources to compete for office. It should be understood first as a conflict between two interpretations of free choice. The liberty of candidates and their supporters does not look so incontestable if it is weighed against another liberty—the liberty of citizens to participate in an electoral process that is not dominated by pecuniary influences. At least citizens should have the opportunity to make the choice of the kind of system they want, and to make it freely in an environment not already dominated by the same influences that are at issue.

A third norm of deliberation suggests that in assessing electoral practices we should adopt an institutional perspective. Such a perspective brings out significant considerations that are otherwise likely to be neglected. It can reveal the expressive meaning of electoral practices—the importance of having one's vote counted as much as having it count, the significance of the shape of electoral districts and the criteria for drawing them, and more generally the implications of the reasons given to justify any electoral practice. The institutional perspective emphasizes the collective consequences of individual conduct and the need for collective action to achieve individual goals. Leaving the choice to individuals does little to control the effects of exit polls or the influence of money.

From an institutional perspective we can see more clearly that in designing and reforming electoral practices we inevitably make choices about what conception of democratic representation we wish to promote. Maintaining a majoritarian system rather than adopting one of the proportional electoral methods such as single transferable vote or cumulative voting obviously implies a commitment to a particular conception of representation. If citizens and their representatives adopt the institutional perspective more consistently, they may begin to take alternative electoral systems more seriously. In their deliberations, they will be more likely to consider experimenting with different types of voting systems, and reconsider retaining the institutions that now exist.

Yet equally fundamental choices about representation arise within existing institutions and systems. Deciding to put certain notations on the ballot or permitting candidates to be listed as representing more than one party favors one kind of representation over others. Some electoral practices tend toward a mandatory conception of representation by permitting voters in effect to give specific instructions to their legislators. More justifiably, other electoral practices favor discretionary forms of representation. In all these and similar cases we should always view the institutional context broadly, attending to legislative as well as electoral institutions. When we think institutionally, we are more likely to see the systemwide effects of what might otherwise seem to be an isolated change in a single electoral practice.

A fourth norm prescribes taking into account the distinctive institutional characteristics of elections. Three such characteristics are worth emphasizing. First, unlike political activity outside government, elections come to a definite conclusion at a particular moment and result in decisions that bind all citizens until the next election. Elections are therefore more appropriately treated as part of government, and may be regulated more rigorously than the parts of the political process that stand outside of government. One implication of this difference between electoral and ordinary politics is that candidate advocacy, which is more relevant in an election, may be subject to more stringent regulation than issue advocacy, which is no less relevant at other times.

The simultaneous nature of elections is a second institutional characteristic to keep in mind in deliberating about electoral justice. Citizens cast their ballots as if they were acting at the same time: they do not adjust their final decisions in light of information about how others are voting. In this way, information about voting is equally available to all, and the value of each citizen's opportunity to make a free choice is the same as that of any other citizen. Also, when citizens go to the polls on the same day, the election more fully expresses equal respect because citizens participate on the same terms in a common experience of civic engagement. To maintain the simultaneous character of elections, we should resist publishing the results of exit polls, granting legislatures the authority to select presidential electors on their own schedule, and expanding the use of absentee balloting.

Voting thus differs from deliberating itself—whether the deliberating is about the election or electoral justice. When citizens deliberate, they offer justifications that are intended to influence others and to invite others to influence them. As deliberators, citizens modify their views in response to the views voiced by others. When citizens vote, they simply record their own conclusions. They do not change them in response to anyone. Citizens may of course declare their voting intentions before the election, but if they do they are still participating in a deliberative process. Their declarations can influence others and enable others to influence them. But once they have cast their ballots, they can no longer take part in the electoral process on the same terms with those fellow citizens who have not yet voted.

A third institutional characteristic of elections relevant in deliberation about electoral justice is their mixture of democratic and aristocratic modes of governing. Everyone can vote, but only those with special qualities are selected. This creates an irony that Madison exploited when he argued against imposing any substantial qualifications for members of Congress. In principle anyone should be allowed to run (the democratic element) but in practice only those with special qualities are likely to win (the aristocratic element). Opponents of term limits today often use the same conceptual strategy. They argue that requiring only minimal qualifications for office (rejecting term limits) increases the chances that more qualified candidates will win. If more incumbents can run, more candidates with greater experience in government are likely to be elected. The mixed character of elections is also manifested—more insidiously—in the current system of campaign finance. Here the idea of superior qualification implied by the aristocratic element has been transmuted into superior wealth. The special qualities that distinguish the winners in this system include, most prominently, the capacity to raise money.

FORUMS OF DELIBERATION

In the wake of the 2000 election, issues of electoral justice gained greater prominence. But most of the public debate, in both the media and the academy, has not shown much respect for the norms of deliberation. It has not given high priority to the need for principled justification of electoral practices. It has rarely considered fundamental principles at all. The focus has been on the mechanics of the electoral process—questions such as how to make voting technology more efficient and accurate. Most democratic theorists also have ignored the underlying values at stake in electoral procedures. Many treat elections as mechanisms for aggregating preferences, and concentrate on the methods of public choice rather than the principles of political justice. Nor have political philosophers rushed to correct the neglect of normative questions. They take seriously questions about the justice of the basic structures and background conditions of the societies in which elections take place. But they usually regard the choice of electoral procedures as a matter of political judgment best left to social scientists, if not politicians.

The midrange of electoral disagreement—the vast territory explored in previous chapters—has received sustained attention from only a relatively small group of specialists: the practitioners who operate and monitor the electoral system, and the scholars in law and political science who write about it. Yet that system stands at the core of democratic government. It is too important to be left only to specialists. It is the only means that citizens have to choose those who make the decisions and pass the laws under which they all must live. Those who govern that system ultimately control who governs.

Electoral justice should have a more prominent place not only on the intellectual agenda of democratic theory, but also on the political agenda of democratic citizens and their representatives. Because the principles of electoral justice govern relationships in a common scheme of cooperation, their content should be decided in a common process of deliberation. The principles substantially define the terms on which citizens cooperate and manifestly express the values on which their institutions rest. All should therefore have a say in defining the terms and values, even if some object to those that are adopted at a particular time. That citizens are likely to disagree about electoral justice is not a reason to resist deliberating about its principles and their institutional implications. On the contrary, it is a reason to encourage more deliberation. The aim should be not only to reach agreement on the procedures so that citizens can accept the results of elections as just. It should also be to understand better the nature of the disagreements that inevitably persist so that citizens can find a basis for cooperating to make their electoral process as just as it can be.

Because electoral justice is the concern of all citizens, it should be debated in a wider range of forums than have been employed in the past. Too much of the responsibility for raising and resolving the questions of principle about electoral justice has been left to courts and legislatures. Judicial forums limit the range of the discussion: the rules of standing, the respect for precedent, and the stress on individual rights make it difficult for courts to attend to the institutional dimensions of electoral justice. Legislative deliberation is not limited enough. On the question of who should be a legislator, legislators are distinctly interested parties, prone to the institutional vice of self-perpetuation against which Madison wisely cautioned. So are justices on the Supreme Court when they undertake to decide a presidential election.

Commissions are a more promising way to elevate the public discussion, but they too should be designed as a stimulus for a wider debate, not as a surrogate for it. The aim should be to widen the scope and multiply the forums for deliberation about electoral justice. Initiative campaigns, party conferences, voluntary associations, Internet chat rooms, high school classrooms, even talk shows—these and other sites provide opportunities for encouraging a more extensive public dialogue that could help citizens regain control of the vital process by which they choose their political leaders.

By continuing and deepening their deliberations about electoral justice, citizens can more constructively confront the conflicts of value that their electoral practices create. They can more productively deal with those conflicts on terms that are mutually justifiable to all who are bound by the results of elections. Guided by well-considered principles of electoral justice, citizens and their representatives are more likely to make well-founded electoral laws on which they can rely.

Notes

INTRODUCTION

1. James Madison, *The Federalist* No. 57, ed. Benjamin Fletcher Wright (Cambridge: Harvard University Press, 1961), 383.

2. The goal of obtaining the best representatives is now the function of prospective voting, and keeping those representatives virtuous has become the job of retrospective voting. Political scientists argue about which kind of voting is more common, whether elections are best seen as selecting or sanctioning representatives, whether these functions conflict with one another, whether elections can be considered mandates, and the extent to which they actually achieve these various purposes. For a sample of the most important work in this genre, see Adam Przeworski, Susan C. Stokes, and Bernard Manin, eds., *Democracy, Accountability and Representation* (New York: Cambridge University Press, 1999), especially chapters by James Fearon and John Ferejohn and the works cited; G. Bingham Powell Jr., *Elections as Instruments of Democracy* (New Haven: Yale University Press, 2000); Morris Fiorina, *Retrospective Voting in American National Elections* (New Haven: Yale University Press, 1981); Stanley Kelley Jr., *Interpreting Elections* (Princeton: Princeton University Press, 1983); and V. O. Key Jr., *The Responsible Electorate* (New York: Vintage, 1966). As valuable as these studies are, they cannot provide the basis for the principle of electoral justice. They focus on outcomes (and procedures mainly as they relate to outcomes). Electoral justice by its nature must consider procedures independently of outcomes. Also, these studies are primarily empirical. Although the analysis of electoral justice should make use of empirical studies and identify questions for further empirical research, it must maintain an essentially normative orientation.

3. The Gallup Organization, "The Florida Recount Controversy from the Public's Perspective: 25 Insights," 22 December 2000, available online: <http://www.gallup.com/poll/releases/pr001222b.asp> (4 February 2002). Also see David W. Moore, "Eight in Ten Americans to Accept Bush as 'Legitimate' President," Gallup News Service, Princeton, N.J., 14 December 2000, available online: <http://www.gallup.com/poll/releases/pr001214.asp> (4 February 2002).

4. See, e.g., Richard A. Posner, "*Bush v. Gore:* Prolegomenon to an Assessment," in *The Vote: Bush, Gore and the Supreme Court,* ed. Cass R. Sunstein and Richard A. Epstein

(Chicago: University of Chicago Press, 2001), 165–71. According to a comprehensive analysis by a consortium of news organizations, Gore could have won only if there had been a statewide recount of all disputed ballots, not simply the recount of ballots ordered by the Florida Supreme Court and not even of those in the four counties in which Gore had requested a recount. See Ford Fessenden and John M. Broder, "Study of Disputed Florida Ballots Finds Justices Did Not Cast the Deciding Vote," *New York Times*, 12 November 2001, sec. A, p. 1. But another report suggests that if the recount had gone forward, the circuit judge supervising it would have ordered the counting not only of undervotes but also the overvotes, which would have resulted in a slim victory for Gore. Hendrik Hertzberg, "Recounted Out," *New Yorker*, 24 and 31 December 2001, 41–42.

5. Gallup Organization, "Florida Recount Controversy." Relatively few voters questioned the fairness of the election in 1996. For a comparison between the two elections on this point, and an analysis that suggests that these reactions in 2000 were not "partisan sour grapes," see John Mark Hansen, Task Force on the Federal Election System, "Sizing the Problem," in *To Assure Pride and Confidence in the Electoral Process: The Final Report of the Commission's Task Force*, National Commission on Federal Election Reform, 4–8, available online: <http://www.reformelections.org/task/t1/t1_reports.php> (7 May 2002).

6. The Constitution as interpreted by the courts still grants only a conditional right to vote. As the Supreme Court observed in *Bush v. Gore*: "The individual citizen has no federal constitutional right to vote for electors for the President of the United States unless and until the state legislature chooses a statewide election as the means to implement its power to appoint members of the Electoral College." 531 U.S. 98, 104 (2000). For some qualifications to this conclusion and further analysis of the current status of the constitutional right to vote, see Samuel Issacharoff, Pamela S. Karlan, and Richard H. Pildes, *The Law of Democracy: Legal Structure of the Political Process*, 2d ed. (Westbury, N.Y.: Foundation Press, 2001), 16–20, 72–74.

7. *The Works of John Adams, Second President of the United States*, ed. Charles Francis Adams (Boston: Little, Brown, 1856), 9:377–78, quoted in Alexander Keyssar, *The Right to Vote: The Contested History of Democracy in the United States* (New York: Basic Books, 2000), 1, 13.

8. Keyssar, *Right to Vote*, 12–13, 44, 98, 187–88. For recent discussions of individualist conceptions of voting, see the extensive list of citations in Heather Gerken, "Understanding the Right to an Undiluted Vote," *Harvard Law Review* 114 (April 2001): 1677 n. 46.

9. The objections raised in the text against the individualist approach also apply generally against group-based views, which also tend to ignore institutional context. The distinction that these objections assume is between individualist and institutional approaches, not individualist and group approaches. An individualist approach is not limited to views that treat individuals in isolation from others or outside of groups. In the study of elections, individuals are most commonly considered in groups, and the analysis of representation cannot proceed without reference to groups. As Justice Lewis Powell observed, the "concept of 'representation' necessarily applies to groups: groups of voters elect representatives, individual voters do not." *Davis v. Bandemer*, 478 U.S. 109, 167 (1986).

10. Testimony of Joan Konner, House Committee on Energy and Commerce, *Hearings on Election Night Coverage*, 107th Cong., 1st Sess., 14 February 2001, 69.

11. Joseph Schumpeter, *Capitalism, Socialism and Democracy*, 3d ed. (New York:

Harper and Row, 1950), 269. For subsequent work in this tradition, see chapter 2, note 64.

12. Reuters, "A Coin, Then Cards, and Finally a Mayor," *New York Times,* 8 March 1998, sec. 1, p. 29. New Mexico law gives the power to choose which kind of game to a committee consisting of the candidates, the county chairs of the political parties, and the district judge (New Mexico Stat. Ann. ch. 1, art. 13, § 11). The law actually specifies only that the decision be made "by lot," but in many counties, as well as in more than a dozen other western states that have similar laws, the practice of using a game of chance has been common. Richard Smolka, editor of *Election Administration Reports,* telephone interview by Judy Hensley, 17 July 2001.

13. See Laurence Tribe's comments, Transcript of Oral Argument, *Bush v. Palm Beach Country Canvassing Bd.,* 531 U.S. 70 (2000), 2000 WL 1763666, at 44–45 (1 December 2000).

14. Senator Jeff Sessions (R–AL), *Congressional Record,* 107th Cong., 1st Sess., 19 March 2001, vol. 147, S2463.

15. Senator Michael DeWine (R–OH), ibid., S2464.

16. The conflict between competitiveness and justice can be seen vividly in the efforts to protect the newly acquired political power of blacks after the Civil War. Because congressional representatives then faced stiff electoral competition, they could not reach bipartisan compromises on racial issues as easily as could their successors in the 1950s and 1960s, who enjoyed greater electoral margins in their districts. See J. Morgan Kousser, *Colorblind Injustice: Minority Voting Rights and the Undoing of the Second Reconstruction* (Chapel Hill: University of North Carolina Press, 1999), 40–49, 53.

17. John Rawls, *A Theory of Justice,* rev. ed. (Cambridge: Harvard University Press, 1999). The principles of electoral justice developed here leave more open to democratic deliberation than Rawls's theory does, and also treat as questions of justice some issues that Rawls would leave as matters of political judgment. For the concept of mutual justification, see T. M. Scanlon, "Contractualism and Utilitarianism," in *Utilitarianism and Beyond,* ed. Amartya Sen and Bernard Williams (Cambridge: Cambridge University Press, 1982), 103–28.

18. On the importance of distinguishing the "second-order question of who should decide" from "first-order questions" about the "procedural devices of democracy," see Frederick Schauer, "Judicial Review and the Devices of Democracy," *Columbia Law Review* 94 (May 1994): 1326–47.

19. An important way to expose the injustices in any current system is to contrast it with alternative systems (such as forms of proportional representation). This comparative approach can be not only consistent with but also supportive of the different approach followed here, provided it does not neglect ways to make the current system less unjust. Lani Guinier and Gerald Torres, for example, demonstrate the force of such a critique of the current system by emphasizing "missing elements" of representation. But when they suggest that in any system with territorial districts and winner-take-all rules no "true representation" at all can exist, they run the risk of disabling internal criticisms of the current system, and dismissing reforms that could remove or at least ameliorate some significant injustices. Lani Guinier and Gerald Torres, *The Miner's Canary: Enlisting Race, Resisting Power, Transforming Democracy* (Cambridge: Harvard University Press, 2002), 170, and generally 168–222.

20. For the theory of deliberative democracy on which this argument draws, see Amy Gutmann and Dennis Thompson, *Democracy and Disagreement* (Cambridge: Harvard

University Press, 1996). For criticisms and responses, see Stephen Macedo, ed., *Deliberative Politics: Essays on* Democracy and Disagreement (New York: Oxford University Press, 1999). Deliberative theory requires that citizens or their representatives justify decisions and policies by mutually acceptable reasons. It is often contrasted with aggregative theory, which requires only that citizens or their representatives express individual preferences. Aggregative theory typically relies on voting to turn these individual preferences into collective outcomes, and emphasizes the technical or formal rather than the moral problems of the procedures. But because voting is associated with aggregative theory and often explicitly opposed to deliberation ("arguing"), even deliberative theory has a tendency to neglect the moral aspects of electoral procedures. On the distinction between deliberative and aggregative theory, see Joshua Cohen, "Procedure and Substance in Deliberative Democracy," in *Deliberative Democracy: Essays on Reason and Politics*, ed. James Boham and William Rehg (Cambridge: MIT Press, 1997), 410–11; and Frank Cunningham, *Theories of Democracy* (London: Routledge, 2002), 164–65. On the contrast between voting and arguing, see Jon Elster, introduction to *Deliberative Democracy*, ed. Jon Elster (Cambridge: Cambridge University Press, 1998), 5–8.

21. Caltech/MIT Voting Technology Project, *Voting: What Is, What Could Be,* July 2001, 17–25, available online: <http://web.mit.edu/voting/> (4 February 2002). The National Commission study questions the need for optical scanners, and emphasizes other reforms such as establishing "benchmarks" for performance, permitting provisional voting, and making election day a national holiday. National Commission on Federal Election Reform, *To Assure Pride and Confidence in the Electoral Process* (Charlottesville, Va.: Miller Center of Public Affairs, University of Virginia; New York: Century Foundation, August 2001), 35–37, 40–42, 51–53. Also see Henry E. Brady et al., "Counting All the Votes: The Performance of Voting Technology in the United States," Department of Political Science, Survey Research Center, University of California, Berkeley, September 2001, available online: <http://ucdata.berkeley.edu/> (7 May 2002). For an example of the fascination with technological solutions, see Edward Tenner, "The Perils of High-Tech Voting," *New York Times,* 5 February 2001, sec. A, p. 21; and the Senate Committee on Governmental Affairs, *Hearings,* 107th Cong., 1st Sess., 9 May 2001. As Representative Maxine Waters remarked: "Machines are easy. . . . It'll get tougher when we get to the strategies and tactics we believe disenfranchise voters." Wayne Washington, "Election Reform Lags in Divided Congress," *Boston Globe,* 8 May 2001, p. A1.

22. Rawls writes that the "idea of justice as fairness is to use the notion of pure procedural justice to handle the contingencies of particular situations. The social system is to be designed so that the resulting distribution is just however things turn out." Rawls, *Theory of Justice,* 242–43. See also Brian Barry, *Justice as Impartiality* (New York: Oxford University Press, 1995), 213–16.

23. Citizens as well as theorists may still be warranted in considering the outcome unjust. Strictly speaking, most outcomes are cases of what Rawls calls "quasi-pure procedural justice." The "outcome does not literally define the right result. It is simply that those who disagree with the decision made cannot convincingly establish their point within the framework of the public conception of justice." Rawls, *Theory of Justice,* 318.

24. Some theorists seek an even purer proceduralism: they propose a principle such as majority rule that they believe does not presuppose any substantive views about justice and thus avoids the objection they bring against theories such as Rawls' (namely, that such theories assume agreement on a conception of justice about which there is legitimate dispute). See Jeremy Waldron, *The Dignity of Legislation* (Cambridge: Cambridge

University Press, 1999), 70–73, 158–61, 161–62. However, the justification of any functional procedural principle, including majority rule, cannot avoid appealing to moral values such as equal respect. When applied to electoral institutions these principles raise many of the same questions of justice that the purer proceduralists sought to avoid. Furthermore, as chapter 3 shows, the practical meaning of majority rule itself is indeterminate until we decide among the conflicting claims of various majorities.

25. Rawls, *Theory of Justice,* 195.

26. Ibid., 199, 313. For example, Rawls writes that the balance between limiting majority rule and preventing entrenched minorities is a question of "political judgment and does not belong to the theory of justice" (313). But he believes that his theory has implications for some institutional issues, such as campaign finance reform. See his *Political Liberalism* (New York: Columbia University Press, 1993), 326–27, 359–63, and the discussion in chapter 2, pages 107–8.

CHAPTER ONE

1. Don Van Natta Jr., "Counting the Vote: Palm Beach County," *New York Times,* 15 November 2000, sec. A, p. 1. In Duvall county, fifteen voters had the opposite experience: their votes counted twice. By mistake, officials counted both their preliminary and final absentee ballots. One of the double voters, informed that both his votes had been recorded, "reacted with jubilation. . . . He raised both arms as if he had just scored a touchdown and savored the two votes he had delivered to George W. Bush. 'Yes' he said, beaming." David Barstow and Don Van Natta Jr., "How Bush Took Florida: Mining the Overseas Absentee Vote," *New York Times,* 15 July 2001, sec. 1, pp. 1, 16.

2. Judith Shklar, *American Citizenship* (Cambridge: Harvard University Press, 1991), 56.

3. John Rawls's principle of equal participation holds that "all citizens are to have an equal right to take part in, and to determine the outcome of, the constitutional process that establishes the laws with which they are to comply." Rawls, *A Theory of Justice,* rev. ed. (Cambridge: Harvard University Press, 1999), 194. For Rawls, the only permissible departures from strict equality are "compromises" to adjust to "existing conditions": the process should "preserve the equal representation of the original position to the degree that this is *practicable*" (emphasis added, 195). Rawls's principle disallows all gerrymandering, and seems to require that redistricting be random (196). His principle is not adopted here because it casts doubt on some electoral inequalities that may be completely justifiable, and because it conceals or settles in advance some questions about the meaning of electoral justice that should be subject to reasonable disagreement. As explained in the introduction, however, the principle of equal respect developed here is grounded in Rawls's moral conception of citizens as "free and equal" persons, and treats equal respect as more fundamental than equality in the distribution of goods. Ibid., 131–32, 475–76, 447.

4. For an argument showing why the concepts of "equal power," "equal prospects of electoral success," and "equal weight" do not provide satisfactory standards of political equality, see Charles R. Beitz, *Political Equality: An Essay in Democratic Theory* (Princeton: Princeton University Press, 1989), esp. 9–11. More generally, the argument in the text is indebted to Beitz's analysis of the concept of political equality, in particular his critique of "simple" theories that assume that procedural equality is "an unambiguous and univocal requirement" (ibid., 16); and his discussion of the "deliberative interest" that political equality promotes (113–16). However, his theory of complex procedural-

ism seems to understate the expressive aspects of electoral institutions, and conflates the values of equal respect and free choice.

5. Beitz makes a similar distinction: the idea of equality operates as a constraint on "the reasons that may be given to explain why we should accept one rather than another conception of fair terms of participation [as distinct from] a direct constraint on the structure for democratic processes themselves." Beitz, *Political Equality,* 17–18. In the view developed here, however, the "reasons" refer to why institutional inequalities should be accepted or rejected, and they become part of the expressive meaning of the institutions in question.

6. *Harper v. Virginia Bd. of Elections,* 383 U.S. 663 (1966).

7. Nelson Polsby and Aaron Wildavsky, *Presidential Elections,* 10th ed. (New York: Chatham House, 2000), 7–8. For a critical survey of the rational choice theories of voting, see Donald P. Green and Ian Shapiro, *Pathologies of Rational Choice: A Critique of Applications in Political Science* (New Haven: Yale University Press, 1994), 47–71.

8. John Mark Hansen, Task Force on the Federal Election System, "Sizing the Problem," in *To Assure Pride and Confidence in the Electoral Process: The Final Report of the Commission's Task Force,* National Commission on Federal Election Reform, August 2001, 11–15, available online: <http://www.reformelections.org/task/t1/t1_reports.php> (7 May 2002).

9. The classic statement of this function of voting—now variously called educative, developmental, or constitutive—is by John Stuart Mill, who was influenced by his reading of Alexis de Tocqueville's account of American politics. Mill and other theorists who emphasize the importance of this function also insist that voting does not have this value unless citizens also participate more regularly and more intensely in a wide variety of political activities. See John Stuart Mill, "Considerations on Representative Government," in *Essays on Politics and Society, Collected Works,* ed. J. M. Robson (London: Routledge, 1977), 19:399–412, 467–81; Mill, "De Tocqueville on Democracy in America (II)," in ibid., 18:153–204; and Alexis de Tocqueville, *Democracy in America,* ed. J. P. Mayer, trans. George Lawrence (Garden City, N.Y.: Doubleday, 1969), 1:199–203, 2:235–37. Also see Dennis F. Thompson, *John Stuart Mill and Representative Government* (Princeton: Princeton University Press, 1976), 28–57. For a sample of contemporary versions, see Carole Pateman, *Participation and Democratic Theory* (Cambridge: Cambridge University Press, 1970), 1–44; Dennis F. Thompson, *The Democratic Citizen: Social Science and Democratic Theory in the 20th Century* (Cambridge: Cambridge University Press, 1970), 10–29, 53–85; and C. B. Macpherson, *Life and Times of Liberal Democracy* (Oxford: Oxford University Press, 1977), 44–76, 93–115. For the application of a similar conception specifically to voting rights and deliberative democracy, see Frank Michelman, "Conceptions of Democracy in American Constitutional Argument: Voting Rights," *Florida Law Review* 41 (summer 1989): 443–90. A wide-ranging discussion that links voting to an appeal for more extensive participation at the grassroots level is Lani Guinier and Gerald Torres, *The Miner's Canary: Enlisting Race, Resisting Power, Transforming Democracy* (Cambridge: Harvard University Press, 2002), esp. 202–7.

10. The expressivist view holds that the meaning of the act of voting itself has value and purpose distinct from its effects on the outcome of the election. But unlike the constitutive view (with which it is sometimes confused), the expressivist view does not limit itself to considering intrinsic values but also takes into account the wider consequences of the act. Unlike outcome-oriented views, the consequences on which it focuses are the effects of the meanings—the expressive consequences for social meanings, such as norms

or values that characterize political life more generally. As several examples in this chapter show, expressivist meaning often cannot be determined without considering such consequences. The most comprehensive discussion of the expressivist approach in law is: Elizabeth S. Anderson and Richard H. Pildes, "Expressive Theories of Law: A General Restatement," *University of Pennsylvania Law Review* 148 (May 2000): 1503–75. Also see Cass Sunstein, "Law, Economics and Norms: On the Expressive Function of Law," *University of Pennsylvania Law Review* 144 (May 1996): esp. 2045–49; Larry Lessig, "The Regulation of Social Meaning," *University of Chicago Law Review* 62 (summer 1995): 943–1045; Rae Langton, "Speech Acts and Unspeakable Acts," *Philosophy and Public Affairs* 22 (autumn 1993): 293–330; Robert Nozick, *The Nature of Rationality* (Princeton: Princeton University Press, 1993), 26–35; Adam Winkler, "Expressive Voting," *New York University Law Review* 68 (May 1993): 330–88; Robert Nozick, *Philosophical Explanations* (Cambridge: Harvard University Press, 1981), 370–80; and Joel Feinberg, *Doing and Deserving* (Princeton: Princeton University Press, 1970), 95–118.

11. Classical philosophers clearly recognized that constitutional provisions could express the character of a regime. Aristotle specifically emphasized the importance of incentives for political participation in determining the nature of the political regime. His best practicable constitution, a mixed regime or *politea,* combined an aristocratic element (fining the rich for not participating) with a democratic element (paying the poor to participate). Like most earlier theorists, Aristotle considered elections to be aristocratic and selection by lot democratic. *The Politics of Aristotle,* ed. and trans. Ernest Barker (New York: Oxford University Press, 1962), bk. 4, chap. 9, p. 177. Also see the discussion in chapter 3, pages 129–31.

12. Jeremy Waldron, *Law and Disagreement* (Oxford: Oxford University Press, 1999), 239–41. Also see Jon Elster, *Sour Grapes: Studies in Rationality and Irrationality* (Cambridge: Cambridge University Press, 1983), 99. Beitz objects to the expressivist approach for a different reason. He argues that institutional expressions of equal respect do not necessarily correspond to institutional equality or to institutional procedural fairness. Beitz, *Political Equality,* 93–95. But an expressivist approach does not have to claim that equal respect always requires institutional equality. Justifications of institutional inequalities are part of the expressive meaning of the institutions, and if the justifications are respectful, the inequalities are acceptable. It is true that equal respect does not capture all forms of procedural unfairness (for example, biases in electoral competition), but that limitation is a virtue because it separates more clearly the values at stake, specifically those of equal respect and free choice.

13. G. Bingham Powell Jr., *Elections as Instruments of Democracy* (New Haven: Yale University Press, 2000), 3–19.

14. Samuel Issacharoff, Pamela S. Karlan, and Richard H. Pildes, *The Law of Democracy: Legal Structure of the Political Process,* 2d ed. (Westbury, N.Y.: Foundation Press, 2001), 360.

15. *Burdick v. Takushi,* 504 U.S. 428, 445 (1992).

16. Ibid., 438, quoting *Storer v. Brown,* 415 U.S. 724, 735 (1974).

17. Other restrictions on how voters mark the ballots—directed not at expressive but outcome-oriented voting—also may run afoul of the equal respect principle. For example, prohibitions on "bullet" voting (selecting only one candidate for a multimember council) were sometimes intended to prevent strategic voting by black minorities in the southern states, who could increase the chances of electing at least one of their candidates by not voting for any of the other candidates on the ballot. See U.S. Commission on Civil

Rights, *The Voting Rights Act: Ten Years After* (Washington, D.C.: Commission on Civil Rights, 1975), 206–7.

18. *Life and Writings of Frederick Douglass,* ed. Philip S. Foner (New York: International Publishers, 1955), 4:159–60, quoted in Shklar, *American Citizenship,* 56.

19. For a description and critique of the "progressive or triumphalist" view, see Alexander Keyssar, *The Right to Vote* (New York: Basic Books, 2000), esp. xvii–xx.

20. Tocqueville, *Democracy in America,* 1:59–60.

21. Groups that for a time lost political rights that they previously enjoyed include women in New Jersey in the early nineteenth century, blacks in the mid-Atlantic states before 1860 and in the south after 1890, naturalized Irish immigrants during the Know-Nothing period, aliens in the late nineteenth and early twentieth centuries, and men and women who were on public relief in Maine in the 1930s. Keyssar, *The Right to Vote,* 318; also see ibid., 126–29, 316–17.

22. Tocqueville, *Democracy in America,* 1:60.

23. Issacharoff, Karlan, and Pildes, *The Law of Democracy,* 45–46; Keyssar, *The Right to Vote,* 302–8; and Alexander Keyssar, "The Right to Vote and Election 2000," in *The Unfinished Election of 2000,* ed. Jack N. Rakove (New York: Basic Books, 2001), 85–88.

24. Issacharoff, Karlan, and Pildes, *The Law of Democracy,* 45.

25. Note, "The Disenfranchisement of Ex-felons: Citizenship, Criminality, and 'the Purity of the Ballot Box,'" *Harvard Law Review* 102 (April 1989): 1300–17.

26. Keyssar, "The Right to Vote and Election 2000," 83.

27. Ibid., 87–88.

28. Keyssar, *The Right to Vote,* 308–11.

29. Martin Hedemann-Robinson, "An Overview of Recent Legal Developments at the Community Level in Relation to Third Country Nationals Resident within the European Union, with Particular Reference to the Case Law of the European Court of Justice," *Common Market Law Review* 38 (June 2001): 582.

30. See U.S. Census Bureau, *Voting and Registration in the Election of November 1996,* July 1998; and *Voting and Registration in the Election of November 1998,* August 2000, available online: <http://www.census.gov/population/www/socdemo/voting.html> (7 May 2002); and U.S. Census Bureau, *Current Population Survey, Voter Supplement, November 2000* (Washington, D.C.: U.S. Census Bureau, 2001). (Analysis by Jonathan Hoffman, University of California, Berkeley.)

31. Most of the registration laws were first enacted in the states in the period between the Civil War and World War I, usually promoted by a coalition of Republicans and middle-class, reform-minded independents who sought to contain the electoral influence and corruption of urban political machines. The available evidence does not definitively show whether registration laws were "primarily weapons in the battle against election fraud, or . . . techniques for diminishing the breadth of democracy." Keyssar, *The Right to Vote,* 159. What is clearer is that the laws "reduced fraudulent voting and that they kept large numbers (probably millions) of eligible voters from the polls" (158). Furthermore, the laws were "likely to have a disproportionate impact on poor, foreign-born, uneducated or mobile voters" (157). Also see Dayna L. Cunningham, "Who Are to Be the Electors? A Reflection on the History of Voter Registration in the United States," *Yale Law and Policy Review* 9 (1991): 370, 380–85.

32. The seminal studies are Stanley Kelley Jr., Richard E. Ayres, and William G. Bowen, "Registration and Voting: Putting First Things First," *American Political Science Review* 61 (June 1967): 359–79; Steven J. Rosenstone and Raymond E. Wolfinger, "The

Effects of Registration Laws on Voter Turnout," *American Political Science Review* 72 (March 1978): 22–45; and Frances Fox Piven and Richard Cloward, *Why Americans Don't Vote* (New York: Pantheon Books, 1988). For more recent data, see Frances Fox Piven and Richard Cloward, *Why Americans Still Don't Vote* (Boston: Beacon Press, 2000); and Committee for the Study of the American Electorate, *Final Post Election Report,* 9 February 1999, available online: <http://www.gspm.org/csae/cgans5.html> (7 May 2002). Benjamin Highton finds that easier registration makes a difference but not as much as many have assumed; he concludes that although turnout in states that have election-day registration is higher than in other states, it does not approach the turnout of registered voters in the rest of the country. "Easy Registration and Voter Turnout," *Journal of Politics* 59 (May 1997): 565–75. For cross-national studies of the extent and causes of unequal participation, see Arend Lijphart, "Unequal Participation: Democracy's Unresolved Dilemma," *American Political Science Review* 91 (March 1997): 1–14; G. Bingham Powell Jr., "American Voter Turnout in Comparative Perspective," *American Political Science Review* 80 (March 1986): 17–43; and Sidney Verba, Norman H. Nie, and Jae-On Kim, *Participation and Political Equality: A Seven-Nation Comparison* (Cambridge: Cambridge University Press, 1978).

33. Comparing turnout in states that have same-day registration with other states, Highton finds that "while registration does contribute to the upscale character of voters, there are substantial differences for which registration laws are not responsible." "Easy Registration," 565. It is plausible to assume that the effects are unequal simply because better-off citizens are more likely to comply with the registration requirements. However, the National Voter Registration Act (ironically) made it more difficult than before to estimate accurately not only the socioeconomic distribution but even the total number of registered voters. Official figures include an undetermined number of voters who have moved or died, and the Act prohibits states from "cleaning" the rolls as regularly as in the past. Committee for the Study of the American Electorate, *Final Post Election Report.* One result is that the Federal Election Commission's charts show registration rates as high as 104 percent (Alaska, 1998) and 106 percent (Maine, 1996). These problems can be overcome but only by carefully analyzing the data from the National Election Study at the University of Michigan and the Voter Supplement of the Census Bureau's Current Population Survey. See Peverill Squire, Raymond E. Wolfinger, and David P. Glass, "Residential Mobility and Voter Turnout," *American Political Science Review* 81 (March 1987): 46–47, 50–51.

34. Senator Mitch McConnell (R–KY) acknowledged that North Dakota has "never had a recorded case of fraud [but] I think they all know each other, anyway. It is quite a small State." *Congressional Record,* 103rd Cong., 1st Sess., 11 March 1993, vol. 139, S2746. Instituting same-day registration could create major administrative problems for the larger states. Partly for this reason the National Commission on Federal Election Reform, although seeking to increase registration, declined to recommend that a same-day provision be established nationwide: *To Assure Pride and Confidence in the Electoral Process* (Charlottesville, Va.: Miller Center of Public Affairs, University of Virginia; New York: Century Foundation, August 2001), 38–39.

35. *National Voter Registration Act of 1993,* 42 U.S.C. § 1973gg. The law also requires states to offer registration by mail. States that have no registration requirements for federal elections or permit same-day registration are exempted from the provisions of this Act.

36. *Congressional Record,* 103rd Cong., 1st Sess., 11 March 1993, vol. 139, S2743.

37. James DeNardo, "Turnout and the Vote: The Joke's on the Democrats," *American Political Science Review* 74 (June 1980): 406–20; Harvey J. Tucker, Arnold Vedlitz, and James DeNardo, "Does Heavy Turnout Help Democrats in Presidential Elections?" *American Political Science Review* 80 (December 1986): 1292–1304.

38. Ruy A. Teixeira, *The Disappearing American Voter* (Washington, D.C.: Brookings Institution, 1992), 86–101; Stephen Earl Bennett and David Resnick, "The Implications of Nonvoting for Democracy in the United States," *American Journal of Political Science* 34 (1990): 771, 779; Benjamin Highton and Raymond E. Wolfinger, "The Political Implications of Higher Turnout," paper presented at the meeting of the American Political Science Association, Boston, September 1998; and Issacharoff, Karlan, and Pildes, *The Law of Democracy,* 136, 139–40.

39. "Why does this bill force State agencies that provide public assistance, unemployment compensation, and related services, to register people to vote and yet does not require the tax office to do it? [T]hese are people who, as obviously our dear colleagues on the left believe, with some justification, are going to vote for them. On the other hand, there are many over here who believe that the people who are going to the tax office are likely to vote for us." *Congressional Record,* 103rd Cong., 1st Sess., 11 March 1993, vol. 139, S2745.

40. See e.g. comments of Senators Alan Simpson (R–WY), Alfonse D'Amato (R–NY), and John Chafee (R–RI), *Congressional Record,* 103rd Cong., 1st Sess., 16 March 1993, vol. 139, S2905–9, S2913.

41. Comments of Senators Alan Simpson and Alfonse D'Amato, ibid., S2906, S2908.

42. *Congressional Record,* 103rd Cong., 1st Sess., 11 March 1993, vol. 139, S2744.

43. Senator John McCain (R–AR), *Congressional Record,* 103rd Cong., 1st Sess., 17 March 1993, vol. 139, S2990.

44. Senator Wendell Ford (D–KY), ibid., S2291.

45. Ibid., S2990. Ford objected to taking away the responsibility not only of voters but also electoral officials.

46. Brief on the Merits of Respondents Katherine Harris . . . , at 10, *Bush v. Palm Beach County Canvassing Bd.,* 531 U.S. 70 (2000). See also Justice O'Connor's questions during oral argument in Transcript of Oral Argument, *Bush v. Gore,* 531 U.S. 98 (2000), 2000 WL 1804429, at 58 (11 December 2000): "[W]hy isn't the standard the one that voters are instructed to follow, for goodness sakes?" and Chief Justice Rehnquist's concurring opinion in *Bush v. Gore,* 531 U.S. at 118–20.

47. Piven and Cloward, *Why Americans Don't Vote,* 222.

48. Raymond E. Wolfinger and Jonathan Hoffman, "Registering and Voting with Motor Voter," *PS* (March 2001): 80–81.

49. See, e.g., *Condon v. Reno,* 913 F. Supp. 946 (D.S.C. 1995).

50. Squire, Wolfinger, and Glass, "Residential Mobility and Voter Turnout," 57–61.

51. Committee for the Study of the American Electorate, *Final Post Election Report.* Also see Federal Election Commission, *The Impact of the National Voter Registration Act of 1993 on the Administration of Elections for Federal Office, 1999–2000,* A Report to the 107th Congress (Washington, D.C.: June 2001). For the most careful comparison of people who used the National Voter Registration Act to register and those who used more traditional methods, see Wolfinger and Hoffman, " Registering and Voting with Motor Voter," 85–92. Also see Piven and Cloward, *Why Americans Still Don't Vote,* 265–72.

52. Significantly, all three of the major studies prompted by the 2000 election recommended against increasing absentee voting. National Commission on Federal Election

Reform, *To Assure Pride,* 43–44; Caltech/MIT Voting Technology Project, *Voting: What Is, What Could Be,* July 2001, 36–41, available online: <http://web.mit.edu/voting/> (7 May 2002); and the Constitution Project, Forum on Election Reform, *Building Consensus on Election Reform* (Washington, D.C.: Election Reform Initiative, August 2001), 16–17.

53. For this data and further analysis, see John Mark Hansen, Task Force on the Federal Election System, "Early Voting, Unrestricted Absentee Voting, and Voting by Mail," in *To Assure Pride, Task Force,* National Commission on Federal Election Reform, 57–72. Nationally, an overwhelming majority of voters still cast their ballots in presidential elections on election day: 90 percent in 2000, and 86 percent in 1996. U.S. Census Bureau, *Current Population Survey, Voter Supplement.* (Analysis by Jonathan Hoffman, University of California, Berkeley.)

54. Hansen, "Early Voting," 62–63.

55. California law permits giving financial incentives to voters but only in state elections and only if the incentives are not intended to discourage voting or to encourage voting for or against a particular candidate or ballot measure. Richard Hasen, "Vote Buying," *California Law Review* 88 (October 2000): 1355.

56. The lottery scheme has been suggested by Nolan Bowie. See Pamela S. Karlan, "Not by Money but by Virtue Won? Vote Trafficking and the Voting Rights System," *Virginia Law Review* 80 (October 1994): 1472.

57. The National Commission recommends that in even-numbered years the Veterans Day national holiday be held on the Tuesday next after the first Monday in November and serve also as election day. National Commission on Federal Election Reform, *To Assure Pride,* 40–41. Because most people who are registered already go to the polls on election day, making election day a national holiday is not likely to increase turnout. It could even reduce turnout if people decide to travel instead of vote. However, the main aim of the reform is to not improve turnout but to increase the number of election workers and polling locations. The enhanced facilities promote equal respect by making voting more accessible. Part of the aim is also to strengthen the sense of participation in a shared civic activity.

58. John Stuart Mill, "Considerations," 488–89. Modern commentators make a similar point: Margaret J. Radin, "Market-Inalienability," *Harvard Law Review* 100 (1987): 1854.

59. Mill, "Considerations," 476–77, 489–91.

60. See Thompson, *Mill,* 98–101.

61. *Naron v. Prestage,* 469 So. 2d 83, 86 (Miss. 1985). The court also commented that the lotteries are undesirable because, if they become common in campaigns, they will further disadvantage candidates of "modest means" (469 So. 2d at 86). Nevertheless, the court permitted the lottery in this case because the candidate "expressly disclaimed any attempt to influence the direction of that vote" (469 So. 2d at 87). The candidate, Ellis L. Prestage, had distributed some four thousand postcards to registered voters with this offer:

WIN $2,000.00 CASH. Congratulations, I have checked the voter list at the courthouse and found that you are a registered voter. Would you like to be 1 of 10 voters who will win $100.00 cash on election day? Would you like to be THE voter who will win $1,000.00 cash on election day? If so, bring this card with you to the Expo Building on election day, September 18, 1984. After you vote, drop this card in the 'Concerned Voter Box' . . . This is a voter turnout drive sponsored by ELLIS L. PRESTAGE, candidate for Supervisor, District 4. You do not have to vote for Ellis L. Prestage to be eligible to win. Ellis L. Prestage encourages you to vote for the candidate of your choice. (469 So. 2d at 87)

62. See Larry J. Sabato and Glenn R. Simpson, *Dirty Little Secrets: The Persistence of Corruption in American Politics* (New York: Times Books, 1996), 205.

63. To mitigate the commodification problem, Pamela Karlan (who favors financial incentives to increase equality in voting) suggests giving citizens vouchers for use on public transportation, admission to public events, or for transferring to charitable organizations. Karlan, "Not by Money," 1473.

64. John Locke, *Two Treatises of Government, Second Treatise,* ed. Peter Laslett, student ed. (Cambridge: Cambridge University Press, 1988), chap. 13, secs. 157–58, pp. 390–91.

65. *Baker v. Carr,* 369 U.S. 186 (1962); *Gray v. Sanders,* 372 U.S. 368 (1963); *Wesbury v. Sanders,* 376 U.S. 1 (1964); *Reynolds v. Sims,* 377 U.S. 533 (1964); and *Lucas v. 44th General Assembly of Colorado,* 377 U.S. 713 (1964). *Baker* started the revolution by declaring that malapportioned districts could be the subject of judicial scrutiny and challenged under the constitutional requirement of equal protection. But it was *Reynolds* that most broadly and clearly established the standard of "one person, one vote."

66. John Moeller argues that the standard "ignores our Madisonian political tradition. Most Americans identify with one or more groups, and those groups, representing varying constituencies, compete with each other for advantage." Moeller, "The Supreme Court's Quest for Fair Politics," *Constitutional Commentary* 1 (1984): 203, 213. Also see Alexander M. Bickel, *The Supreme Court and the Idea of Progress* (New Haven: Yale University Press, 1978), 108–13.

67. Daniel Hays Lowenstein, "Bandemer's Gap: Gerrymandering and Equal Protection," in *Political Gerrymandering and the Courts,* ed. Bernard Grofman (New York: Agathon Press, 1990), 107.

68. See the references in chapter 3, note 134.

69. An electoral system violates the standard only if "it will consistently degrade a voter's or a group of voters' influence on the political process as a whole." *Davis v. Bandemer,* 478 U.S. 109, 110 (1986). See Lowenstein, "Bandemer's Gap," 135–38; and Issacharoff, Karlan and Pildes, *The Law of Democracy,* 868–89. On the fundamental similarities of partisan and racial gerrymandering, see note 79 below.

70. See the literature cited by Issacharoff, Karlan, and Pildes, *The Law of Democracy,* 906–7. Although most of the controversy about racial gerrymandering has concerned blacks, the Voting Rights Act covers other protected minorities. The principle of equal respect also applies to those minorities—for example, Latinos—although to the extent that they experienced less discrimination in the past, they may need less protection in the present.

71. The Act applies mostly to only jurisdictions in the Deep South. For discussion of the coverage of the Act, see Issacharoff, Karlan, and Pildes, *The Law of Democracy,* 556–71.

72. Robert Pear, "Race Takes Back Seat as States Prepare to Redistrict," *New York Times,* 4 February 2001, sec. 1, p. 17.

73. For a critique of compactness and the need for districting to serve many different values, see the early article, David R. Mayhew, "Congressional Representation: Theory and Practice in Drawing the Districts," in *Reapportionment in the 1970s,* ed. Nelson W.

Polsby (Berkeley: University of California Press, 1971), esp. 253–73. Although the examples and evidence in this article are dated, the conceptual categories and political judgments are still quite relevant.

74. See Thompson, *Mill*, 102–11. The academic enthusiasm for proportional representation (PR) (especially the single transferable vote system) exceeds its political popularity. Recent proponents include Douglas J. Amy, *Real Choices/New Voices: The Case for Proportional Representation Elections in the United States* (New York: Columbia University Press, 1996); Thomas Christiano, *The Rule of the Many: Fundamental Issues in Democratic Theory* (Boulder: Westview Press, 1996), 224–40, 258–61; and Kathleen Barber, *A Right to Representation: Proportional Election Systems for the 21st Century* (Columbus: Ohio University Press, 2001). On the advantages of various forms of PR for group representation, see Lani Guinier, *The Tyranny of the Majority: Fundamental Fairness in Representative Democracy* (New York: Free Press, 1994), 41–118; and more generally, Guinier and Torres, *Miner's Canary*, 209–13.

75. Eben Moglen and Pamela S. Karlan, "The Soul of a New Political Machine: The Online, the Color Line, and Electronic Democracy," *Loyola of Los Angeles Law Review* 34 (2001): 1099. "As we spend greater and more meaningful portions of our lives in computer-mediated communications with other people . . . location doesn't matter, our interests determine our communities, and we don't have to use our feet to vote with them" (1098). Internet democracy may create its own problem of electoral justice; to the extent that access to Internet technology is greater for already advantaged citizens, equal respect would be violated.

76. For an analysis showing that "in important ways territorial identities cannot be freely chosen," and raising more general doubts about treating territorial districting as less suspect than racial districting, see Richard T. Ford, "Law's Territory (A History of Jurisdiction)," *Michigan Law Review* 97 (February 1999): 843–929; and "Geography and Sovereignty: Jurisdictional Formation and Racial Segregation," *Stanford Law Review* 49 (July 1997): 1365–1445. For a general critique of the idea that "representatives should be elected by aggregations of individuals that may have nothing more in common than geographical proximity," see Guinier and Torres, *Miner's Canary*, 170, 168–222.

77. Jeffrey C. Kubin, "The Case for Redistricting Commissions," *Texas Law Review* 75 (March 1997): 841–51. Generally, a redistricting bill passed by the legislature must still be signed by the governor.

78. Partisan gerrymandering can, however, make it more difficult to accomplish constitutionally acceptable racial gerrymandering. When legislators are trying to protect incumbents, they do not have as many possibilities for creating majority-minority districts, and are more likely to draw unusual and irregular boundaries. The "bizarre" shape of the notorious majority-black District 12 in North Carolina, cited by the Supreme Court in finding the redistricting unconstitutional, could have been avoided if the state had not given such a high priority to protecting incumbents. See Justice White's dissent in *Shaw v. Reno*, 509 U.S. 630, 674 n. 10 (1993).

79. Some critics argue that the "representational harms" caused by partisan gerrymandering should be treated like the harms caused by racial redistricting, and therefore regarded as violations of equal protection (and presumably equal respect). In both cases, individuals are said to be harmed because they are assigned to districts in which they have no realistic prospects of electing a candidate of their choice. But for the principle of equal respect the critical difference lies in the reason for the assignment—whether it is based on an ascriptive characteristic such as race or a political attribute such as party affiliation.

For the argument that racial and partisan gerrymandering should be treated similarly in some important respects, see Megan Creek Frient, "Similar Harm Means Similar Claims: Doing Away with *Davis v. Bandemer*'s Discriminatory Effect Requirement in Political Gerrymandering Cases," *Case Western Reserve Law Review* 48 (spring 1998): 617–58. For an argument that partisan gerrymandering does not violate any equality principle (at least none that should be adjudicated by the courts), see Peter H. Schuck, "The Thickest Thicket: Partisan Gerrymandering and Judicial Regulation of Politics, *Columbia Law Review* 87 (November 1987): 1325–84. Guinier and Torres argue that if partisan districting is justified, then to achieve "formal equality" so is racial districting. *Miner's Canary*, 176–83, 194–202. But they suggest that both are flawed because they do not "challenge the idea that a single representative can effectively stand in for a complex whole . . . and the idea that elected officials" should choose "the units of electoral control" (200).

80. For a wide-ranging study of racial considerations in political ethics, including a discussion of redistricting, see K. Anthony Appiah and Amy Gutmann, *Color Conscious: The Political Morality of Race* (Princeton: Princeton University Press, 1996), esp. 151–62.

81. *Shaw v. Reno*, 509 U.S. at 658.

82. One district was compared to a "Rorschach ink-blot test" and a "bug splattered on a windshield." The other, with its 160-mile-long "snake-like" shape, was even more unusual: "if you drove down the interstate with both car doors open, you'd kill most of the people in the district." *Shaw v. Reno*, 509 U.S. at 635.

83. The most cogent expressivist interpretation of the opinion is Richard Pildes and Richard Niemi, "Expressive Harms, 'Bizarre Districts,' and Voting Rights: Evaluating Election-District Appearances after *Shaw v. Reno*," *Michigan Law Review* 92 (December 1993): 483–587. Although the discussion in the text follows Pildes and Niemi in emphasizing the expressivist aspect of the opinion, it does not accept their account of what is expressed by the electoral scheme. They suggest that *Shaw* is "best understood . . . as an opinion condemning value reductionism"—using only one value (race) instead of seeking to "realize a plurality of values" (500). Even if race were the predominant value in designing this scheme (and that is in question), the scheme could still be justified by showing that race must have more weight here to compensate for its neglect in other aspects of the political process (and society as a whole). The justification itself would be a form of value pluralism, applied more generally to the political process and society rather than to a particular redistricting scheme. To object that this is still value reductionism, one would have to require that each decision about particular features of institutions reflect a plurality of values. It does not seem plausible to attribute such a rigid view to the Court majority.

84. *Shaw v. Reno*, 509 U.S. at 647, 648 (emphasis added). Also: "[R]eapportionment legislation that cannot be understood as anything other than an effort to classify and separate voters by race injures voters in other ways. It reinforces racial stereotypes and threatens to undermine our system of representative democracy by *signaling* to elected officials that they represent a particular racial group rather than their constituency as a whole." 509 U.S. at 650.

85. In his dissent Justice Souter remarked that "it seems utterly implausible to me to presume . . . that North Carolina's creation of this strangely shaped majority-minority district 'generates' within the white plaintiffs here anything comparable to 'a feeling of inferiority as to their status in the community that may affect their hearts and minds in a way unlikely ever to be undone.'" *Shaw v. Reno*, 509 U.S. at 686 n. 9, quoting *Brown v. Board of Education*, 347 U.S. 483, 494 (1954). It would be less implausible to presume

that blacks suffer from the racial stereotyping implied by redistricting, but they were not plaintiffs in the case and they were expected to benefit from the scheme.

86. We need to know even more in order to decide whether a redistricting scheme passes the current test of constitutionality—whether race was the "predominant" factor in drawing the boundaries. In the most recent incarnation of *Shaw*, Justice Breyer (writing for the Court majority) analyzes in detail the empirical evidence provided by expert witnesses and attorneys for the parties, before concluding that the district court erred in finding that the legislature's motive was predominantly racial, not political. *Easley v. Cromartie*, 532 U.S. 234, 237–58 (2001) [originally *Hunt v. Cromartie*].

87. *Shaw v. Reno*, 509 U.S. at 673–74.

88. Ibid., 679. To refuse to permit racial redistricting in this case is to send what Justice Blackmun sees as an "ironic" message: the case in which the majority "chooses to abandon settled law . . . is a challenge by white voters to the plan under which North Carolina has sent black representatives to Congress for the first time since Reconstruction." 509 U.S. at 676.

89. David Lublin, *The Paradox of Representation: Racial Gerrymandering and Minority Interests in Congress* (Princeton: Princeton University Press, 1997), 72–119; and Richard H. Pildes, "The Politics of Race: Quiet Revolution in the South," *Harvard Law Review* 108 (April 1995): esp. 1376–92. For a more critical view of the bleaching claims and an incisive analysis of the literature, see Pamela S. Karlan, "Loss and Redemption: Voting Rights at the Turn of a Century," *Vanderbilt Law Review* 50 (March 1997): 291–325.

90. Claudine Gay, "The Effect of Black Congressional Representation on Political Participation," *American Political Science Review* 95 (September 2001): 589–602.

91. Donald Horowitz, Senate Committee on the Judiciary, *Hearings before the Subcommittee on the Constitution on S. 53, S. 1761, S. 1975, and S. 1992, Bills to Amend the Voting Rights Act of 1965*, 97th Cong., 2d Sess., January–March 1982, 1327–28 (emphasis added).

92. *Rural West Tennessee African-American Affairs Council, Inc., et al. v. Ned McWherter et al.*, 877 F. Supp. 1096 (W.D. Tenn.), *summarily aff'd*, 516 U.S. 801 (1995). The earlier case was *Rural West Tennessee African-American Affairs Council, Inc., et al. v. Ned McWherter et al.*, 836 F. Supp. 453 (W.D. Tenn. 1993).

93. Transcript of Trial before Honorable Chief Judge Gilbert Merritt . . . , Memphis, Tennessee, *Rural West v. McWherter et al.*, 877 F. Supp. 1096, vol. 5, no. 92–2407-TUBRO, at 833–961 (28 June 1993). During the trial, the court instructed witnesses that testimony should focus on the responsiveness of the Senate as an institution to blacks, not that of individual legislators (at 891). The legislators who testified were not to take personal credit for any of their own efforts to promote black interests. This limitation, running so palpably against the natural instincts of politicians, predictably proved difficult to enforce and prompted repeated objections (e.g., at 916–17).

94. Ibid., 920.

95. Ibid., 920–21. See also ibid., 913–14, 953–54.

96. Ibid., 854.

97. Ibid., 850.

98. *Rural West v. McWherter et al.*, 877 F. Supp. 1096.

99. The district court cited another Supreme Court opinion in support of its conclusion, but the key passage in that opinion refers only to cross-racial coalitions among voters within a district, not within the legislature: "[T]here are communities in which minority citizens are able to form collations with voters from other racial and ethnic

groups, having no need to be a majority within a single district in order to elect candidates of their choice." *Johnson v. De Grandy,* 512 U.S 977, 1020 (1994). Coincidentally, in the middle of the trial in *Rural West,* one of the attorneys announced to the court that he had been told on the phone that the Supreme Court had just handed down its decision in *Shaw,* and asked permission to file a supplemental brief. 877 F. Supp. 1096, Transcript of Trial, at 896–97.

100. Karlan, "Loss and Redemption," 312. The account in this paragraph is based on Karlan's discussion.

101. "New Jersey's Redistricting," *New York Times,* 9 May 2001, sec. A, p. 30. For an account of the politics of the process, see Barbara Fitzgerald, "In Control, but Losing a Grip," *New York Times,* 3 June 2001, sec. 14NJ, p. 1. For the subsequent legal controversy, see *McNeil v. Legislative Apportionment Comm'n of New Jersey,* MER-L-1442–01 (N.J. Super., 17 May 2001), *appeal pending,* No. A-1027–01T5 (N.J. Super. Ct. App. Div., 30 October 2001).

102. This is so even for what might seem to be the more objective evidence—the statistical analyses. Each side has its own expert witnesses, and although a dispassionate appraisal might show some expert conclusions to be more cogent than others, the courts find themselves confronting a battle of experts, seemingly without end. In the oral argument in a later incarnation of the *Shaw* case, *Easley v. Cromartie,* the justices devoted more time to discussing the disputes between and about the expert witnesses than to any other issue. At the end of the argument, the U.S. solicitor general remarked, "So you really have an expert who is making political judgments." Transcript of Oral Argument, *Easley v. Cromartie,* 532 U.S. 234 (2001), 2000 WL 1742700, at 45 (27 November 2000).

103. *Rural West,* Transcript of Trial, at 955.

104. O'Connor and Stevens respectively, *Shaw v. Reno,* 509 U.S. at 647, 648.

105. For example, Lublin, *The Paradox of Representation,* 12.

106. For a defense of descriptive representation, see Melissa S. Williams, *Voice, Trust, and Memory: Marginalized Groups and the Failings of Liberal Representation* (Princeton: Princeton University Press, 1998).

107. For a clear and critical statement of the distinction, see Keith J. Bybee, *Mistaken Identity: The Supreme Court and the Politics of Minority Representation* (Princeton: Princeton University Press, 1998), 147–54.

108. *Shaw v. Reno,* 509 U.S. at 648.

109. See, for example, Senator Orrin Hatch (R–UT), quoted in Abigail M. Thernstrom, *Whose Votes Count? Affirmative Action and Minority Voting Rights* (Cambridge: Harvard University Press, 1987), 123.

110. The distinction does not track precisely the traditional distinction between trustee and delegate theories of representation, though the two distinctions share some common features. Both the discretionary and the trustee conceptions give representatives considerable discretion in making independent judgments, but unlike trustees, the discretionary representatives do not necessarily follow their conscience or promote the national interest. They may use their discretion to advance the best interests of their constituents (or only their stated preferences). The mandatory and the delegate representatives are more similar: both are bound by their constituents' views, though the delegate is usually assumed to have discretion to make compromises in the legislature if that will further the constituents' goals. For further analysis of the role of the representative (using somewhat different terminology), see Dennis F. Thompson, *Political Ethics and Public Office* (Cambridge: Harvard University Press, 1987), 96–122.

111. On the importance of taking account of the legislative process in a theory of representation, see Dennis Thompson, "Representatives in the Welfare State," in *Democracy and the Welfare State*, ed. Amy Gutmann (Princeton: Princeton University Press, 1988), 131–55.

112. One of the few studies to examine the relationship between majority-black districts and styles of legislative behavior finds that such districts can provide significant representation for blacks and at the same time permit building biracial coalitions in the legislature. See David T. Canon, *Race, Redistricting, and Representation* (Chicago: University of Chicago Press, 1999), 243–64.

113. Keith J. Bybee is one of the few scholars to stress the need for a deliberative approach to redistricting, but he is primarily interested in devising a "judicial standard," which seems to be purely procedural, since it rejects substantive standards such as "reciprocity," and requires only "sufficient diversity" and "deliberative procedures" in the legislature. *Mistaken Identity*, 154–72.

114. Lani Guinier, *Tyranny of the Majority*, 14–16, 107–8, 94–95; and Issacharoff, Karlan, and Pildes, *The Law of Democracy*, 1099–1132 (and the works cited there).

115. Since 1980, the Justice Department has evaluated more than fifty such systems in the United States (plus another dozen similar "limited voting" systems) as part of the preclearance process under the Voting Rights Act. Testimony of Anita Hodgkiss, Deputy Asst. Attorney General, House Committee on the Judiciary, *Hearings before the Subcommittee on the Constitution on States' Choice of Voting Systems Act, H.R. 1173*, 106th Cong., 1st Sess., 23 September 1999, 57. The requirement of single-member districts, first enacted in 1842, lapsed in 1929, but was reinstated only in 1967.

116. *United States v. Hays*, 515 U.S. 737 (1995).

117. Pildes and Niemi, "Expresssive Harms," 513–16; and Samuel Issacharoff and Pamela S. Karlan, "Commentary: Standing and Misunderstanding in Voting Rights Law," *Harvard Law Review* 111 (June 1998): 2276–92.

118. O'Connor and Stevens respectively, *Shaw v. Reno*, 509 U.S. at 647, 648.

119. 42 U.S.C. § 1973l(c)(3) (1965).

120. *Delahunt v. Johnston*, 423 Mass. 731 (1996). The dispute involved what are now known as "pregnant" or "dimpled" chads—in the court's words, "the presence of a discernible impression made by a stylus as clear indication of a voter's intent" (423 Mass. at 733–34). The court concluded that "a vote should be recorded for a candidate if the chad was not removed but an impression was made on or near it" (423 Mass. at 733). The court went on to explain: "It is, of course, true that a voter who failed to push a stylus through the ballot and thereby create a hole in it could have done a better job of expressing his or her intent. Such a voter should not automatically be disqualified, however, like a litigant or one seeking favors from the government, because he or she failed to comply strictly with announced procedures. The voters are the owners of the government, and our rule that we seek to discern the voter's intention and to give it effect reflects the proper relation between government and those to whom it is responsible" (423 Mass. at 733).

121. *Bush v. Gore*, 531 U.S. 98, 111 (2000). Justice Breyer was not so explicit on this point as most commentators assume, and perhaps should not be counted as part of the seven member majority on this question: "[B]asic principles of fairness *may* well have counseled the adoption of a uniform standard . . . but I *need not decide* whether, or the text to which, as a remedial matter, the *constitution* would place limits upon the content of the uniform standard" (531 U.S. at 146, emphasis added).

122. Per curiam, *Bush v. Gore*, 531 U.S. at 106–7.

123. Richard A. Posner, "Florida 2000: A Legal and Statistical Analysis of the Election Deadlock and the Ensuing Litigation," *Supreme Court Review* (2000): 40–41. Posner believes that the decision can be defended but on grounds that the majority did not use: he argues that Article II of the Constitution bars the Florida court from ordering any recount at all. "Florida 2000," 47; and Posner, *Breaking the Deadlock: The 2000 Election, the Constitution, and the Courts* (Princeton: Princeton University Press, 2001), 128–32, 167–68. In contrast, Pamela Karlan, a critic of the decision, believes that the Court's use of equal protection in this case is at a deeper level quite consistent with some earlier decisions—in particular the racial redistricting cases. In both the recent and the earlier decisions, the Court, she suggests, mistakenly tried to regulate the structure of the political process instead of attending to the protection of individual rights. Karlan, "The Newest Equal Protection: Regressive Doctrine on a Changeable Court," in *The Vote: Bush, Gore and the Supreme Court,* ed. Cass R. Sunstein and Richard A. Epstein (Chicago: University of Chicago Press, 2001), 77–97. Another important critique of the equal protection argument in this case is Laurence H. Tribe, "Comment: *Bush v. Gore* and Its Disguises: Freeing *Bush v. Gore* from Its Hall of Mirrors," *Harvard Law Review* 115 (November 2001): 217–74.

124. See Justice Stevens's dissent, *Bush v. Gore*, 531 U.S. at 126; and David Boies in Transcript of Oral Argument, *Bush v. Gore*, 2000 WL 1804429, at 72–73 (11 December 2000). Also note this conclusion of a study by a political scientist: "By any reckoning, the machine variability in undervotes and overvotes exceeds the variability due to different standards by factors of ten to twenty." Henry E. Brady, "Equal Protection for Votes," in *The Longest Night: Polemics and Perspectives on Election 2000,* ed. Arthur Jacobson and Michel Rosenfeld (Berkeley: University of California Press, forthcoming).

125. Transcript of Oral Argument, *Bush v. Gore*, 2000 WL 1804429, at 52.

126. The majority in their opinion carried this a step further (almost turning the point on its head) by suggesting that because "intent of the voter" is subjective and too easily permits variation that is not easily challenged, officials should be required to adopt objective standards when they are available. When the "factfinder confronts a thing, not a person . . . the search for intent can be confined by specific rules designed to ensure uniform treatment" (*Bush v. Gore*, 531 U.S. at 106).

127. The demand for uniform treatment could also be justified as necessary to express respect toward voters in two other ways: a uniform rule functions as a prophylactic to reduce the occurrence of hard-to-detect discrimination, and it gives voters greater confidence that their votes will be accurately and fairly counted even if no discrimination takes place. See Heather K. Gerken, "New Wine in Old Bottles: A Comment on Richard Hasen's and Richard Briffault's Essays on *Bush v. Gore,*" *Florida State University Law Review* 29 (February 2002), 409–13.

128. See note 46 above.

129. *Bush v. Gore*, 531 U.S. at 109.

130. Samuel Issacharoff, "The Court's Legacy for Voting Rights," *New York Times,* 14 December 2000, sec. A, p. 39. A former attorney general of Florida who also served as secretary of state testified to the Civil Rights Commission that the Court's decision "strongly suggested" that "we need uniform technology statewide and procedures" to avoid "equal protection" challenges. U.S. Commission on Civil Rights, *Hearings on Allegations of Election-Day Irregularities in Florida,* 11 January 2001, 160.

131. David Abel, "Bush v. Gore Case Compels Scholars to Alter Courses at US Law

Schools," *Boston Globe,* 3 February 2001, p. A1. Also see William Glaberson, "Court Battle for Presidency Rages On in Legal Circles," *New York Times,* 1 February 2001, sec. A, p. 14. Whether the decision is unprincipled or merely indefensible depends significantly on how the Court itself in the future treats it. See Tribe, "ɘɿoⅭ ʌ ɥƨu8 and Its Disguises," 268–73.

132. Caltech/MIT Voting Technology Project, *Voting: What Is, What Could Be,* 17–25. The National Commission report takes a more skeptical view of the use of optical scanners. National Commission on Federal Election Reform, *To Assure Pride,* 51–52. The most careful comparison of voting methods concludes that "much more testing of the available systems is needed before making any final judgments about the suitability of one system over another." Henry E. Brady et al., "Counting All the Votes: The Performance of Voting Technology in the United States," Department of Political Science, Survey Research Center, University of California, Berkeley, September 2001, 7, 49, available online: <http://ucdata.berkeley.edu/> (7 May 2002).

133. Issacharoff, Karlan, and Pildes, *The Law of Democracy,* 307–9.

134. U.S. General Accounting Office, *Elections: A Framework for Evaluating Reform Proposals,* Report GAO-02-90, 15 October 2001, 38–39, available online: <http://www.gao.gov/new.items/d0290.pdf> (7 May 2002).

135. U.S. Commission on Civil Rights, *Hearings,* 11 January 2001, 187 (Darryl Paulson). See also ibid., 12 January 2001, 50–52, 78 (Ion Sancho); and 328–29 (Susan Caplowe). Other witnesses observed that this pattern of disparities shows up in districts throughout the United States. Ibid., 12 January 2001, 199 (Jackson Chin). In the final report, a majority of the commission concluded that blacks in Florida were ten times more likely than other voters to have had their ballots rejected. The dissenters on the commission argued that "voter error, not disenfranchisement" was the "central problem." U.S. Commission on Civil Rights, *Voting Irregularities in Florida during the 2000 Presidential Election* (June 2001), chap. 9.

136. Even the major report that concentrates most on making improvements in technology recognizes the importance of recruiting and training competent support staff at the polls. See Caltech/MIT Voting Technology Project, *Voting: What Is, What Could Be,* 35.

137. Most of the states that permit provisional voting limit its application to only certain categories of voters. See John Mark Hansen, Task Force on the Federal Election System, "Provisional Balloting," in *To Assure Pride: Task Force,* National Commission on Federal Election Reform, 82–88. See also National Commission on Federal Election Reform, *To Assure Pride,* 35–37; Caltech/MIT Voting Technology Project, *Voting: What Is, What Could Be,* 29–30; and Constitution Project, *Building Consensus on Election Reform,* 8–9.

138. Florida Statute, tit. 9, § 102.166(5): "If the manual recount indicates an error in the vote tabulation which could affect the outcome of the election, the county canvassing board shall: (a) Correct the error and recount the remaining precincts with the vote tabulation system; (b) Request the Department of State to verify the tabulation software; or (c) Manually recount all ballots." If a board decides to go forward with a manual recount, they must follow the elaborate procedure described in the next sections of the statute, which clearly anticipate the likelihood of disputes about the "intent of the voter"—not merely about whether the voter has spoiled his ballot or in other ways failed to follow instructions.

139. Posner, "Florida 2000," 26. Also see cites in note 46 above.

140. U.S. Commission on Civil Rights, *Hearings*, 11 January 2001, 52–82. At least one commissioner (Linda Howell) denied that these problems occurred disproportionately in counties or precincts in which minority voters were concentrated. Ibid., 12 January 2001, 95–96.

141. Posner, "Florida 2000," 58. Posner's support of improving the clarity and ease of use of the ballot is conditional: "*if* it is considered important as a matter of democratic theory or social peace to facilitate" voting by "the confused, inept or inexperienced" citizen (ibid., 19, emphasis added).

142. U.S. Commission on Civil Rights, *Hearings*, 12 January 2001, 283–86.

143. Ibid., 286.

CHAPTER TWO

1. The secret ballot was adopted in the United States only in the last decade of the nineteenth century. Some democratic theorists initially opposed it because it seemed to express a message that voting is a private matter instead of a public trust. On John Stuart Mill's opposition to the secret ballot, see Dennis F. Thompson, *John Stuart Mill and Representative Government* (Princeton: Princeton University Press, 1976), 98–99. On the introduction of the secret ballot in the United States, see Alexander Keyssar, *The Right to Vote* (New York: Basic Books, 2000), 142–43. For an argument sympathetic to public voting, see Geoffrey Brennan and Philip Pettit, "Unveiling the Vote," *British Journal of Political Science* 20 (July 1990): 311–34.

2. Leon Epstein, *Political Parties in the American Mold* (Madison: University of Wisconsin Press, 1986), 158. Also see Samuel Issacharoff, Pamela S. Karlan, and Richard H. Pildes, *The Law of Democracy: Legal Structure of the Political Process*, 2d ed. (Westbury, N.Y.: Foundation Press: 2001), 398.

3. Jefferson, Letter to Francis Hopkinson, 13 March 1789, in *The Life and Selected Writings of Thomas Jefferson,* ed. Adrienne Koch and William Peden (New York: Modern Library, 1993), 424.

4. James Madison, *The Federalist* No. 10, ed. Benjamin Fletcher Wright (Cambridge: Harvard University Press, 1961), 130. Madison used "faction" and "party" as near synonyms—as in "the spirit of party and faction" (131)—though he did not have in mind a mass organization like the political parties that developed later.

5. Epstein, *Political Parties,* 159.

6. Adam Winkler, "Voters' Rights and Parties' Wrongs: Early Political Party Regulation in the State Courts, 1886–1915," *Columbia Law Review* 100 (April 2000): 892. The recognition of the public character of parties did not continue in an unbroken line from the founders to these turn-of-the-century cases. In the mid-nineteenth century some observers and some courts tended to treat parties as more like a "meeting of citizens" or a "private corporation" than a public entity. Ibid., 878–79.

7. For a valuable discussion arguing that the distinction between private and public is not helpful in deciding the relative scope of the freedom of parties, see Daniel Hays Lowenstein, "Associational Rights of Major Political Parties: A Skeptical Inquiry," *Texas Law Review* 71 (June 1993): 1741–91. For a broader view of the role of parties in civil society, emphasizing their "civic educational effects" and their internal processes, see Nancy L. Rosenblum, "Political Parties as Membership Groups," *Columbia Law Review* 100 (April 2000): 813–44.

8. Winkler, "Voters' Rights," 892–93.

9. Daniel Maxmanian, *Third Parties in Presidential Elections* (Washington, D.C.:

Brookings, 1974); Steven J. Rosenstone, Roy Behr, and Edward Lazarus, *Third Parties in America* (Princeton: Princeton University Press, 1984); and Nelson Polsby and Aaron Wildavsky, *Presidential Elections,* 10th ed. (New York: Chatham House, 2000), 48–51.

10. The fusion ban "imposes a Hobson's choice between political efficacy and conviction." Brief for Respondents, *Timmons v. Twin Cities Area New Party,* 520 U.S. 351 (1997), 1996 WL 501955, at 10 (30 August 1996). Strictly speaking, a Hobson's choice offers no alternative: the seventeenth-century English keeper of a livery stable who gave the choice its name insisted that his customers take either the horse nearest the stable door or none.

11. In a common version of this system, the first-place preferences are counted, and any candidate who receives the predetermined quota (typically the number of total votes divided by seats plus one) is elected. Any surplus votes the elected candidate accumulates are then distributed to the candidates who appear as the second preference on these ballots. This process of redistribution continues through the third and lower choices until all the seats are filled. The classic proponent of this system was John Stuart Mill; see Thompson, *Mill,* 102–11. More recent discussions include Douglas J. Amy, *Real Choices/New Voices: The Case for Proportional Representation Elections in the United States* (New York: Columbia University Press, 1996); Thomas Christiano, *The Rule of the Many: Fundamental Issues in Democratic Theory* (Boulder: Westview Press, 1996), 224–40, 258–61; and Kathleen Barber, *A Right to Representation: Proportional Election Systems for the 21st Century* (Columbus: Ohio University Press, 2001). For a survey of the debate and alternatives, see Arend Lijphart and Bernard Grofman, eds., *Choosing an Electoral System: Issues and Alternatives* (Westport, Conn.: Praeger, 1984); and David M. Farrell, *Electoral Systems: A Comparative Introduction* (New York: Palgrave, 2001).

12. See chapter 1, page 52.

13. Lani Guinier and Gerald Torres, *The Miner's Canary: Enlisting Race, Resisting Power, Transforming Democracy* (Cambridge: Harvard University Press, 2002), 170–72.

14. For an argument that equality does not require proportional representation, see Charles R. Beitz, *Political Equality: An Essay in Democratic Theory* (Princeton: Princeton University Press, 1989), 132–40.

15. See, e.g., *Final Report of the Vermont Commission to Study Instant Runoff Voting,* presented to the Vermont House of Representatives pursuant to H.R. 37, January 1999, available online: <http://www.fairvote.org/irv/vermont/index.html> (7 May 2002). For a description of the system in other countries, as well as a survey of alternative methods, see Farrell, *Electoral Systems.*

16. William R. Kirschner, "Fusion and the Associational Rights of Minor Political Parties," *Columbia Law Review* 95 (1995): 683; and Note, "Fusion Candidacies, Disaggregation, and Freedom of Association," *Harvard Law Review* 109 (April 1996): 1302–37. For a historical perspective, see Peter H. Argersinger, " 'A Place on the Ballot': Fusion Politics and Antifusion Laws," *American Historical Review* 85 (April 1980): 287–306.

17. Only four states expressly permit fusion, and the laws of three would allow it, but only in New York does it play a significant political role. Note, "Fusion Candidacies," 1303–4 n. 14.

18. Argersinger, " 'A Place on the Ballot,' " 296.

19. E. E. Schattschneider, *The Semisovereign People* (New York: Holt, Rinehart and Winston, 1960), 78–85; Walter Dean Burnham, "The System of 1896: An Analysis," in *The Evolution of American Electoral Systems,* ed. P. Kleppner (Westport, Conn.: Greenwood Press, 1981), 152–65; and Argersinger, " 'A Place on the Ballot,' " 287–306.

20. Argersinger, " 'A Place on the Ballot,' " 303–5; and Frank Smallwood, *The Other Candidates: Third Parties in Presidential Elections* (Hanover, N.H.: University Press of New England for Dartmouth College, 1983), 250–54. For a more skeptical view of the role of fusion in the fortunes of third parties, see James Gray Pope, "Fusion, Timmons v. Twin Cities Area New Party, and the Future of Third Parties in the United States," *Rutgers Law Review* 50 (winter 1998): 473–506.

21. *Twin Cities Area New Party v. McKenna*, 73 F.3d 196 (8th Cir. 1996).

22. Ibid., 199.

23. *Timmons v. Twin Cities Area New Party*, 520 U.S. 351, 369–70 (1997). The Court thus rejected the party's claim that the ban violated its rights under the First and Fourteenth Amendments.

24. Ibid., 361, 365, 366–67.

25. Richard Slowes, Assistant Solicitor General for the state of Minnesota, Transcript of Oral Argument, *Timmons v. Twin Cities Area New Party*, 520 U.S. 351 (1997), 1996 WL 709359, at 6 (4 December 1996).

26. Ibid., 7. Justice Scalia felt compelled to add: "For the record, I was being facetious" (23).

27. *Timmons v. Twin Cities Area New Party*, 520 U.S. at 370 n. 13.

28. Brief for Petitioners, *Timmons v. Twin Cities Area New Party*, 520 U.S. 351 (1997), 1996 WL 435927, at 17, 44 (1 August 1996).

29. Transcript of Oral Argument, *Timmons*, 1996 WL 709359, at 31.

30. Ibid., 27, 29.

31. Ibid., 27 (emphasis added).

32. Ibid., 38.

33. Ibid., 40. This prompted Justice Scalia to complain: "Why does this make any difference? It's sort of like saying you can paint the whole building green but you can't paint the window frets green" (40).

34. Ibid., 41.

35. Generally, see Issacharoff, Karlan, and Pildes, *The Law of Democracy*, 417–22. Compare the Court's comment in *Storer v. Brown*, 415 U.S. 724, 730 (1974): "[T]he rule fashioned by the Court . . . provides no litmus-paper test for separating those restrictions that are valid from those that are invidious . . . the rule is not self-executing and is no substitute for the hard judgments that must be a 'matter of degree.' . . . What the result of this process will be in any specific case may be very difficult to predict with great assurance."

36. Samuel Issacharoff and Richard Pildes, "Politics as Markets: Partisan Lockups of the Democratic Process," *Stanford Law Review* 50 (February 1998): 643–717. Although the authors' emphasis on institutional context and open competition is consistent with the principle of free choice developed here, their use of the market analogy carries the implication (criticized in chapter 3) that the main concern is competition among interests or preferences, rather than among principles or ideas. Their economic categories, especially the analogies with corporate law, make their conception seem less a marketplace of ideas than a market in political pressure.

37. The bill was introduced by Representative Gene Pelowski of the Democratic Farmer-Labor Party. Minnesota House of Representatives, floor session, 19 March 1996, House File 3123, audio tape; and Minnesota Senate, floor session, 11 March 1996. Also see description of final bill, Minnesota House, *Session Weekly*, 12 April 1996, vol. 13.

38. Minnesota House Committee on General Legislation, Veteran Affairs and Elec-

tions (Karen Lotofsky), 8 February 1996, House File 3132, audio tape. Also see Minnesota Senate Ethics and Campaign Reform Committee, 6 February 1996, Senate File 2720, audio tape; Minnesota House, Ways and Means Committee, 8 March 1996; and Minnesota House, *Session Weekly,* 9 February, 15 March, 22 March, 29 March, and 12 April 1996, vol. 13.

39. Senator John Marty (Democratic Farmer-Labor Party), Minnesota Senate, floor session, 11 March 1996, Senate File 2720, audio tape.

40. Minnesota House, *Session Weekly,* 22 March 1996, vol. 13.

41. About two-fifths of the states currently have open primaries. Three states besides California have some form of blanket primary: Alaska, Washington, and Louisiana (which has a nonpartisan variant). It is not easy to classify many of the other states, because the difference between open and closed primaries begins to disappear the closer the deadline for declaring party membership is to election day.

42. Statement of support included in the ballot pamphlet, quoted in *California Democratic Party v. Jones,* 169 F.3d 646, 649 (9th Cir. 1999) (internal quotation marks omitted). Supporters argued that the blanket primary would increase voter participation in the primary election, restore healthy competition, make elected officials more responsive to voters than to party officials, reduce the influence of special interest groups, and strengthen the major political parties by encouraging them to nominate candidates with broader bases of support.

43. Ibid. (internal quotation marks omitted).

44. Ibid.

45. Richard L. Hasen, "Law and Political Parties: Parties Take the Initiative (and Vice Versa)," *Columbia Law Review* 100 (April 2000): 747. The Democrats spent less than five thousand dollars, and the Republicans about fifty thousand, opposing the initiative (748 n. 71).

46. *California Democratic Party v. Jones,* 169 F.3d at 646. The appeals court adopted the district court judge's opinion as its own.

47. *California Democratic Party v. Jones,* 530 U.S. 567, 568 (2000).

48. Testimony of Martin Wattenberg, Reporter's Transcript, 576, quoted in Brief for Respondents, *California Democratic Party v. Jones,* 530 U.S. 567 (2000), 2000 WL 340273, at 43 (31 March 2000).

49. *California Democratic Party v. Jones,* 169 F.3d at 646.

50. See *Tashjian v. Republican Party of Connecticut,* 479 U.S. 208, 222–24 (1986); *Eu v. San Francisco County Democratic Cent. Comm.,* 489 U.S. 214, 227–28 (1989).

51. For a "functional approach" consistent with the argument here, see Samuel Issacharoff, "Private Parties with Public Purposes: Political Parties, Associational Freedoms, and Partisan Competition," *Columbia Law Review* 101 (March 2001): 308–13. Other valuable analyses, which explicitly discuss blanket primaries, are Bruce E. Cain, "Point-Counterpoint: Party Autonomy and Two-Party Electoral Competition," *University of Pennsylvania Law Review* 149 (January 2001): 793–814; and Richard L. Hasen, "Do the Parties or the People Own the Electoral Process?" *University of Pennsylvania Law Review* 149 (January 2001): 815–41.

52. See Justice Stevens's dissent in *California Democratic Party v. Jones,* 530 U.S. at 593.

53. The Supreme Court majority in the blanket primary case recognized that a party's right of free association is not absolute, but they treated the ability to select the party's nominee as an essential part of associational freedom, which could not be outweighed by

any of the substantial interests that a blanket primary was claimed to promote. *California Democratic Party v. Jones,* 530 U.S. at 572–77.

54. Notice that the trial judge who upheld the California law decided only that blanket primaries were constitutional, not that they were desirable: "[T]he court does not decide whether a blanket primary is a good idea; it may prove to be a bad idea, in which case the people of the State presumably will act to reform the system in the future as they have in the past" (*California Democratic Party v. Jones,* 169 F.3d at 662).

55. The consensus among political scientists who testified in the California case is that nearly all cross-over voters "invade a party's primary to vote for a preferred candidate," and "not to vote for a candidate who they will oppose in the general election and who they believe will be easier to defeat in that election." Constantini Report, Reporter's Transcript, 485–86, cited in *California Democratic Party v. Jones,* 169 F.3d at 656. The experience of Washington state, which has used the blanket primary since 1935, also confirms that this strategic voting (sometimes called raiding) is rare, and almost never affects the outcome.

56. *California Democratic Party v. Jones,* 530 U.S. at 584.

57. Ibid., 579.

58. Brief for Respondents, *California Democratic Party v. Jones,* 530 U.S. 567 (2000), 2000 WL 340273, at 39–41 (31 March 2000). A more recent careful study of the June 1998 California primary concludes that "the evidence strongly suggests that the overall net effect of the blanket primary was to produce more moderate candidates." Elisabeth R. Gerber, "Strategic Voting and Candidate Policy Positions," in *Voting at the Political Fault Line: California's Experiment with the Blanket Primary,* ed. Bruce E. Cain and Elisabeth R. Gerber (Berkeley: University of California Press, 2002), 210.

59. *California Democratic Party v. Jones,* 169 F.3d at 658.

60. Ibid., 662. Typical of Madison's criticisms of factions is this comment: "A zeal for different opinions . . . attachment to different leaders . . . have, in turn, divided mankind into parties, inflamed them with mutual animosity, and rendered them much more disposed to vex and oppress each other than to co-operate for their common good" (*The Federalist* No. 10, 131).

61. Brief of Amici Curiae Eagle Forum Education and Legal Defense Fund and the Claremont Institute Center for Constitutional Jurisprudence, *California Democratic Party v. Jones,* 530 U.S. 567 (2000), 2000 WL 486738, at 7 (3 March 2000). In Madison's words: "[T]he public good is disregarded in the conflicts of rival parties, and . . . measures are too often decided, not according to the rules of justice and the rights of the minor party, but by the superior force of an interested and overbearing majority . . . . When a majority is included in a faction, the form of popular government . . . enables it to sacrifice to its ruling passion or interest both the public good and the rights of other citizens" (*The Federalist* No. 10, 129–30, 132).

62. Compare Justice Scalia's comment that "the net effect of this scheme . . . is to *reduce* the scope of choice, by assuring a range of candidates who are all more 'centrist.' This may well be described as broadening the range of choice *favored by the majority*— but that is hardly a compelling state interest, if indeed it is even a legitimate one" (*California Democratic Party v. Jones,* 530 U.S. at 584).

63. Nathaniel Persily and Bruce E. Cain, "The Legal Status of Political Parties: A Reassessment of Competing Paradigms," *Columbia Law Review* 100 (April 2000): 802.

64. The classic statement of this view is Anthony Downs, *An Economic Theory of Democracy* (New York: Harper and Row, 1957). The theory has been subjected to con-

siderable criticism over the years, and requires extensive revision to accommodate subsequent empirical findings. But in a judicious review of the literature, Bernard Grofman concludes that "although the notion of Tweedledum-Tweedledee politics (implied by the Downsian model) is fundamentally flawed . . . Downs is in some ways fundamentally right in treating two-party competition as a quest for the center" ("Toward an Institution-Rich Theory of Political Competition," in *Information, Participation, and Choice,* ed. Bernard Grofman [Ann Arbor: University of Michigan Press, 1993], 193). See also John H. Aldrich, *Why Parties? The Origin and Transformation of Political Parties in America* (Chicago: University of Chicago Press, 1995); and Anders Westholm, "Distance versus Direction: The Illusory Defeat of the Proximity Theory of Electoral Choice," *American Political Science Review* 91 (December 1997): 865–83. The convergence is more pronounced in the United States than in other two-party democracies, but even in the United States the role of party activists and multiple stages of selection of candidates and policies may keep one or more of the parties from coming to rest at the center of the political spectrum. G. Bingham Powell Jr., *Elections as Instruments of Democracy* (New Haven: Yale University Press, 2000), 176–78, 183.

65. Stephen Earl Bennett, "Trends in Americans' Political Information, 1967–1987," *American Politics Quarterly* 17 (October 1989): 422–35; Stephen Earl Bennett, " 'Know-Nothings' Revisited: The Meaning of Political Ignorance Today," *Social Science Quarterly* 69 (June 1988): 476–90; Michael X. Delli Carpini and Scott Keeter, *What Americans Know about Politics and Why It Matters* (New Haven: Yale University Press, 1996), 62–104; and R. Michael Alvarez, *Information and Elections* (Ann Arbor: University of Michigan Press, 1998), 7–23.

66. Delli Carpini and Keeter, *What Americans Know,* 73–86. See also "Political Knowledge (House and Senate) Set E5–E7," in *National Election Studies, 2000: Pre-/Post-Election Study,* ed. Nancy Burns et al. (Ann Arbor: University of Michigan Center for Political Studies, 2001).

67. Alexis de Tocqueville, *Democracy in America,* ed. J. P. Mayer, trans. George Lawrence (Garden City, N.Y.: Doubleday, 1969), 1:198.

68. Except as indicated all quotations in this and the following paragraphs are from Tocqueville, *Democracy in America,* 1:198–201.

69. Thompson, *Mill,* 28–53.

70. Tocqueville, *Democracy in America,* 1:194.

71. W. Russell Neuman, *The Paradox of Mass Politics: Knowledge and Opinion the American Electorate* (Cambridge: Harvard University Press, 1986); and Arthur Lupia and Mathew D. McCubbins, *The Democratic Dilemma: Can Citizens Learn What They Need to Know?* (New York: Cambridge University Press, 1998). More broadly, see John Zaller, *The Nature and Origins of Mass Opinion* (New York: Cambridge University Press, 1992), esp. 6–28, 216–64, 266–74.

72. Benjamin I. Page and Robert Y. Shapiro, *The Rational Public: Fifty Years of Trends in American's Policy Preferences* (Chicago: University of Chicago Press, 1992), 387–88. See also Richard D. McKelvey and Peter C. Ordeshook, "Information, Electoral Equilibria, and the Democratic Ideal," *Journal of Politics* 48 (November 1986): 909–37; John A. Ferejohn, "Information and Electoral Processes," in *Information and Democratic Processes,* ed. John A. Ferejohn and James H. Kuklinski (Urbana: University of Illinois Press, 1990), 1–19; Samuel L. Popkin, *The Reasoning Voter: Communication and Persuasion in Presidential Campaigns* (Chicago: University of Chicago Press, 1991). For a more skeptical view of the heuristics approach, see Larry M. Bartels, "Uninformed Votes: Informa-

tion Effects in Presidential Elections," *American Journal of Political Science* 40 (February 1996): 194–230; and James H. Kuklinski and Paul J. Quirk, "Reconsidering the Rational Public: Cognition, Heuristics and Mass Opinion," in *Elements of Reason: Cognition, Choice and the Bounds of Rationality,* ed. Arthur Lupia, Mathew D. McCubbins, and Samuel L. Popkin (Cambridge: Cambridge University Press, 2000), 153–82.

73. On party identification as a shortcut, see Popkin, *The Reasoning Voter,* 13–14, 50–60. On "likability," see Paul M. Sniderman, "Taking Sides: A Fixed Choice Theory of Political Reasoning," in *Elements of Reason,* 69–74.

74. On retrospective evaluations of the economy, see Morris P. Fiorina, *Retrospective Voting in American National Elections* (New Haven: Yale University Press, 1981). The tamale example is from Popkin, *The Reasoning Voter,* 111: During the 1976 campaign when "President Ford tried to eat an unshucked tamale, he committed a faux pas far more serious than spilling mustard on his tie or ice cream on his shirt. To Hispanic voters in Texas, he betrayed an unfamiliarity with their food which suggested a lack of familiarity with their whole culture. Further, tamales were a way of projecting from the personal to the political, of assuming that personal familiarity with a culture and the acceptability of a candidate's polices to a group were linked." Personal foibles (such as President Clinton's alleged cheating at golf) may be politically significant, but only when they are considered part of a pattern of conduct directly relevant to office. Compare Frederick Schauer, "Can Public Figures Have Private Lives?" *Social Philosophy and Policy* 17 (2000): 299–300; and Dennis F. Thompson, "Private Life and Public Office," *Public Integrity* 3 (spring 2001): 163–76.

75. Bartels, "Uninformed Votes," 199–202, 215–22; and Scott Althaus, "Information Effects in Collective Preferences," *American Political Science Review* 92 (September 1998): 545–58.

76. Sniderman, "Taking Sides," 68. Also see Arthur Lupia, "What We Should Know: The Case for Voter Competence," in *Ordinary People, Extraordinary Choices: How Citizens Make Fundamental Political Decisions,* ed. Pierre Martin and Richard Nadeau (forthcoming).

77. For a sample of the vast critical literature, see Shanto Iyengar and Donald R. Kinder, *News That Matters: Television and American Opinion* (Chicago: University of Chicago Press, 1987), 112–33; Robert Entman, *Democracy without Citizens: Media and the Decay of American Politics* (New York: Oxford University Press, 1989); Shanto Iyengar, *Is Anyone Responsible? How Television Frames Political Issues* (Chicago: University of Chicago Press, 1991); Kathleen Hall Jamieson, *Dirty Politics: Deception, Distraction, and Democracy* (Oxford: Oxford University Press, 1992), 163–99; Thomas Patterson, *Out of Order* (New York: Knopf, 1993); Benjamin I. Page, *Who Deliberates? Mass Media in Modern Democracy* (Chicago: University of Chicago Press, 1996), esp. 6–11; and James M. Fallows, *Breaking the News: How the Media Undermine American Democracy* (New York: Vintage Books, 1997).

78. Tocqueville, *Democracy in America,* 1:200. The idea of an institutional filter is also quite consistent with Madison's theory: the effect of representation in a republic is "to refine and enlarge the public views, by passing them through the medium of a chosen body of citizens, whose wisdom may best discern the true interest of their country" (*The Federalist* No. 10, 134).

79. For a philosophical analysis of the value of limiting information, see Alvin Goldman, "Epistemic Paternalism: Communication Control in Law and Society," *Journal of Philosophy* 88 (March 1991): 113–31.

80. The seminal modern statement is Isaiah Berlin, "Two Concepts of Liberty," in *Liberty*, ed. David Miller (Oxford: Oxford University Press, 1991), 33–35. Also see Gerald C. MacCallum Jr., "Negative and Positive Freedom," in *Liberty*, 100–22. John Locke's concept of law similarly suggests that constraints can enhance freedom: "[F]or Law, in its true Notion, is not so much the Limitation as the direction of a free and intelligent agent to his proper Interest, and prescribes no farther than is for the general Good of those under that Law: could they be happier without it, the Law, as an useless thing, would of itself vanish; and that ill deserves the Name of Confinement which hedges us in only from Bogs and Precipices" (*Two Treatises of Government, Second Treatise*, ed. Peter Laslett, student ed. [Cambridge: Cambridge University Press, 1988], chap. 13, sec. 57, p. 323).

81. Jon Elster, *Ulysses and the Sirens: Studies in Rationality and Irrationality* (Cambridge: Cambridge University Press, 1979), 36–111. In a later more extended study of precommitment, Elster acknowledges that the individual and institutional cases may differ significantly because in the latter case the self-binding restricts not only one self, but other selves, who may not wish to be bound. Elster, *Ulysses Unbound: Studies in Rationality, Precommitment, and Constraints* (Cambridge: Cambridge University Press, 2000), 88–174.

82. Eight states (Alaska, Arkansas, Colorado, Idaho, Maine, Nebraska, Nevada, and South Dakota) adopted ballot notations in 1996, and a ninth (California) joined them in 1998. Oklahoma's initiative was declared invalid before it took place. Brief for Respondents, *Cook v. Gralike*, 531 U.S. 510 (2001), 2000 WL 1409741, at 6–7 (14 August 2000).

83. Representative Barney Frank (D–MA), *Congressional Record*, 105th Cong., 1st Sess., 12 February 1997, vol. 143, H487. Frank had fun with the differences that did exist: "[T]he second speaker . . . said the voice of the people is the voice of God . . . if it is Vox Populi, Vox Dei, why do we have a different 'vox' when you cross the river between Nebraska and Colorado? [no one asked: what river?] [T]here are some very important differences [in the versions from Arkansas and Colorado even though] they both have the same limits. In Arkansas it is section A, B and C, whereas in Colorado it is section 1, 2, and 3. Certainly the gentleman from Colorado would not want to betray the voice of God in Colorado by adopting the voice of God in Arkansas because apparently God says A, B, C in Arkansas and God says 1, 2, 3 in Colorado. Now religious wars have been fought over less, so I understand the gentleman's scrupulosity" (H489). He also mocked the differences in periods: "Some [members] are going to vote for 6 [year limits] and not 12, some are going to vote for 12 and not 8, some are going to vote for 8 and not 6. . . . Whatever happened to 10? Apparently there is some numerological fetish on the majority side which makes 10 terra infirma" (H487).

84. Representative Michael Crapo (R–Idaho), ibid., H490.

85. The example comes from the Missouri state constitution (art. VIII, §§ 15–22), declared unconstitutional in *Cook v. Gralike*, 531 U.S. at 510. Challengers who refused to take a "term limit pledge" were branded with this notation: "DECLINED TO PLEDGE TO SUPPORT TERM LIMITS."

86. *Congressional Record*, 105th Cong., 1st Sess., 12 February 1997, vol. 143, H487.

87. Representative Bill McCollum (R–FL), ibid., H510.

88. Elisabeth Garrett presents the most cogent case in favor of ballot notation, though she stops short of endorsing the practice. "The Law and Economics of 'Informed Voter' Ballot Notations," *Virginia Law Review* 85 (November 1999): 1533–87.

89. Joanne M. Miller and Jon A. Krosnick, "The Impact of Candidate Name Order on Election Outcomes," *Public Opinion Quarterly* 62 (autumn 1998): 291–330.

90. The Board of Election Commissioners refused to allow the alderman to appear on the ballot under her new name. In a case titled *None of the Above v. Hardy*, 377 So. 2d 385 (La. Ct. App. 1979), the court disallowed "None of the Above." As Low-Tax Looper's political career sank even lower than the taxes he favored, he was arrested and indicted for murdering his opponent in the election. See Garrett, " 'Informed Voter' Ballot Notations," 1535 nn. 6, 7.

91. Garrett, " 'Informed Voter' Ballot Notations," 1555–56.

92. Ibid., 1560–64.

93. Ibid., 1573–76.

94. The Court, 9–0, struck down the Missouri ballot notation law in *Cook v. Gralike*. Although the court's opinion and one of the three concurring opinions express disapproval of ballot notations in general, the main grounds on which the justices agreed concerned the authority of states to regulate congressional elections. Under the Elections Clause of the Constitution, states may regulate only the "time, place and manner" of elections; that authority does not include the right to require ballot notations, which do not merely inform voters but disadvantage candidates (531 U.S. at 522–27). In his concurring opinion, Justice Kennedy objected to the Missouri law on the grounds that could be consistent with a federal ballot notations law. He argued that the "idea of federalism" and the "theory of representative government" require that individual voters, not the states as intermediaries, "hold federal legislators to account for the conduct of their office" (531 U.S. at 528).

95. Brief for Respondents, *Cook*, 2000 WL 1409741, at 8. The district, appeals, and Supreme Court all seemed to accept this claim in varying degrees: see *Gralike v. Cook*, 996 F. Supp. 901, 905–17 (W.D. Mo. 1998); and *Cook v. Gralike*, 531 U.S. at 524–26.

96. Transcript of Oral Argument, *Cook v. Gralike*, 531 U.S. 510 (2001), 2000 WL 1673928, at 41–42 (6 November 2000).

97. For an analysis that shows that what counts as coercive depends on a moral evaluation of the "baseline" circumstances in which it takes place, see Alan Wertheimer, *Coercion* (Princeton: Princeton University Press, 1987).

98. Justice Rehnquist, joined by Justice O'Connor, concurring in the judgment in *Cook v. Gralike*, 531 U.S. at 530–31.

99. Bruce E. Cain, "Garrett's Temptation," *Virginia Law Review* 85 (November 1999): 1597. Cain evidently does not base his objection only on the alleged violation of candidates' rights; his justification for candidates' rights seems to rest at least partly on the consequences for the democratic system as a whole.

100. *Cook v. Gralike*, 531 U.S. at 525.

101. See chapter 1, pages 49–50.

102. Mo. Const. art. VIII, §§ 17(2)(a)–(h), cited in Brief for Respondents, *Cook*, 2000 WL 1409741, at 3–4.

103. Brief for Respondents, *Cook*, 2000 WL 1409741, at 22–33.

104. *Annals of the Congress of the U.S.*, ed. Joseph Gales (Washington, D.C.: Gales and Seaton, 1834–56), 1:766–67.

105. Cf. Cain, "Garrett's Temptation," 1592.

106. John E. Jackson, "Election Night Reporting and Voter Turnout," *American Journal of Political Science* 27 (November 1983): 615.

107. Jackson, "Election Night Reporting," 615; and "Note: Exit Polls and the First Amendment," *Harvard Law Review* 98 (June 1985): 1928.

108. Iyengar and Kinder, *News That Matters,* 106–10.

109. Jackson, "Election Night Reporting," 615–35. Jackson presents one of the few analyses based on information about individuals (using the American National Election Study, University of Michigan). The studies that do not find this effect on turnout mostly use aggregate data, which ignore the large regional differences in the campaigns, relative salience of issues, and variations in the weather. Jackson acknowledges that early reporting of projections may affect turnout only in elections in which the projections differ from prior expectations, as when people expect a close race but the projections indicate a clear victory (632). See also the more recent analysis by John Mark Hansen, Task Force on the Federal Election System, "Uniform Poll Closing and Uniform Closing," in *To Assure Pride and Confidence in the Electoral Process: The Final Report of the Commission's Task Force,* National Commission on Federal Election Reform, August 2001, 96–100, 106–10, available online: <http://www.reformelections.org/task/t1/t1_reports.php> (7 May 2002).

110. For example: "Concurrent resolution expressing the sense of Congress with respect to the adverse impact of early projections of election results by the news media," 98th Cong., 2d Sess., H. Con. Res. 321, *Congressional Record,* 18 June 1984, vol. 130, H16885. To see how little the positions on this issue have changed, compare the most recent hearings in Congress with any of the earlier hearings in Congress: House Task Force on Elections, Committee on House Administration and Subcommittee of the Committee on Energy and Commerce, *Hearings on Election Day Practices and Election Projections,* 97th Cong., 1st and 2d Sess., 15 December 1981 and 21 September 1982; and House Committee on Energy and Commerce, *Hearings on Election Night Coverage,* 107th Cong., 1st Sess., 14 February 2001.

111. Testimony of Roger Ailes (Chairman of Fox News), House Committee, *Hearings on Election Night Coverage,* 14 February 2001. Previously, the general policy of the networks was to wait only until "a great majority" of the polls were closed in a state. Although the new policy is an improvement, it does not prevent the networks' declarations in presidential elections from influencing voters in other states.

112. Colin C. J. Feasby, "Public Opinion Poll Restrictions, Elections, and the Charter," *University of Toronto Faculty of Law Review* 55 (spring 1997): 242.

113. Jackson, "Election Night Reporting," 629–31.

114. See especially the testimony of Paul Biemer and exchanges with members. House Committee, *Hearings on Election Night Coverage,* 14 February 2001, 52–67.

115. Ibid., 11; and Political Staff of the Washington Post, *Deadlock: The Inside Story of America's Closet Election* (New York: Public Affairs Press, 2001), 242–45.

116. Political Staff of the Washington Post, *Deadlock: The Inside Story,* 243–44; Correspondents of the New York Times, *36 Days: The Complete Chronicle of the 2000 Presidential Election Crisis* (New York: Times Books; New York: Henry Holt, 2001), 2.

117. House Committee, *Hearings on Election Night Coverage,* 14 February 2001, 105 (Louis Boccardi, AP), 111 (David Westin, ABC), 113 (Andrew Heyward, CBS), 116 (Tom Johnson, CNN), 116 (Roger Ailes, Fox), and 120 (Andrew Lack, NBC).

118. Joan Konner, James Risser, and Ben Wattenberg, *Television's Performance on Election Night 2000: A Report for CNN* (CNN: 29 January 2001), 5–7.

119. The TV executives seemed more resigned than eager in their of support of uni-

form poll closing legislation, as these responses in the hearings suggests. Louis Boccardi (AP): "[T]he reason I support . . . the uniform poll closing is that any perception that there might be [voter suppression] should be avoided. . . . And to the extent that this legislation can put an end to it and put a rest to the whole subject, I'm fully supportive of it for that reason." David Westin (ABC News): "I think we think if you pass this law, we'll stop having to answer the question." House Committee, *Hearings on Election Night Coverage,* 14 February 2001, 141.

120. Ibid., 106.

121. Anthony M. Barlow, "Restricting Election Day Exit Polling: Freedom of Expression vs. the Right to Vote," *University of Cincinnati Law Review* 58 (1990): 1020. Barlow does believe that some "remedial actions" may be necessary, however (1020–21). The claim that reports of exit polls do not restrict voters' choice is frequently made in legislative forums: "[I]t is up to a voter to vote . . . the polls are open; the voter may vote. It's just that simple. [It is] their responsibility, whether or not to be influenced [by the reports of exit polls]" (Testimony of Joan Konner, House Committee, *Hearings on Election Night Coverage,* 14 February 2001, 69).

122. A more recent bill seeks to mitigate this difficulty by extending daylight savings time in the Pacific time zone, but it still ignores the problem of Hawaii. See the Uniform Poll Closing Act (H.R. 5678), 106th Cong., 2d Sess., introduced 15 December 2000 by Representative Edward Markey (D–MA). The bill would require polls in all fifty states to close at 9:00 P.M. eastern standard time during presidential elections, which would be 7:00 P.M. Pacific daylight time. The House passed uniform poll closing bills in 1988 (H.R. 435) and 1989 (H.R. 18), but they died for lack of action in the Senate.

123. Hansen, Task Force, "Uniform Poll Closing and Uniform Closing," in *To Assure Pride: Task Force,* 100–106.

124. *Arkansas Educ. Television Comm'n v. Forbes,* 523 U.S. 666, 681–82 (1998). Also see Frederick Schauer and Richard Pildes, "Electoral Exceptionalism and the First Amendment," *Texas Law Review* 77 (June 1999): 1803–36; and Owen M. Fiss, "The Censorship of Television," *Northwestern University Law Review* (summer 1999): 1215–38.

125. Issacharoff, Karlan and Pildes, *The Law of Democracy,* 444–45.

126. For a sampling of the debate, see Anthony Corrado et al., eds., *Campaign Finance Reform: A Sourcebook* (Washington, D.C.: Brookings Institution, 1997); Annelise Anderson, ed., *Political Money: Deregulating American Politics: Selected Writings on Campaign Finance Reform* (Stanford, Calif.: Hoover Institution Press, 2000); and Diana Dwyre and Victoria A. Farrar-Myers, *Legislative Labyrinth: Congress and Campaign Finance Reform* (Washington, D.C.: CQ Press, 2001). The Brookings Institution maintains a website with useful sources and updated reports of developments in Congress and the states: <http://www.brook.edu/gs/cf/cf_hp.htm> (7 May 2002).

127. Anthony Corrado, "Money and Politics: A History of Federal Campaign Finance Law," in *Campaign Finance Reform,* 32–33, 53–55; and more generally, Robert E. Mutch, *Campaigns, Congress, and Courts: The Making of Federal Campaign Finance Law* (New York: Praeger, 1988). The 1974 reforms amended the more modest Federal Elections Campaign Act of 1971, which had prohibited contributions from corporations and unions and limited expenditures made by candidates from their personal or family funds. The amendments not only imposed limits on contributions to federal campaigns by individuals and political committees, but they also regulated total spending by presidential, Senate, and House candidates, and independent expenditures intended to support or oppose a federal candidate.

128. *Buckley v. Valeo,* 424 U.S. 1 (1976) (per curiam). For a brief survey, see Thomas Mann, "The U.S. Campaign Finance System Under Strain," in *Setting National Priorities: The 2000 Election and Beyond* (Washington, D.C.: Brookings Institution, 1999), chap. 14.

129. The original Senate version is S. 27, An Act to Amend the Federal Election Campaign Act of 1971, 107th Cong., 1st Sess., adopted 2 March 2001. The bill also restricts candidate-specific issue ads run by corporations or unions near an election, and increases hard money contribution limits for individuals. The House version that finally passed is H.R. 2356, sponsored by Christopher Shay (R–CT) and Martin Meehan (D–MA). See *Congressional Record,* 107th Cong., 2nd Sess., 13 February 2002, H339–55.

130. *Congressional Record,* 107th Cong., 1st Sess., 2 April 2001, vol. 147, S3247.

131. The largest and almost only significant predictor of monetary contributions, not surprisingly, is income. See Sidney Verba, Kay Lehman Schlozman, and Henry E. Brady, *Voice and Equality: Civic Voluntarism in American Politics* (Cambridge: Harvard University Press, 1995), 28–29; and Steven J. Rosenstone and John Mark Hansen, *Mobilization, Participation, and Democracy in America* (New York: Macmillan, 1993), 43–44, 134.

132. Senator John Kerry (D–MA), *Congressional Record,* 107th Cong., 1st Sess., 27 March 2001, vol. 147, S2930.

133. Senator Orrin Hatch (R–Utah), *Congressional Record,* 107th Cong., 1st Sess., 28 March 2001, vol. 147, S3039.

134. The Court did not itself defend its decision as a compromise between liberty and equality, but several commentators have suggested that such a compromise is the most plausible way to understand the decision. See most notably Kathleen Sullivan, "Against Campaign Finance Reform," *Utah Law Review* (1998): 313; and "Political Money and Freedom of Speech," *U.C. Davis Law Review* 30 (spring 1997): 665–68.

135. The Court itself later identified a "different type of corruption in the political arena"—corporate political expenditures. *Austin v. Michigan Chamber of Commerce,* 494 U.S. 652 (1990).

136. As a result, the controlling opinions in recent cases have continued to accept the distinction as fundamental. See Justice Breyer's opinion in *Colorado Republican Campaign Committee v. FEC,* 518 U.S. 604, 611–18 (1996).

137. John Rawls, *Political Liberalism* (New York: Columbia University Press, 1993), 326–27, 359–63. Also see Ronald Dworkin, "The Curse of American Politics," *New York Review of Books* (17 October 1996), 19–24; Cass R. Sunstein, *Democracy and the Problem of Free Speech* (New York: Free Press, 1993), 94–101; and David A. Strauss, "Corruption, Equality, and Campaign Finance Reform," *Columbia Law Review* 94 (May 1994): 1369–89.

138. Rawls, *Political Liberalism,* 327.

139. *Buckley v. Valeo,* 424 U.S. at 49–51.

140. Rawls, *Political Liberalism,* 360–61.

141. Ibid., 361 (emphasis added).

142. Elsewhere Rawls recognizes that limitations on liberty should be assessed according to how they affect the "scheme of basic liberties" or "system of liberty" as a whole. See *Political Liberalism,* 331–40; and *A Theory of Justice,* rev. ed. (Cambridge: Harvard University Press, 1999), 201–2, 213, 220.

143. See Laura I. Langbein, "Money and Access: Some Empirical Evidence," *Journal of Politics* 48 (November 1986): 1052–62; Richard L. Hall and Frank W. Wayman, "Buying Time: Moneyed Interests and the Mobilization of Bias in Congressional Committees," *American Political Science Review* 84 (September 1990): 797–820. For a critical review

contending that contributors exercise more influence than much of the social science literature implies, see Daniel Hays Lowenstein, "On Campaign Finance Reform: The Root of All Evil is Deeply Rooted," *Hofstra Law Review* 18 (fall 1989): 313–35. More generally, see Morris P. Fiorina, *Congress: Keystone of the Washington Establishment,* 2d ed. (New Haven: Yale University Press, 1989), 129; and Frank Sorauf, *Inside Campaign Finance: Myths and Realities* (New Haven: Yale University Press, 1992).

144. Senator Bill Frist (R–TN), *Congressional Record,* 107th Cong., 1st Sess., 27 March 2001, vol. 147, S2931.

145. Senator J. Bennett Johnston (D–LA), *Congressional Record,* daily ed., 103rd Cong., 2d Sess., 4 May 1994, S5157. For a more sophisticated argument suggesting that disclosure is the proper remedy for most forms of potential deception that would otherwise impair free choice, see Samuel Issacharoff and Pamela S. Karlan, "The Hydraulics of Campaign Finance Reform," *Texas Law Review* 77 (June 1999): 1718–23.

146. Dennis F. Thompson, *Ethics in Congress: From Individual to Institutional Corruption* (Washington, D.C.: Brookings Institution, 1995), 137–43.

147. Ironically, Feingold won reelection to the Senate in 1998 to continue to fight for reform only because his supporters in the campaign acted contrary to his stated position on reform. After voluntarily limiting his expenditures in the spirit of the reform he favored, Feingold fell far behind in the polls. His opponent's massive advertising drive would have defeated him had not his supporters financed, without his approval, a counterdrive in the last days of the campaign. See Glenn R. Simpson, "Late Storm of Issue-Ad Spending Sweeps Places Like Wisconsin, Chills a Senator," *Wall Street Journal,* 29 October 1998, sec. A, p. 24; and Thomas W. Still, "Some Winners, Some Losers as Dust Settles," *Wisconsin State Journal,* 5 November 1998, p. 13A. A similar irony may be found in McCain's effort to persuade some House Republicans to support the Senate version of McCain–Feingold by reminding them of his help in raising funds for their campaign. Philip Shenon, "House Critics Call McCain a Bully on Campaign Bill," *New York Times,* 9 July 2001, sec. A, p. 8. In neither case does the irony reveal hypocrisy or inconsistency, but rather it illustrates a common dilemma of reform—namely, the necessity of exploiting the defects in a system now in order to eliminate them later.

148. For the view that dealing in political offices should be a "blocked exchange," see Michael Walzer, *Spheres of Justice: A Defense of Pluralism and Equality* (New York: Basic Books, 1983), 95–128. On the claim that money is a "unique political resource because it can be converted into many other political resources," see Lowenstein, "On Campaign Finance Reform," 301–2, and the citations there.

149. "Senate OKs Lifting Individual Donation Limits to Candidates," *St. Louis Post–Dispatch,* 29 March 2001, p. A1.

150. See Baron de Montesquieu, *The Spirit of Laws,* ed. David Wallace Carrithers, trans. Thomas Nugent (Berkeley: University of California Press, 1977), pt. 1, bk. 5, chap. 19; and Jeremy Bentham, "The Rationale of Reward," in *The Works of Jeremy Bentham,* ed. John Bowring (Edinburgh: William Tait, 1843), 5:246–48. More generally, see Albert O. Hirschman, *The Passions and the Interests: Political Arguments for Capitalism before Its Triumph* (Princeton: Princeton University Press, 1977).

151. Frank J. Sorauf, *Inside Campaign Finance: Myths and Realities* (New Haven: Yale University Press, 1992), 187.

152. David B. Magleby and Candice J. Nelson, *The Money Chase: Congressional Campaign Finance Reform* (Washington, D.C.: Brookings Institution, 1990), 47.

153. For some earlier proposals, see Joel Fleishman and Pope McCorkle, "Level-Up Rather Than Level-Down: Toward a New Theory of Campaign Finance Reform," *Journal of Law and Politics* 1 (spring 1984): 275–98; and Gary C. Jacobson, *The Politics of Congressional Elections*, 3d ed. (New York: HarperCollins, 1992), 63–79. It should be noted, however, that providing public funding without imposing any ceilings could result in simply increasing the total cost of campaigns, without changing the advantage that incumbents enjoy over challengers.

154. Joseph E. Cantor, Denise S. Rutkus, and Kevin B. Greely, *Free and Reduced-Rate Television Time for Political Candidates* (Washington, D.C.: Congressional Research Service, Library of Congress, 7 July 1997).

155. Their effect on free choice is not the only serious problem with fundraising practices. See Thompson, *Ethics in Congress*, 115–24.

156. Sullivan, "Against Campaign Finance Reform," 317–20.

157. Richard Briffault, "Issue Advocacy: Redrawing the Elections/Politics Line," *Texas Law Review* 77 (June 1999): 1753–54.

158. Ibid., 1764–66. Other important contributions to developing the idea of an electoral domain distinct from ordinary politics are Schauer and Pildes, "Electoral Exceptionalism and the First Amendment"; and C. Edwin Baker, "Campaign Expenditures and Free Speech," *Harvard Civil Rights-Civil Liberties Law Review* 33 (winter 1998): 1–55.

159. Issacharoff, Karlan, and Pildes, *The Law of Democracy*, 533–45. Also see Brennan Center for Justice Policy Committee on Political Advertising, "Five New Ideas to Deal with the Problems Posed by Campaign Appeals Masquerading as Issue Advocacy," May 2000, available online: <http://www.brennancenter.org/programs/cmag_temp/cmag_recs.html> (7 May 2002).

160. Some form of this general objection may be found in: Sullivan, "Political Money," 680–82; Issacharoff and Karlan, "Hydraulics of Campaign Finance Reform," 1724–25; Daniel R. Ortiz, "The Democratic Paradox of Campaign Finance Reform," *Stanford Law Review* 50 (February 1998): 893–914; and Bruce E. Cain, "Moralism and Realism in Campaign Finance Reform," *University of Chicago Legal Forum* 1995: 122–23.

161. Me. Rev. Stat. Ann. tit. 21-A, §§ 1001–20A and 1121–28. (Legislative materials were generously provided by the Maine State Law and Legislative Reference Library, Augusta, Maine.) See Theodore Lazarus, "The Maine Clean Election Act: Cleansing Public Institutions of Private Money," *Columbia Journal of Law and Social Problems* 34 (fall 2000): 79–132; Deborah E. Schneider, "As Goes Maine? The 1996 Maine Clean Election Act: Innovations and Implications for Future Campaign Finance Reforms at the State and Federal Level," *Washington University Journal of Urban and Contemporary Law* 55 (winter 1999): 235–72; and Michael E. Campion, "Note: The Maine Clean Election Act: The Future of Campaign Finance Reform," *Fordham Law Review* 66 (May 1998): 2391–2434.

162. Rick Klein, "Clean Elections Act Alters Terrain in Maine," *Boston Globe*, 26 February 2001, p. A1.

163. Ibid.

164. State Committeeman Leo Robichaud (Republican), Maine House of Representatives, *Legislative Record*, 30 March 1996, H2003.

165. *Daggett v. Commission on Governmental Ethics and Election Practices*, 205 F.3d 445 (2000). See "Public Financing Grants," in *Report of the Commission*, Governor's Blue-Ribbon Commission on Campaign Finance Reform, State of Wisconsin (May 1997),

1:26–29; and Wisconsin Democracy Campaign, "Reform Coalition Calls on Finance Committee to Act on Ellis–George Campaign Finance Reform Bill," 23 October 2001, available online: <http://www.wisdc.org/sb104jfcrelease.htm> (7 May 2002).

166. James Madison, *The Federalist* No. 51, 356. The concept of pluralism of pressures is not simply an application but an extension of Madison's policy (with which he justifies the separation of powers) because it applies to candidates and voters as well as officials, and because it emphasizes that individuals and institutions act on mixed motives (not only an institutionally determined "ambition").

CHAPTER THREE

1. James Madison, *The Federalist* No. 63, ed. Benjamin Fletcher Wright (Cambridge: Harvard University Press, 1961), 417.

2. James Madison, *The Federalist* No. 39, 280–81. Like Tocqueville later, Madison defended indirect elections—"the policy of refining popular appointments by successive filtrations." But he worried that this policy "might be pushed too far," and argued strongly for direct election of members of the House. The Constitution would be "more stable and durable if it should rest on the solid foundation of the people themselves, than if it should stand merely on the pillars of the Legislatures." *The Records of the Federal Convention of 1787*, ed. Max Farrand (New Haven: Yale University Press, 1966), 31 May 1787, 1:50.

3. *Vera v. Richards*, 861 F. Supp. 1304, 1334 (S.D. Tex. 1994). The quotation comes from the opinion of Judge Edith H. Jones in a district court decision that struck down racial districting in three congressional districts in Texas. She wrote that "the Legislature obligingly carved out districts of apparent supporters of incumbents, as suggested by the incumbents, and then added appendages to connect their residences to those districts. . . . The final result seems not one in which the people select their representatives, but in which the representatives have selected the people." 861 F. Supp. at 1334.

4. For a defense of the moral basis of majority rule, see Jeremy Waldron, *The Dignity of Legislation* (Cambridge: Cambridge University Press, 1999), 147–50. For other analyses of the justification of majority rule, see Charles R. Beitz, *Political Equality: An Essay in Democratic Theory* (Princeton: Princeton University Press, 1989), 58–67; Robert Dahl, *Democracy and Its Critics* (New Haven: Yale University Press, 1989), 139–41; Bruce Ackerman, *Social Justice in the Liberal State* (New Haven: Yale University Press, 1980), 277–93; and Amartya Sen, *Collective Choice and Social Welfare* (San Francisco: Holden-Day, 1970), 71–73. For more on the limits of majority rule, see Amy Gutmann and Dennis Thompson, *Democracy and Disagreement* (Cambridge: Harvard University Press, 1996), 27–33.

5. Thomas E. Cronin, *Direct Democracy: The Politics of Initiative, Referendum and Recall* (Cambridge: Harvard University Press, 1999), 38–59. The initiative should be distinguished from the referendum: in the former a majority of citizens can directly enact a law, whereas in the latter citizens ratify or reject a proposal already adopted by the legislature. An initiative sometimes has the effect of a referendum, as when voters overturn a law enacted earlier by the legislature.

6. The source of the numbers in this paragraph is the Initiative and Referendum Institute, whose website provides up-to-date information and analysis of these practices in the United States: <http://www.iandrinstitute.org/> (7 May 2002).

7. The amendment limited the terms of state representatives to three terms (six years), state senators to two terms (eight years), U.S. representatives to three terms, and U.S. sen-

ators from Arkansas to two terms. Also, executives in the state government were limited to four-year terms. Ark. Const. amend. 73, §§ 1–3 (§ 3 superseded by amend. 76).

8. When the case reached the U.S. Supreme Court, most of the oral argument was devoted to the question whether term limits are a qualification (which the states could not regulate) or a "manner" of election (which they could), or some "third something-or-other" (which no one could quite categorize). Transcript of Oral Argument, *U.S. Term Limits, Inc. v. Thornton*, 514 U.S. 779 (1995), 1994 WL 714634, at 17 (29 November 1994).

9. Justice Robert H. Dudley in dissent, *U.S. Term Limits, Inc. v. Hill*, 316 Ark. 251, 267–70 (1994).

10. From the preamble to the "Term Limitation Amendment," adopted 3 November 1992. Ark. Const. amend. 73, §§ 1–3 (§ 3 superseded by amend. 76).

11. For a thoughtful critical analysis of the popular and academic arguments (from the perspective of a proponent), see Einer Elhauge, "Are Term Limits Undemocratic?" *University of Chicago Law Review* (winter 1997): 83–203. See also George F. Will, *Restoration: Congress, Term Limits and the Recovery of Deliberative Democracy* (New York: Free Press, 1992); Gerald Benjamin and Michael J. Malbin, eds., *Limiting Legislative Terms* (Washington, D.C.: Congressional Quarterly, 1992); Elizabeth Garrett, "Term Limitations and the Myth of the Citizen-Legislator," *Cornell Law Review* 81 (March 1996): 623–97; and Bernard Grofman, ed., *Legislative Term Limits: Public Choice Perspectives* (Boston: Kluwer, 1996).

12. *U.S. Term Limits, Inc. v. Hill.*

13. *U.S. Term Limits, Inc. v. Thornton.*

14. Ibid., 790–820, 884–925.

15. "The majority and dissent battled fiercely over text and history, but to a draw." Kathleen M. Sullivan, "Dueling Sovereignties: *U.S. Term Limits, Inc. v. Thornton*," *Harvard Law Review* 109 (November 1995): 80. See also Mark Killenbeck and Steve Sheppard, "Another Such Victory? Term Limits, Section 2 of the Fourteenth Amendment, and the Right to Presentation," *Hastings Law Journal* 45 (July 1994): 1121–1221.

16. Farrand, *Records of the Federal Convention*, 10 August 1787, 2:249–50.

17. Ibid., 250.

18. Justice Thomas writing in dissent, *U.S. Term Limits, Inc. v. Thornton*, 514 U.S. at 877.

19. Ibid., 871.

20. *U.S. Term Limits, Inc. v. Thornton*, 514 U.S. at 783, 793, 795, 818, 845. Both sides in the judicial dispute cited Hamilton's formulation (which should not be confused with the "Hamiltonian proviso" described later in this chapter). See *Elliot's Debates* (*The debates in the several state conventions on the adoption of the federal Constitution*), ed. Jonathan Elliot, vol. 2 (Philadelphia: J. B. Lippincott, 1836–59), 257. Neither side mentioned that Hamilton (speaking in the New York convention during the ratification debates) was addressing a proposal to enlarge the size of the House of Representatives, not the question of the regulation of elections.

21. Transcript of Oral Argument, *U.S. Term Limits, Inc. v. Thornton*, 1994 WL 714634, at 7–8.

22. Ibid., 17.

23. Ibid., 18.

24. Bernard Manin, *The Principles of Representative Government* (Cambridge: Cambridge University Press, 1997), 132–60.

25. *The Politics of Aristotle,* ed. and trans. Ernest Barker (New York: Oxford University Press, 1962), bk. 4, chap. 9, p. 177; Jean Jacques Rousseau, *The Social Contract,* trans. Maurice Cranston (New York: Penguin, 1987), bk. 4, chap. 3; and Baron de Montesquieu, *The Spirit of Laws,* ed. David Wallace Carrithers, trans. Thomas Nugent (Berkeley: University of California Press, 1977), pt. 1, bk. 2.

26. The only significant proposal to use lot was never voted on: James Wilson's suggestion that the president be chosen by a college of electors, who themselves would be chosen by lot from members of Congress. Wilson himself admitted that this is "not a digested idea and might be liable to strong objection." Elbridge Gerry immediately objected, with presumably unintended irony, "[T]his is committing too much to chance." The motion was indefinitely postponed. See Farrand, *Records of the Federal Convention,* 24 July 1787, 2:99, 103, 105.

27. Madison, *The Federalist* No. 57, 384 (quoted, from a different edition, by Justice Stevens in *U.S. Term Limits, Inc. v. Thornton*).

28. Ibid., 383.

29. Manin, *Principles of Representative Government,* 114–16.

30. John A. Ferejohn, "On the Decline of Competition in Congressional Elections," *American Political Science Review* 71 (March 1977): 166–76; Glenn R. Parker, "The Advantage of Incumbency in House Elections," *American Politics Quarterly* 8 (October 1980): 449–64; Andrew Gelman and Gary King, "Estimating Incumbency Advantage without Bias," *American Journal of Political Science* 34 (November 1990): 1142–64; James C. Garand, "Electoral Marginality in State Legislative Elections, 1968–1986," *Legislative Studies Quarterly* 16 (February 1991): 7–28; Gary W. Cox and Jonathan N. Katz, "Why Did the Incumbency Advantage in U.S. House Elections Grow?" *American Journal of Political Science* 40 (May 1996): 478–97; Ronald Keith Gaddie and Lesli E. McCollum, "Money and the Incumbency Advantage in U.S. House Elections," in *The U.S. House of Representatives: Reform or Rebuild?* ed. Joseph F. Zimmerman and Wilma Rule (Westport, Conn.: Praeger, 2000), 71–87; and William D. Berry, Michael B. Berkman, and Stuart Schneiderman, "Legislative Professionalism and Incumbent Reelection," *American Political Science Review* 94 (December 2000): 859–74.

31. *U.S. Term Limits, Inc. v. Thornton,* 514 U.S. at 820, 846.

32. Sullivan, "Dueling Sovereignties," 78–109.

33. Farrand, *Records of the Federal Convention,* 10 August 1787, 2:249–50.

34. On fusion candidacies, see chapter 2, pages 70–80. Also see Samuel Issacharoff and Richard Pildes, "Politics as Markets: Partisan Lockups of the Democratic Process," *Stanford Law Review* 50 (February 1998): 643–717, esp. 651.

35. Bruce Ackerman, "The Court Packs Itself," *American Prospect* 12 (12 February 2001): 48.

36. Elhauge, "Are Term Limits Undemocratic?" 114–41. States sought to overcome this collective action problem in various ways—for example, by specifying that the limits would not go into effect until twenty-one or more states had adopted them, and by stipulating a delayed effective date. See John M. Carey, *Term Limits and Legislative Representation* (Cambridge: Cambridge University Press, 1998), 12–13.

37. Linda Cohen and Matthew Spitzer, "Positive Political Theory and Political Law: Term Limits," *Georgetown Law Journal* 80 (February 1992): 477–521. Also see Morris P. Fiorina, *Retrospective Voting in American National Elections* (New Haven: Yale University Press, 1981), 25–43; Jeffrey S. Banks, Linda R. Cohen, and Roger G. Noll, "The Politics of Commercial R&D Programs," in *The Technology Pork Barrel,* ed. Linda R. Cohen and

Roger G. Noll (Washington, D.C.: Brookings Institution, 1991), 53, 61; and Linda R. Cohen and Roger G. Noll, *The Political Discount Rate* (Stanford: Center for Economic Policy Research, 1990).

38. Alexander Hamilton, *The Federalist* No. 59, 394–95.

39. Ibid., 394.

40. "If the qualifications set forth in the text of the Constitution are to be changed, that text must be amended." *U.S. Term Limits, Inc. v. Thornton,* 514 U.S. at 783.

41. See Donald S. Lutz, "Toward a Theory of Constitutional Amendment," in *Responding to Imperfection: The Theory and Practice of Constitutional Amendment,* ed. Sanford Levinson (Princeton: Princeton University Press, 1995), 237–74, esp. 261, table 11. On Lutz's "index of difficulty" of amendment, the U.S. Constitution ranks at the top, while most U.S. state constitutions rank near the bottom.

42. U.S. Const. art. V offers two ways to amend the Constitution: a proposal passed by two-thirds of both the Senate and the House, and ratified by three-quarters of the states; or a proposal passed by the conventions in the two-thirds of the states, and ratified by three-quarters of the states. The second method has never been used. On the amendment process generally, see Levinson, *Responding to Imperfection.*

43. The amendments were the Seventeenth (instituting direct election of senators), Nineteenth (granting women the right to vote), Twenty-Second (limiting presidents to two terms), Twenty-Fourth (abolishing poll taxes), Twenty-Fifth (granting residents of the District of Columbia the right to vote), and the Twenty-Sixth (lowering the voting age to eighteen). For a history of some of these amendments (as well as earlier ones), see Alexander Keyssar, *The Right to Vote* (New York: Basic Books, 2000), 26–27, 42–43, 175–76, 184–89, 278–81.

44. Gerald Benjamin and Thomas Gais, "Constitutional Conventionphobia," *Hofstra Law and Policy Symposium* 1 (1996): 62, 69–72.

45. Jefferson to John Wayles Eppes, 24 June 1813, *The Writings of Thomas Jefferson,* ed. Andrew A. Lipscomb and Albert Ellery Bergh, memorial ed. (Washington, D.C.: Thomas Jefferson Memorial Association, 1903–4), 13:270. The Madisonian proviso is grounded in some beliefs that Jefferson held even more strongly than did Madison: the value of encouraging political change and opposing entrenched majorities. On Jefferson's generational argument, see Herbert E. Sloan, *Principle and Interest: Thomas Jefferson and the Problem of Debt* (New York: Oxford University Press, 1995).

46. Jefferson to Samuel Kercheval, 12 July 1816, *The Writings of Thomas Jefferson,* 15:42. For an analysis of Jefferson's attitudes toward constitutional change, see John R. Vile, *The Constitutional Amending Process in American Thought* (New York: Praeger, 1992), 59–78.

47. See the essays in Levinson, *Responding to Imperfection;* and Benjamin and Gais, "Constitutional Conventionphobia," 53–77.

48. For criticisms consistent with popular sovereignty (including versions of those presented here), see Hans A. Linde, "Taking Oregon's Initiative toward a New Century," *Willamette Law Review* 34 (summer/fall 1998): 391–419; Hans A. Linde, "Practicing Theory: The Forgotten Law of Initiative Lawmaking," *UCLA Law Review* 45 (August 1998): 1735–60; and Sherman Clark, "A Popular Critique of Direct Democracy," *Harvard Law Review* 112 (December 1998): 434–81.

49. Thomas E. Cronin, *Direct Democracy,* 70–77; Shaun Bowler and Todd Donovan, *Demanding Choices: Opinion, Voting and Direct Democracy* (Ann Arbor: University of Michigan Press, 1998), 7–20; and Elizabeth Garrett, "Who Directs Direct Democracy?"

University of Chicago Law School Roundtable 4 (1997): 17–36. Initiatives are less often translated into public policy than is generally assumed. See Elisabeth R. Gerber et al., *Stealing the Initiative: How State Government Responds to Direct Democracy* (Upper Saddle River, N.J.: Prentice-Hall, 2001), 15–26. To the extent that governments do not comply with initiatives, their undesirable policy consequences are obviously avoided, but their value as a process for the expression of popular will is also lost.

50. In oral argument in the U.S. Supreme Court in the Colorado case discussed later in this section, one justice asked: "How many of these election gypsies are there who wander around from State to State?" The attorney general replied: "[I]n any given petition there can be several hundred." Transcript of Oral Argument, *Buckley v. American Constitutional Law Found.*, 525 U.S. 182 (1999), 1998 WL 731585, at 15 (14 October 1998).

51. *Meyer v. Grant*, 486 U.S. 414 (1988).

52. Colo. Const. art. V, § 1(6), 1981 Colorado Sessions Laws, chap. 56, § 4.

53. Peter G. Chronis, "Law Impedes Right to Petition, Lawsuit Claims," *Denver Post*, 15 July 1993, p. B-05.

54. *Buckley v. American Constitutional Law Found.* The Court protected anonymous speech more generally in *McIntyre v. Ohio Elections Comm'n*, 514 U.S. 334 (1995).

55. *Buckley v. American Constitutional Law Found.*, 525 U.S. at 199.

56. For the first point, see the remark by one justice: "You know, if, in fact, someone sits at a shopping center and waits for people to come up to them, and they're anxious to get as many signatures as they can, one would suspect that there's not much debate. If someone is going to say, I don't like that proposition, the petition circulator just says, okay, go on. I want someone who will sign." Transcript of Oral Argument, *Buckley*, 1998 WL 731585, at 17. For the other point, see Justice Kennedy's remark: "It seems to me that this promotes free speech rather than retards it. It gives the voter who's considering signing the petition added information." Ibid., 44.

57. *Buckley v. American Constitutional Law Found.*, 525 U.S. at 195, quoting *Meyer v. Grant*, 486 U.S. at 422–23.

58. This exchange in the oral argument is illustrative:

Question: Isn't there something in the record that suggests that it's easier to determine whether someone is a registered voter than it is to determine whether they're a resident?
[Colorado attorney general Gale] Norton: We have specific lists of registered voters. We do not have lists of people who are otherwise residents. It gives us a concrete place to answer that question.

Transcript of Oral Argument, *Buckley*, 1998 WL 731585, at 9–10.

59. Trial testimony, quoted in *Buckley v. American Constitutional Law Found.*, 525 U.S. at 194.

60. Trial testimony, quoted in ibid., 219.

61. See the comments of Justices O'Connor and Rehnquist in ibid., 218, 228.

62. In the oral argument the state's attorney general briefly defended the registration requirement as providing a way to demonstrate a "commitment to the Colorado lawmaking process"— which could be interpreted as a nascent version of the argument presented in the text. Transcript of Oral Argument, *Buckley*, 1998 WL 731585, at 10.

63. *Buckley v. American Constitutional Law Found.*, 525 U.S. at 228.

64. Alexis de Tocqueville, *Democracy in America*, ed. J. P. Mayer, trans. George Lawrence (Garden City, N.Y.: Doubleday, 1969), 1:89, 95, 89–90.

65. See, e.g., the comments of Representative Melvin Watt (D–NC) (the states have "a lot closer first-hand experience"), and Robinson Everett, one of the witnesses ("leaving intact the boundaries of existing political subdivisions . . . enhance[s] participation by voters in the political process"). House Committee on the Judiciary, *States' Choice of Voting Systems Act: Hearings before the Subcommittee on the Constitution on H.R. 1173*, 106th Cong., 1st Sess., 23 September 1999, 68, 35.

66. Congressman Bob Barr (R–GA), House Committee, *States' Choice of Voting Systems Act: Hearings*, 77.

67. See, e.g., *Final Report of the Vermont Commission to Study Instant Runoff Voting*, presented to the Vermont House of Representatives pursuant to H.R. 37, January 1999, available online: <http://www.fairvote.org/irv/vermont/index.html> (7 May 2002).

68. See, e.g., *The Voter's Choice Act* (H.R. 1189), introduced by Representative Cynthia McKinney (D–GA) on 22 March 2001. It would permit states to institute multiseat districts with proportional representation; it would also express the sense of Congress in favor of using instant runoff voting in presidential elections.

69. *States' Choice of Voting Systems Act*, 106th Cong., 1st Sess., H.R. 1173.

70. Tom Campbell (R–CA), House Committee, *States' Choice of Voting Systems Act: Hearings*, 18–20.

71. See chapter 1, page 52.

72. House Committee, *States' Choice of Voting Systems Act: Hearings*, 12.

73. Testimony of Katharine Inglis Butler (professor of law, University of South Carolina), ibid., 160.

74. House Committee, *States' Choice of Voting Systems Act: Hearings*, 72–74, 59–61.

75. Testimony of Roger Clegg, Center for Equal Opportunity, ibid., 86.

76. Ibid.

77. This objection is usually combined with criticism of cumulative voting, but at least one witness made clear that what she opposed is the mixture of the two systems: "The issue here . . . is not the merits of interest group representation via cumulative voting versus territorial representation via single member districts. Rather it is whether Congress can fairly permit a system that provides for direct interest group representation for some citizens, but not all." Testimony of Katharine Inglis Butler, House Committee, *States' Choice of Voting Systems Act: Hearings*, 161.

78. Before 1842, members of Congress were elected in a mixed system. The larger states used district-based elections while the smaller states used at-large elections. The different systems corresponded to different conceptions of representation; the larger states emphasized demographic aggregation of interests, the smaller states, geographic combinations. See Rosemarie Zagarri, *The Politics of Size: Representation in the United States, 1776–1850* (Ithaca: Cornell University Press, 1987).

79. Testimony of Katharine Inglis Butler, House Committee, *States' Choice of Voting Systems Act: Hearings*, 161.

80. Edmund Burke, *Burke's Politics*, ed. Ross Hoffman and Paul Levack (New York: Knopf, 1959), 116.

81. See, e.g., the testimony of Theodore Arrington: this proposal is "giving some States the authority to experiment. . . . If they are not successful . . . they will disappear. If they are successful, the other States will copy them. That is the laboratory that our Federal system is." House Committee, *States' Choice of Voting Systems Act: Hearings*, 96.

82. Representative Gaston I. Cantens (R–Miami), State of Florida, *Journal of the House of Representatives,* First Special Session, "A" of 2000–2002 (12 December 2000), 52.

83. Representative Mike Fasano (R–New Port Richey), ibid., 35.

84. Representative Paula Bono Dockery (R–Lakeland): "You are not here to determine the next president . . . you are here to ensure that Florida's 25 electoral votes are included along with the other 49 states to determine who the next president will be" (ibid., 31).

85. For example, Representative Bendross-Mindingall (D–Miami), ibid., 41; and Representative Dorothy Cusack (D–Leland), ibid., 47. The Republicans also complained about disenfranchisement—but of the absentee voters, whose ballots the Democrats had challenged, and whose votes were expected to go heavily for Bush: the Democrats are trying "to systematically strip service men and women of their right to vote. [W]e certainly shouldn't forget the Americans who serve us overseas. [We must] include votes cast by American defenders of liberty on guard around the world." Representative Jerry Louis Maygarden (R–Pensacola), ibid., 36.

86. Representative Timothy Ryan (D–Dania Beach), ibid., 46. Another opponent similarly declared that "the people . . . don't want politicians in the state legislature deciding who's going to be their next president." Representative Kenneth A. Gottlieb (D–Miramar), ibid., 53.

87. Ibid., 55. Also see Representative Lois Frankel (D–West Palm Beach), ibid., 59.

88. "Each State shall appoint, in such Manner as the Legislature thereof may direct, a Number of Electors." U.S. Const. art. I, § 1.

89. Michael J. Glennon, *When No Majority Rules: The Electoral College and Presidential Succession* (Washington, D.C.: Congressional Quarterly, 1992), 10–12.

90. Representative Henry R. Storrs (New York), *Register of Debates,* 19th Cong., 1st Sess., 17 February 1826, 1405.

91. Samuel Issacharoff, Pamela S. Karlan, and Richard H. Pildes, *When Elections Go Bad: The Law of Democracy and the Presidential Election of 2000* (New York: Foundation Press, 2001), 105–7.

92. The fullest argument in the debate was presented by Representative J. Dudley Goodlette (R–Naples), Florida, *Journal of House* (12 December 2000), 28–29. For the most incisive constitutional argument, see the Brief of the Florida Senate and House as Amici Curiae in Support of Neither Party, *Bush v. Palm Beach County Canvassing Bd.,* 531 U.S. 70 (2000).

93. 3 U.S.C. § 2 (1948).

94. Some members also invoked another statute (the so-called safe harbor provision) that would require Congress to accept Florida's electors if they were selected by a process that remained unchanged after election day. But as opponents pointed out, the disputes about the election were about whether the process had changed, and therefore the "safe harbor" had already been lost. "There is no question the safe harbor is gone, we are out of the harbor folks. [I]t doesn't exist because there is a contest." Representative Dan Gelber (D–Miami Beach), Florida, *Journal of House* (12 December 2000), 33.

95. Ibid., 32.

96. The certification is arguably insufficient. During the legislative hearings prior to this session, the Republicans' expert witness, Einer Elhauge, contended that the relevant statute (tit. 3, § 5) refers to the "final determination of any controversy or contest," and therefore means that the "mere fact that a contest is pending and not finally adjudicated by December 12th would deprive the election of conclusivity when it is judged by

congress." Florida Legislature, Select Joint Committee on the Manner of Appointment of Presidential Electors, *Proceedings,* 28 November 2000, p. 11, lines 6, 10–14.

97. Florida, *Journal of House* (12 December 2000), 32.

98. Testimony of Einer Elhauge, Florida Legislature, Select Joint Committee, *Proceedings,* 28 November 2000, p. 24, lines 9–16.

99. Representative J. D. Alexander (R–Winter Haven), Florida, *Journal of House* (12 December 2000), 29–30. Also see remarks of Representative Marco Rubio (R–Miami), ibid., 45.

100. For example, Representative Lois Frankel (D–West Palm Beach), ibid., 31–32.

101. *Bush v. Gore,* 531 U.S. 98 (2000). The separate concurrence by three justices asserted, while the dissenters denied, that the Florida Supreme Court had changed the law. But the per curiam opinion of the court decided the case on other grounds (namely, that the variation in standards for the manual recounts violated the equal protection clause).

102. "Without the intervention of the State legislatures, the president . . . cannot be elected at all. They must in all cases have a great share in his appointment, and will, perhaps, in most cases, of themselves determine it." Madison, *The Federalist* No. 45, 327. In the Florida debate, Madison was invoked by J. Dudley Goodlette (R–Naples), Florida, *Journal of House* (12 December 2000), 29.

103. "The difficulty of finding an unexceptionable process for appointing the Executive Organ of a Government such as that of the U. S., was deeply felt by the Convention; and as the final arrangement of it took place in the latter stage of the Session, it was not exempt from a degree of the hurrying influence produced by fatigue and impatience in all such Bodies: tho' the degree was much less than usually prevails in them." Madison to George Hay, 23 August 1823, in Farrand, *Records of the Federal Convention of 1787,* 3:458–59.

104. "And there is a basic reason that this power was put in the hands of the state Legislatures. They were viewed as the entity closest to the will of the people." Remarks of Einer Elhauge, Florida Legislature, Select Joint Committee, *Proceedings,* 28 November 2000, p. 6, lines 1–3.

105. Brief of the Florida Senate and House as Amici Curiae in Support of Neither Party, at 4–9, *Bush v. Palm Beach County Canvassing Bd.*

106. Hamilton favored keeping the selection process out of the hands of the state legislatures for other reasons as well. Rather than a "pre-established body" like the state legislature, a separate group of individuals "chosen by the people" for the "special purpose" and at the "particular juncture" of a presidential election, is best designed for expressing the "sense of the people." *The Federalist* No. 68, 441. He also believed that a separate group of electors would be less vulnerable to "cabal, intrigue and corruption" and would be more likely to select the best qualified person, one less beholden to those who chose him (441).

107. Congress exercises its authority through the Electoral Count Act of 1887, now codified in 3 U.S.C. § 15 (1948), which lays out a complex set of procedures for counting electoral votes in the event of a dispute about their validity. The Act was a response to the Tilden–Hayes election in which the validity of some of the electoral votes of both candidates was challenged (including the votes from Florida). Although some scholars question whether the Act is consistent with the Constitution's grant of power to the states to choose electors (art. II, § 1), the Act has never been successfully challenged.

108. For example, Representative J. D. Alexander (R–Winter Haven), Florida, *Journal of House* (12 December 2000), 30.

109. Representative Timothy Ryan (D–Dania Beach), ibid., 46.

110. Representative Christopher Smith (D–Ft. Lauderdale), ibid., 38.

111. Laurence Tribe, Transcript of Oral Argument, *Bush v. Palm Beach Country Canvassing Bd.,* 531 U.S. 70 (2000), 2000 WL 1763666, at 44–45 (1 December 2000).

112. "The citizens that voted for us relied . . . on our . . . party affiliations. [W]hy shouldn't we rely on party affiliation to guide us? [L]et us be loyal to the voters who elected us." Representative Carlos Lacasa (R–Miami), Florida, *Journal of House* (12 December 2000), 43.

113. The constitutional requirement that all states hold elections on the same day may be read as an expression of this principle (art. II, § 1).

114. Issacharoff, Karlan, and Pildes, *When Elections Go Bad,* 108–16.

115. Samuel Issacharoff, Pamela S. Karlan, and Richard H. Pildes, *The Law of Democracy: Legal Structure of the Political Process,* 2d ed. (Westbury, N.Y.: Foundation Press, 2001), 1038–88.

116. *Delahunt v. Johnston,* 423 Mass. 731 (1996).

117. The most subtle argument is by Richard A. Posner, *Breaking the Deadlock: The 2000 Election, the Constitution, and the Courts* (Princeton: Princeton University Press, 2001), 92–189. Also see Richard Epstein, " 'In such Manner as the Legislature Thereof May Direct,' " in *The Vote: Bush, Gore and the Supreme Court,* ed. Cass R. Sunstein and Richard A. Epstein (Chicago: University of Chicago Press, 2001), 36–37.

118. Posner, *Breaking the Deadlock,* 109–15, 151–61. In his concurring opinion in *Bush v. Gore,* Chief Justice Rehnquist (joined by Justices Scalia and Thomas) presents a less developed version of the argument, *Bush v. Gore,* 531 U.S. at 111–22 (2000). Also see Einer Elhauge, "Florida's Vote Wasn't 'Irregular,' " *Wall Street Journal,* 13 November 2000, p. A36; and Charles Fried and Ronald Dworkin, "A Badly Flawed Election: An Exchange," *New York Review of Books,* 22 February 2001, p. 8.

119. The Florida election code, ch. 102.111, specified that returns filed after the seven-day deadline "shall be ignored" by the secretary, but ch. 102.112 states that the secretary "may . . . ignore" returns filed after that deadline. Later the Florida legislature amended these provisions. See 2001 Fla. Sess. Law Serv. 2001–40 (West).

120. See the dissent of Florida Supreme Court chief justice Charles T. Wells in *Gore v. Harris,* 772 So. 2d 1243, 1263–64 (Fla. 2000); and Chief Justice Rehnquist's concurring opinion in *Bush v. Gore,* 531 U.S. at 116–22; Posner, *Breaking the Deadlock,* 93–109; and Epstein, " 'In such Manner as the Legislature Thereof May Direct,' " 13–37.

121. Chief Justice Rehnquist concurring in *Bush v. Gore,* 531 U.S. at 124–25; and Posner, *Breaking the Deadlock,* 126–27.

122. Howard Gillman, *The Votes That Counted: How the Court Decided the 2000 Presidential Election* (Chicago: University of Chicago Press, 2001), 185–87; Samuel Issacharoff, "Political Judgments," in *The Vote,* 60–68; and David A. Strauss, "*Bush v. Gore*: What Were They Thinking?" in ibid., 184–204.

123. Laurence H. Tribe, "Comment: ɘɿo⅁ .v ʜƨuꓭ and Its Disguises: Freeing *Bush v. Gore* from Its Hall of Mirrors," *Harvard Law Review* 115 (November 2001): 194–217; and Gillman, *Votes That Counted,* 180–84.

124. *Boardman v. Esteva,* 323 So. 2d 259, 263 (Fla. 1975).

125. Gillman, *Votes That Counted,* 159–60; and Michael W. McConnell, "Two-and-a-Half Cheers for *Bush v. Gore,*" in *The Vote,* 118–20.

126. Posner, *Breaking the Deadlock,* 128–32, 185–89, 255–56; and John C. Yoo, "In Defense of the Court's Legitimacy," in *The Vote,* 239–40. Tribe in effect deploys a "pragmatic" argument to make the opposite argument: the Court should have regarded this case as raising a "political question," which, in order to avoid "the appearance of its own impropriety," it should not have taken at all. "Comment: ɘɿoƆ .v ʜƨuᙠ, " 281–82.

127. Cass R. Sunstein, "Order without Law," in *The Vote,* 221.

128. Ibid., 216–218; and Posner, *Breaking the Deadlock,* 134–39. See also introduction, note 4.

129. Or if he had recused himself, the presidential succession procedures would have been set in motion, leading by a curious sequence of decisions to the appointment of the then secretary of the treasury Lawrence Summers as president. Posner, *Breaking the Deadlock,* 139.

130. Sunstein, "Order without Law," 218.

131. Posner, *Breaking the Deadlock,* 143.

132. Gillman, *Votes That Counted,* 193–96. Also see McConnell, "Two-and-a-Half Cheers for *Bush v. Gore,*" 119–20; Elizabeth Garrett, "Leaving the Decision to Congress," in *The Vote* 50–54; and Tribe, "Comment: ɘɿoƆ .v ʜƨuᙠ," 276–77.

133. Richard A. Epstein, "Afterword: Whither Electoral Reforms in the Wake of *Bush v. Gore?*" in *The Vote,* 241–53; and Posner, *Breaking the Deadlock,* 221–60.

134. For a critique of the electoral college in light of the 2000 election, see Jack N. Rakove, "The E-College in the E-Age," in *The Unfinished Election of 2000,* ed. Jack N. Rakove (New York: Basic Books, 2001), 201–34. For defenses of the institution, see Robert M. Hardaway, *The Electoral College and the Constitution* (Westport, Conn.: Praeger, 1994); and Judith Best, *The Choice of the People?* (Lanham, Md.: Rowman and Littlefield, 1996). A valuable collection on the college and alternative systems is Paul Schumaker and Burdett A. Loomis, eds., *Choosing a President: The Electoral College and Beyond* (New York: Chatham House, 2002). Also see Glennon, *When No Majority Rules.*

135. Garrett, "Leaving the Decision to Congress," 54.

136. Bruce Ackerman goes further: the Court's action undermines the legitimacy of the Court, and Congress should therefore refuse to approve any of the president's nominees. Ackerman, "The Court Packs Itself," 48.

137. Gillman, *Votes That Counted,* 185–206; and Tribe, "Comment: ɘɿoƆ .v ʜƨuᙠ," 292–99.

138. Tribe, "Comment: ɘɿoƆ .v ʜƨuᙠ," 294; and Richard H. Pildes, "Democracy and Disorder," in *The Vote,* 140–64.

139. Robert F. Williams, "Are State Constitutional Conventions Things of the Past? The Increasing Role of the Constitutional Commission in State Constitutional Change," *Hofstra Law and Policy Symposium* 1 (1996): 2–3.

140. Janice C. May, "Amending State Constitutions 1996–97," *Rutgers Law Journal* 30 (1999): 1025–57; Robert F. Williams, "Is Constitutional Revision Success Worth Its Popular Sovereignty Price?" *Florida Law Review* 52 (April 2000): 249–73.

141. An exception is the Delaware constitution, which may be amended by the legislature without a vote by the people. Opinion of the Justices, 264 A.2d 342 (Del. 1970)

142. *Proceedings of the Constitutional Convention of the State of New York* (Albany: New York State Constitutional Convention, 1967), 22 August 1967, 3: 28–29. Mr. Shapiro, a Democrat–liberal and justice of the state supreme court, was a delegate from Queens County. Mr. Cooper, a Republican lawyer, was a delegate from Westchester County. "Directory of Delegates and Staff," in ibid., 1:32, 92. Robert F. Williams called my

attention to this debate. Kathy Wu, the reference Librarian at the University of Rochester, provided copies of the document.

143. Benjamin and Gais, "Constitutional Conventionphobia," 11–12.

144. Ibid., 71–72.

145. Paul Leland Haworth, *The Hayes–Tilden Disputed Presidential Election of 1876* (New York: AMS Press, 1979).

146. Fla. Const. art. IX, § 2 (1999). Generally, see W. Dexter Douglass, "The 1997–98 Constitution Revision Commission: Valuable Lessons from a Successful Commission," *Florida Law Review* 52 (April 2000): 275–83; and Joseph W. Little, "The Need to Revise the Florida Constitution Revision Commission," *Florida Law Review* 52 (April 2000): 475–95.

147. Albert L. Sturm, "The Development of American State Constitutions," *Publius: The Journal of Federalism* 12 (winter 1982): 85; and Little, "Florida Constitution Revision Commission," 488 n. 85.

148. The only revision to fail was an attempt to reverse several state supreme court decisions denying government the authority to make certain tax exemptions. Florida Constitution Revision Commission, *Revision Watch* (March–April 1998): 5.

149. The electoral package won by a 64 percent margin, which was the lowest of any of the winning proposals except for "miscellaneous." Douglass, "1997–98 Constitution Revision Commission," 282 n. 22. Many observers believed that the public financing provision in this package reduced its overall appeal.

150. Douglass, "1997–98 Constitution Revision Commission," 275–83. Douglass was chair of the commission. For a more critical assessment, see Little, "Florida Constitution Revision Commission."

151. Chesterfield H. Smith, in a speech to the Florida legislature on 10 January 1967, quoted in Collins Center for Public Policy, Florida State University, "The Opportunity to Change the Constitution Every 20 Years," available online: <http://www.law.fsu.edu/crc/collins/Opportunity.html> (13 February 2002).

152. Little, "Florida Constitution Revision Commission," 478–80.

153. Florida Constitution Revision Commission, *Meeting Proceedings*, 10 February 1997, 208–9.

154. Ibid., 225–26.

155. Florida Constitution Revision Commission, *Meeting Proceedings*, 15 January 1997, 163–65. See also ibid., 179, 189, 206. In the debate on limiting corporate contributions, Commissioner Chris Corr commented that "in trying to get to some kind of campaign reform during this process . . . we have a unique opportunity as a Constitution Revision Commission to do something that politicians never will" (Revision Commission, *Meeting Proceedings*, 12 December 1997, 111). In the debate on a provision that would prohibit second primaries (which tend to benefit incumbents), Commissioner Frank Morsani spoke in favor: "[I]t has come up many times in the Legislature and they do not and I do not see them changing this on half of the citizenry. It's . . . an incumbency issue" (ibid., 31). See also ibid, 39, 42.

156. The states in the first group are Alaska, Arkansas, Colorado, Missouri, Ohio, and Pennsylvania; in the second group are Arizona, Hawaii, Idaho, Maine, Montana, New Jersey, Rhode Island, and Washington. Vermont's reapportionment board drafts the initial legislative redistricting plan, but the legislature has final authority. Texas has a back-up commission, which acts if the legislature fails to adopt a plan. This information is drawn from the state government websites of the individual states, as of January 2002.

An earlier survey is National Conference of State Legislatures, *Redistricting Law 2000* (Denver, January 1999), Appendices E, F.

157. State of Arizona, Proposition 106, available online: <http://www.sosaz.com/election/2000/info/pubpamphlet/english/prop106.htm> (7 May 2002).

158. For a survey and argument for such commissions, see Jeffrey C. Kubin, "The Case for Redistricting Commissions," *Texas Law Review* 75 (March 1997): 837–72.

159. Secretary of State of Arizona, *2000 Ballot Propositions and Judicial Performance Review: November 7, 2000 General Election* (Phoenix: Office of the Secretary of State, 2000), 59.

160. *Vera v. Richards*, 861 F. Supp. at 1334. Some critics make a broader argument that goes beyond the Madisonian proviso. Lani Guinier and Gerald Torres, for example, object not only to politicians' control over redistricting, but also to geographical districting itself as well as the winner-take-all rule. Guinier and Torres, *The Miner's Canary: Enlisting Race, Resisting Power, Transforming Democracy* (Cambridge: Harvard University Press, 2002), 168–83. Each of these may well stand in the way of fair representation, but each constitutes a distinct (though related) objection. The Madisonian proviso focuses on who should control the redistricting.

161. Secretary of State of Arizona, *2000 Ballot Propositions*, 57–59.

162. Transcript of KAET (Phoenix) broadcast, "Proposition 106: Independent Redistricting Commission," *Horizon*, 19 September 2000, available online: <http://www.kaet.asu.edu/ballot/prop106transcript.html> (7 May 2002).

163. More precisely, redistricting increases responsiveness (the degree to which the partisan composition of the legislature responds to changes in voter partisan preferences), and reduces partisan bias (the degree to which an electoral system favors one political party in the conversion of the total vote into the partisan division in the legislature). See Andrew Gelman and Gary King, "Enhancing Democracy through Legislative Redistricting," *American Political Science Review* 88 (September 1994): 541–59. But partisan control may affect responsiveness and bias. See Gary W. Cox and Jonathan N. Katz, "The Reapportionment Revolution and Bias in U.S. Congressional Elections," *American Journal of Political Science* 43 (July 1999): 828–33.

164. Transcript of KAET (Phoenix) broadcast, "Proposition 106."

165. One of the more sophisticated applications of the market analogy to electoral politics is Issacharoff and Pildes, "Politics as Markets," 643–717. In other writings, the authors recognize the significance of other forms of competition. See, e.g., Pildes, "Democracy and Disorder," 140–64.

166. "Put the Crayons Back in the Box! Redistricting Commission Would Take Voters' Needs, Not Legislators', to Heart," *Arizona Republic*, 27 June 1999, p. B6.

167. See note 30 above.

168. Bengt Säve-Söderbergh, "Broader Lessons of the US Election Drama," Institute for Democracy and Electoral Assistance, November 2000, available online: <http://www.idea.int/press/op_ed_08.htm> (7 May 2002).

169. Political Staff of the Washington Post, *Deadlock: The Inside Story of America's Closet Election* (New York: Public Affairs Press, 2001), 86–89, 99–100, 117–22.

170. Ariz. Const. art. IV, pt. 2, § 1(14).

171. See David Butler and Bruce Cain, *Congressional Redistricting: Comparative and Theoretical Perspectives* (New York: Macmillan, 1992), 65–90.

172. Ariz. Const. art. IV, pt. 2, § 1(15).

173. "The United States shall guaranty to every State in this Union a republican form

of Government, and shall protect each of them against invasion; and, on application of the Legislature, or of the Executive, (when the Legislature cannot be convened), against domestic violence" (U.S. Const. art. IV, § 4). The Court has rarely invoked this clause, generally treating claims that might arise under it as "political questions," not appropriate for judicial resolution. The classic case is *Luther v. Borden*, 48 U.S. (7 Howard) 1 (1849). For an argument that more cases involving political rights should be decided under the guaranty clause, see Michael McConnell, "The Redistricting Cases: Original Mistakes and Current Consequences," *Harvard Journal of Law and Public Policy* 24 (fall 2000): 103–17.

Index

ballot notations (*continued*)
226n94; citations on, 225n88, 226nn90–91,
226n99
ballots: absentee, 34–35, 208–9n52, 209nn53–
54; improvements in, 15, 58, 218n141;
limits on access to, 69; marking, 205–6n17;
role of, 119; secret vs. public, 66, 101,
218n1; states' control over, 144; voter
education on, 59–61. *See also* fusion
candidacies; voting mechanisms
ballots, counting: authority for, 124;
certification of, 153–54, 238–39n96;
commissions' possible role in, 178–
79; disparate treatment in, 55, 56–59;
legislation on, 53–54; partisanship in,
177–78; states' control over, 144. *See also*
vote recounts
Banks, Jeffrey S., 234–35n37
Barber, Kathleen, 211n74
Barlow, Anthony M., 228n121
Barnes, Stan, 176
Barr, Bob, 237n66
Barry, Brian, 202n22
Barstow, David, 203n1
Bartels, Larry M., 223–24n72, 224n75
Behr, Roy, 218–19n9
Beitz, Charles R.: on expressivist approach,
205n12; on majority rule, 232n4; on
political equality, 203–4n4, 204n5, 219n14
Belgium: compulsory voting in, 35
Bendross-Mindingall, Dorothy, 238n85
Benjamin, Gerald, 233n11, 235n44, 235n47,
242n143
Bennett, Stephen Earl, 208n38, 223n65
Bentham, Jeremy, 112–13, 230n150
Berkman, Michael B., 234n30
Berlin, Isaiah, 225n80
Berry, Mary Frances, 60
Berry, William D., 234n30
Best, Judith, 241n134
Bickel, Alexander M., 210n66
Biemer, Paul, 227n114
Blackmun, Harry, 213n88
blacks: commission on votes of, 217n135;
districts with majority of, 5–6, 44–46, 48,
211n78, 215n112; equal respect for, 9–10;
post–Civil War political power of, 201n16;
rights won/lost by, 206n21; on Supreme
Court vote recount decision, 3–4; voting
rights of, 26. *See also* race
blanket primaries: ballot initiative on, 80–87,
221–22n53, 222n54; closed primaries

compared to, 80, 86, 222n58; electoral
choice issues and, 84–87, 120; opposition
to, 80–81, 86, 221n45; states with, 221n41;
support for, 81–82, 83–85, 221n42
Boardman v. Esteva, 240n124
Boccardi, Louis, 227n117, 227–28n119
Boies, David, 55, 216n124
Bowen, William G., 206–7n32
Bowie, Nolan, 209n56
Bowler, Shaun, 235–36n49
Brady, Henry E., 202n21, 216n124, 217n132,
229n131
Brennan, Geoffrey, 218n1
Breyer, Stephen, 76, 77, 213n86, 215n121,
229n136
bribery: free choice vs., 66; regulation of, 116;
for vote, 54
Briffault, Richard, 231nn157–58
Broder, John M., 199–200n4
Brookings Institution, 228n126
Brown v. Board of Education, 212–13n85
Buckley v. American Constitutional Law Found.:
on initiative regulations, 236n50, 236n56,
236n58, 236n62; cited, 236n57, 236n63,
236nn54–55, 236nn59–61
Buckley v. Valeo: opinion in, 107–8, 116; cited,
229n128, 229n139
Burdick v. Takushi, 205n15
Burke, Edmund, 150, 237n80
Burnham, Walter Dean, 219n19
Bush, George W., 2, 3, 100, 123. *See also*
presidential election (2000)
Bush, Jeb, 165
Bush v. Gore: on equal protection violation, 54–
55, 182, 215n121; intent of voter and, 55,
216nn126–27; merits of, 57, 167, 216n123;
right to vote and, 200n6; significance of,
54; on state court as having changed law,
239n101; cited, 208n46, 216n122, 216n125,
216n129, 240n118, 240nn120–21
*Bush v. Palm Beach County Canvassing
Bd.,* 201n13, 208n46, 238n92, 239n105,
240n111
Butler, David, 243n171
Butler, Katharine Inglis, 237n73, 237n77,
237n79
Bybee, Keith J., 214n107, 215n113

Cain, Bruce E.: on ballot notations, 226n99; on
blanket primaries, 221n51; on campaign
finance, 231n160; on redistricting,
243n171; cited, 222n63, 226n105

and, 179–80; redistricting issues and, 176; to term limits debate, 132–38

institutions: adverse incentives in, 154–55; as context for redistricting, 43–44; disparate treatment by, 55, 56, 216nn126–27; equal respect in context of, 52–53, 62–63; excluding discussions of, 15–16; as filters in political information, 88–92, 224n78; final authority in democratic, 134; popular sovereignty and, 183–84, 190–91; rights of, 82–83. *See also* ballot initiatives; commissions; electoral institutions; political parties

intent of voter, 55, 162–63, 216nn126–27

Internet: registration vs. voting on, 34; representation and, 40–41, 211n75

Iranian hostage crisis, 98

Irish immigrants: voting rights of, 206n21

Issacharoff, Samuel: on campaign finance, 230n145, 231n160; on constitutional right to vote, 200n6; on functional approach, 221n51; on fusion candidacies, 234n34; on markets and politics, 220n36, 243n165; cited, 205n14, 206nn23–24, 208n38, 210nn69–71, 215n114, 215n117, 216n130, 217n133, 218n2, 220n35, 228n125, 231n159, 238n91, 240nn114–15, 240n122

Iyengar, Shanto, 224n77, 227n108

Jackson, John E., 226n106, 227n107, 227n109, 227n113

Jacobson, Gary C., 231n153

Jamieson, Kathleen Hall, 224n77

Jefferson, Thomas: on majorities, 137–38; on political parties, 68; cited, 218n3, 235nn45–46

Johnson, Tom, 227n117

Johnson v. DeGrandy, 213–14n99

Johnston, J. Bennett, 110, 230n145

Jones, Edith H., 232n3

jury duty, 37, 141

justice: application of concept, 13; contractarian theories of, 8–9, 201n17; as fairness, 202n22; rights required by, 16–17. *See also* electoral justice; procedural justice; Rawls, John

Karlan, Pamela S.: on "bleaching," 213n89; on campaign finance, 230n145, 231n160; on commodification, 210n63; on constitutional right to vote, 200n6; on possibilities of Internet, 211n75; on

presidential election (2000), 216n123; cited, 205n14, 206nn23–24, 208n38, 209n56, 210nn69–71, 214n100, 215n114, 215n117, 217n133, 218n2, 220n35, 228n125, 231n159, 238n91, 240nn114–15

Katz, Jonathan N., 234n30, 243n163

Keeter, Scott, 223nn65–66

Kelley, Stanley, Jr., 199n2, 206–7n32

Kennedy, Anthony M., 185, 226n94, 236n56

Kerry, John, 106, 229n132

Key, V. O., Jr., 199n2

Keyssar, Alexander: on constitutional amendments, 235n43; on secret ballot, 218n1; on voter registration, 206n31; cited, 200nn7–8, 206n19, 206n23, 206n26, 206n28

Killenbeck, Mark, 233n15

Kim, Jae-On, 206–7n32

Kinder, Donald R., 224n77, 227n108

King, Gary, 234n30, 243n163

Kirschner, William R., 219n16

Klein, Rick, 231nn162–63

Konner, Joan, 200n10, 227n118, 228n121

Kousser, J. Morgan, 201n16

Krosnick, Jon A., 226n89

Kubin, Jeffrey C., 211n77, 243n158

Kuklinski, James H., 223–24n72

Lacasa, Carlos, 240n112

Lack, Andrew, 227n117

Langbein, Laura I., 229–30n143

Langley, Richard, 172

Langton, Rae, 204–5n10

language tests: prohibition of, 27

laws: antifusion, 72–73; on counting ballots, 53–54; as filter of political knowledge, 90–91; on single-member districts, 52, 215n115; on voter registration, 206n31. *See also* courts

Lazarus, Edward, 218–19n9

Lazarus, Theodore, 231n161

League of Women Voters, 127

legal standing, 53–53, 62–63, 78, 143, 182

legislatures: authority of constitutional commission vs., 171–79, 182–83; commission's recommendations approved by, 168, 170; election authority of, 135–36; elector selection and, 151–61, 162; equal representation in, 38; as expression of majority's will, 143–68; institutional features of, 46–47; judicial intervention and, 161–68; Madisonian proviso and, 180;

Wolfinger, Raymond E.: on voter registration, 206–7n32, 207n33; cited, 208n38, 208n48, 208nn50–51
women: rights won/lost by, 206n21; voting rights of, 26. *See also* gender
write-in votes, 24–25, 127–28

Wu, Kathy, 241–42n142

Yoo, John C., 241n126

Zagarri, Rosemarie, 237n78
Zaller, John, 223n71